A NEW WORLD OF KNOWLEDGE

A NEW WORLD OF KNOWLEDGE

Canadian Universities and Globalization

Edited by

Sheryl Bond
and
Jean-Pierre Lemasson

INTERNATIONAL DEVELOPMENT RESEARCH CENTRE
Ottawa • Cairo • Dakar • Johannesburg • Montevideo • Nairobi • New Delhi • Singapore

Published by the International Development Research Centre
PO Box 8500, Ottawa, ON, Canada K1G 3H9

© International Development Research Centre 1999

Canadian Cataloguing in Publication Data

Main entry under title :
A new world of knowledge : Canadian universities and globalization
Issued also in French under title: Un nouveau monde du savoir.
Includes bibliographical references.

ISBN 0-88936-893-7

1. International education — Canada.
2. Education, Higher — Canada — Aims and objectives.
3. Universities and colleges — Canada — International cooperation.
4. Educational assistance — Canada.
I. Bond, Sheryl.
II. Lemasson, Jean-Pierre.
III. International Development Research Centre (Canada)

LC1090.N38 1999   378'.016'0971   C99-980380-8

IDRC Books endeavours to produce environmentally friendly publications. All
paper used is recycled as well as recyclable. All inks and coatings are vegetable-
based products.

Contents

Contents

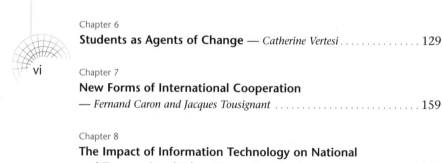

Preface

In any examination of the recent history of Canadian universities, special consideration must be given to their efforts to foster an international dimension, their deliberate outreach beyond their place in domestic affairs, and the integration of new knowledge and perspectives gained as a result. On this score, the Canadian International Development Agency (CIDA), the International Development Research Centre (IDRC), and the Association of Universities and Colleges of Canada share the view that the Canadian university community has an inspiring story to share with Canada — indeed, with the world. Canadian universities can take credit for many early initiatives that opened up new lines of international assistance and shaped the values that have defined Canadian aid. This book documents the university community's leadership, long-held visions, and good and steady efforts in the sphere of international development.

The story of Canadian universities' international dimension is continuously evolving, however, and taking a look at it now from a variety of perspectives is essential, given the speed with which the world is changing and the implications some of these changes have for Canada and particularly for the Canadian university community. In a globalized environment, education is an increasingly valuable commodity and service that determines the winners and losers — states, firms, and individuals — in a competitive world. It is against this background that the discourse on the internationalization of Canadian universities will be engaged. In the mix of higher education (with its stewardship of the research and teaching that underpin the kind of society we want for citizens of Canada and the world) and the call for international outreach, we have to reflect on how far the market approach will take us in the search for sustainable and equitable development. In the chapters that follow, the contributors look at the evolution of the international dimension of Canadian universities from a variety of vantage points. The contributors air issues that anchor the discussion in day-to-day reality and oblige us to confront shortcomings and focus on new challenges, particularly those posed by the new expectations for education and research. The contributors also show, however, that strength can be drawn from the strong tradition of human-centred work that has been the hallmark of the Canadian universities' international endeavour. An understanding of this strong tradition reaffirms the role that the universities have played and must continue to play in Canada's response to globalization: it provides a base from which to confront, with confidence, current and future challenges faced by the faculty, students, and the people in the larger community who look to the universities for guidance.

Those of us who planned and guided the preparation of the book kept several categories of reader in mind: readers in Canada and abroad; members of the university community and those whose work connects with that community; and both the "old hands" and a new generation of scholars and practitioners.

For Canadian university people of all ranks and persuasions — institutional leaders, faculty, students, and support staff — the book offers perspectives on the rich tradition of Canadian accomplishments, which may serve as guideposts for those involved in the internationalization of the institution, now and in the future, and encourage them to champion innovative approaches to the challenges posed by globalization.

Practitioners working in the institutions and agencies engaged in Canada's role on the international scene, such as CIDA and IDRC — as well as a growing range of government departments, nongovernmental organizations, and private firms caught up in international issues — often call on the resources of the university community to

help solve an immediate problem, which inevitably results in a fragmented view of the institution. This constituency will benefit from
the book's stocktaking of past achievements, which have built this
resource, and the discussion of obstacles to be overcome and strengths
to be built on to protect and enhance the unique contribution universities make to Canada's international endeavours.

A very important overseas audience is found in the university
communities in developing and developed countries. For those in the
developing countries who have shared in making the Canadian university community's history of the international-outreach work, those
who are currently involved in this work, and those who will be future
collaborators and partners, we hope that the record of international
work set out in the book demonstrates that Canadian universities
have been worthy partners over five decades of Canadian aid. But we
are equally aware that overseas collaborators know Canadian universities are subject to a range of economic stresses: the need to cope
with government deficit cutting and declining aid budgets and a
greater concern for international competitiveness are forces shaping
the way in which Canadian universities approach international collaboration. Readers will learn how the Canadian university community is coming to terms with these forces while preserving the values
and principles that support an open sharing and exchange of knowledge, as well as concern for equity and justice.

Although mentioned last, one final audience is arguably the most
important. This is the younger generation, in Canada especially, but
also overseas. The book has much to say to students and faculty starting their careers, who need to be reminded that earlier generations
of students and faculty were among the leaders in the internationalization of Canadian universities, bringing a sense of mission, commitment, and energy to the proposition that the universities have a
central role to play in making a better world. That proposition is as
valid today as ever.

Sheryl Bond
Jean-Pierre Lemasson

Acknowledgments

We wish to publicly thank the many and diverse people whose visions and dedication were critical to realizing the publication of this book.

Foremost in our minds are our friends and colleagues from around the world who have shared our passion about the ability of education to transform lives and institutions. They have changed our personal and intellectual lives in significant ways and it was through their openness that we came to see our world through a very different set of eyes. To the many people in the far reaches of the world who opened their homes, shared their lives, and nurtured our ideas of who we are as educators and Canadians, our deepest gratitude.

Closer to home, we wish to thank Eva Egron-Polak of the Association of Universities and Colleges of Canada (AUCC), who was with us at the start of the book, and Chris Smart of IDRC whose good humour and tireless generosity kept us invigorated through the two and one-half years it took to see the result of our collective efforts. We sincerely thank the contributing authors, who, with many demands on their time, joined us in believing that this book had to be written, and that now was the time to do it. Likewise, the members of the Editorial Board — Howard Clark, Jane Knight, Roger Schwass, Olaf Slaymaker, and Janet Wardlaw — deserve our appreciation for their valuable insight and ideas for improving this publication.

We also want to thank the many men and women, at home and abroad, who believe that openness to the world of knowledge is key to building a healthy global world. Our book is about internationalization and in that light the new world that is emerging is the responsibility of all of those who will try to shape it.

Sad news, received as the manuscript of the book was in its final stages, underlined the quality of the work that the Canadian universities and exceptional individuals have contributed to international development. "A Modest 'Man of Action'" was how the National Post headed its obituary for Alexander Angus MacDonald, best known for his work as the Director of the Coady International Institute at St Francis Xavier University. Alex MacDonald's life and work as a thinker and practitioner in university-based development epitomizes the combination of research, teaching, and community service that has contributed to the development of Canada and has been placed at the service of the world's developing regions. Alex was a member of the Editorial Board guiding the preparation of this book.

Sheryl Bond
Jean-Pierre Lemasson

Chapter 1

Introduction: The Internationalization of Canadian Universities

Jean-Pierre Lemasson

Introduction

It has become commonplace to point to the globalization process in the explanation of the changes reshaping our societies on the economic, social, and political fronts. Large corporations increasingly think of their future in global terms, and governments now meet together regularly, whether through international organizations or in more specific groupings (for example, the Group of Seven), in an effort to coordinate a broad agenda of topics of mutual interest, ranging from economic policy, to the prevention of conflict, to the management of epidemics, to the conquest of space. At a more prosaic level, ordinary mortals can now fly off to the ends of the Earth, or, thanks to the explosion of telecommunications and the mass media, feel themselves part of the countless events that, little by little, are reshaping the entire world. Information and decisions from distant continents now make themselves felt swiftly in our daily lives, placing our local existence in an entirely new perspective.

Although there has been a great deal of thinking and theorizing about this phenomenon in terms of economics, politics, and

1

2

communications, relatively little attention has been paid to its implications for education or, more precisely, for higher education. In fact,
the only restraint on the headlong drive for economic integration has
been the exemptions for culture in international trade agreements,
based on national responsibilities in the cultural area. The audiovisual
sector was excluded from the North American Free Trade Agreement,
and, in the case of the General Agreement on Tariffs and Trade,
Canada has aligned itself with the so-called cultural exemption promoted for the francophone world. Generally speaking, education
itself has received no notice, apart from in the European Union,
which has recognized the importance of education through specific
international education cooperation programs.

In Canada, the universities have long been involved on the international front. Like universities everywhere, they see it as their fundamental mission to produce and disseminate knowledge on a
universal scale, and they have supported their researchers' efforts to
integrate themselves into the international scientific community,
publish in the best journals, and secure their place in the many traditional or emerging academic disciplines. One may even say that in
many respects scientific activity was "globalized" long before the
world of business and economics. What economic sector has not benefited from the contributions of researchers in many countries? As an
integral dimension of universities, research has in fact been internationalized since its beginnings, and the universities have been among
the engines of globalization. What, then, are we to make of the importance now attributed to the internationalization of our universities?

To approach this question, it is useful to look first at the relationship between globalization and internationalization. The idea of
globalization refers to the space in which certain institutions carry
out their activities (for example, multinational corporations or the
United Nations agencies). These institutions are, in effect, capable of
operating virtually any place; indeed, they can exist without regard
to location at all. Thus, the universities, as institutions, may well be
engaged in the globalization of higher education, but because they
are rooted in their own home base they are not necessarily international. Internationalization therefore must be seen as something different. Internationalization does not prevent an institution from
acting in any place in the world, but it does not make it a requirement. The predominant thrust is not so much the geographic extension of activity but the internal transformation of the institution
itself. Internationalization is, thus, first to be understood as an institutional process that in some way internalizes the concept of

openness to the world in all the activities and organizational aspects of the university and that may even launch an internal transformation to prepare the university to act more directly on the international or global scene.

Although by definition the scientific mission of universities is international in nature, it is clear that this does not mean that a given institution can be considered "internationalizing" or already "internationalized." For either to be the case, the other two basic missions of a university — teaching and service to the community — must also have an international orientation. All the internal processes of the university must be structured to take into account the international dimension.

The idea of bringing the many and disparate international activities of universities under the umbrella term *internationalization* is a relatively recent one, dating back only to the early 1990s. It has involved a far-reaching reinterpretation of the basic missions of the university, effecting a cultural change directly linked to the growing presence of international influences in our daily lives.

Scientific activity — which has, at least in modern times, always been international — is now developing at an accelerating pace; new fields of specialization are emerging; and sometimes colleagues who are the closest to each other scientifically are in fact the farthest removed from each other physically. Scarcely a single area of scientific investigation, whether in the natural or the social sciences, has escaped being caught up in this momentum to broaden and deepen scientific activity.

Education in all sectors is being transformed to prepare today's students to work in a world that will be undergoing a wide-ranging process of integration and globalization at many levels. To the extent that ever fewer activities will escape restructuring and reorganization on an international scale, education must do better to prepare its beneficiaries to think in both a global and a differentiated context, help them take a cosmopolitan view and be more aware of cultural differences, and promote an open, understanding mind. This becomes even more urgent as the complexity of the world around us seems to grow exponentially.

In fact, the greatest expectations at present focus on teaching and introducing what could be considered a truly international education. Even if this ambition is difficult to define in terms of its subject matter, it is basically an undertaking directly linked to the complexity of our new world and implies the desire to take a more organized approach to offering an educational experience that is cross-cultural

4

and open to "otherness," rather than leaving it to the initiative of a few of the bolder or more inquisitive individuals in the universities, as in the past. Whether in student mobility, language instruction, distance education, or the cogranting of degrees, a new realm of potential collaboration is opening before us, in which our students, too, will be directly invited to chart their educational path. It is clear that the internationalization of universities is not an end in itself, although it poses a number of questions in its own right. Nevertheless, our students are the ones who are seeking to speed up the process of opening the universities to the world, and they are actively engaged in defining this process.

Finally, the community-service questions we must address no longer relate solely to communities in close physical proximity to our universities but also relate to those that are struggling with poverty in ever growing numbers in developing countries. Some go so far as to speak of the internationalization of disease, misery, illiteracy, and poverty, which the internationalization of aid responds to but feebly.

We may say, then, that the internationalization of universities relates to all the objectives, processes, structures, activities, and results that bring elements of international or global information, action, and decision-making to bear on all levels of university life, whether in teaching, research, or service to the community.

This consensus of views on the meaning of the term *internationalization* is the fruit of a slow gestation process, during which one might have believed that nothing was happening in Canadian universities. The purpose of this book is precisely to demonstrate that this is not the case. In fact, we attempt to show how Canadian universities, far from being passive institutions buffeted about in a world beyond their ken or control, have been, and will always strive to be, full players in a broad process to which no one can remain indifferent. We want to make it clear that our universities have made a direct contribution to shaping today's world by pursuing their mission of preparing new generations for a world undergoing rapid change.

How are the universities — whose very purpose has always been to create and disseminate knowledge of universal validity — facing up to their responsibilities in a world in which symbolic frontiers are becoming more important than physical ones? How are they engaging in the process of globalization, in which the opposing forces of competition versus cooperation, marginalization versus equality, are at war? How indeed have the various missions of the universities evolved? How are they now being cast in this swiftly accelerating process?

In this book, we have attempted to go beyond the surface impressions and anecdotal evidence that have been the hallmark of thinking on this issue to date. In light of the lack of hard research data in this area, this book must be regarded as an essay, rather than as a scientific demonstration. We have made use, wherever possible, of quantitative methods, but these serve only as backup to the qualitative analysis, which is primarily of a heuristic nature.

5

Since the pioneering efforts of Norma Walmsley (Walmsley 1970) this book represents the first initiative in Canada to systematically consider the internationalization of the universities within a perspective at once diachronic and synchronic. In effect, we have tried both to offer a global view of the ground covered since our universities first became involved in internationalization and to promote awareness of the great variety of its current forms. Our intent is to offer not only to the universities themselves but also, and more broadly, to all the stakeholders in higher education a common framework to foster discussion of the issues of internationalization at all levels.

Although there was, perhaps, a time when it seemed an easy matter to predict the future, that is certainly not the case today. International realities make themselves felt in so many areas and involve so many sectors that it is not a simple task to discern the major issues at stake. Today, hardly a discipline can make progress without contributions from intellectual communities working on a world scale; moreover, the content of courses, the choice of research subjects, the evolution of teaching methods, and the structure of programs are all profoundly influenced by information flowing in from the four corners of the globe. Everything seems to be in a constant state of flux. It is not easy, then, for institutions seeking to open themselves to the world to maintain the capacity to listen and to assimilate and not to succumb to confusion in the face of so much information. Paradoxically, because the universities can no longer know, assimilate, and transmit everything, they run a greater risk than ever of becoming bound up in their own specifics, institutional personalities, and priorities.

It is a healthy thing that all university stakeholders — whether students, professors, administrators, or lecturers — share a common view of the relevance of the questions and that they each seek the answers that seem to them most appropriate. The university world is not unidimensional, and its prevailing pluralism inevitably sparks debate about values, practical orientations, and day-to-day choices. To the extent that we can help to clarify the Canadian situation and the international challenges facing us and facilitate the choice of options, we believe we will have contributed directly to the broad-based but coherent development of our universities.

Such a common vision is all the more important because the world of the university is far from being the isolated ivory tower so readily denounced by those who know little of university reality. In Canada, government stakeholders are many, and their objectives differ both between the provincial and federal levels and within ministries at the same level. It will be recalled that the federal government has no jurisdiction in the area of education, and the provinces, which have this responsibility, do not necessarily have the same perspective as in countries where the education system is centralized. We find that government agencies often have a fractured, compartmentalized, and incomplete view of universities. This applies not only to teaching but also to research and community service.

Once the international dimension is injected into this scene, questions of coherence and synergy become paramount. We hope, at the very least, to revitalize the kinds of cooperation that have always occurred but that have been partial, limited, and sporadic. But the internationalization of our universities is a major challenge not only to the institutions themselves but also to governments because the collective place of Canadian universities within the international system, with its many economic, cultural, social, and scientific aspects, depends on having the appropriate support policies and programs.

It is also interesting to note that multilateral bodies are showing increasing interest in the implications of the internationalization of universities for international cooperation. For example, the fact that the Organisation for Economic Co-operation and Development (OECD 1996b) is now attempting to draw up a comparative balance sheet of the degree and type of internationalization in universities in diverse countries is a clear sign that governments are taking a greater political interest in the issue. We know that the European Union in particular has made it a political objective to encourage a new European consciousness, using programs for student mobility and language learning, for example. Such topics as international mobility and cross-border recognition of degrees and diplomas have been the focus of international conventions under the aegis of the United Nations Educational, Scientific and Cultural Organization (UNESCO) and the Council of Europe (UNESCO 1997). A declaration was recently adopted at the first World Conference on Higher Education (UNESCO 1998). The declaration contains many references to international cooperation and to certain aspects of internationalization, demonstrating the worldwide interest shown in internationalization.

Internationalizing the basic missions of universities means that the intergovernmental political agenda, at both the bilateral and the multilateral levels, will increasingly include cooperation in the areas of teaching, research, and community services. Canadian universities should at least be clear about the stakes and their own specific strengths and interests. Cooperation does not so much pose a threat of leveling as it offers a tool for the development of institutions.

7

We hope, of course, that our book will be of interest to universities and indeed to all stakeholders in Canada and elsewhere in higher education. Internationalization can offer a unique opportunity for universities on the five continents to draw together and forge lasting links of many kinds. Today, such ties need to be formed at all levels, just as the development of science has allowed us to share a common culture of knowledge. A greater familiarity with Canadian universities among other countries will lead, we may hope, to new partnerships.

Organization of the book

The book has two major parts. The first part offers a summary of the internationalization activities of universities. Chapters 2–4 trace the evolution of the basic university missions: community service, teaching, and research. This seemed to us to provide the most relevant analytical framework, as well as allowing for continuity over time. Moreover, as noted above, the dynamics of the interface with external stakeholders, particularly with governments, varies according to function and generates, as we shall see, specific activities. As well, this framework offers a relatively universal basis for making international comparisons and a quick and ready system of classification. Chapter 5 analyzes the organizational changes that the universities have made to equip themselves with appropriate management tools to fulfil their three broad missions in their international activities.

James Shute opens the book by underlining the importance of development assistance activities carried out in Canadian universities. The importance of those activities and the fact that they have been going on for so long make them an essential point of departure for the reader and the reason why we have chosen to deal with the community-service mission first. Shute, who has pioneered thinking in Canada about this subject, also reviews the impact of development cooperation, both in the field and in our institutions, and discusses the necessary conditions for the universities to maintain their commitments in these difficult times.

Sheryl Bond and Jacquelyn Thayer Scott focus on the internationalization of instruction. The title of their chapter, "From reluctant acceptance to modest embrace," is highly evocative. These authors show clearly that the internationalization of instruction initially had more to do with development assistance than with strictly academic pursuits. It was only after a very gradual evolution that the internationalization of instruction began to be recognized as having importance in its own right. The authors have taken the approach of focusing on instruction from the viewpoint of learning, and this opens an original perspective on internationalization by tying it directly to education, which makes the coming challenges and responsibilities of universities all the more clear.

In Chapter 4, Yves Gingras, Benoît Godin, and Martine Foisy examine the internationalization of university research through an analysis of copublications, giving the reader a unique appreciation of the importance of collaboration between Canadian and foreign researchers in various disciplines. Their research helps us to understand the specific forms that internationalization has taken within each discipline, as well as giving us an idea of the major flows of collaboration, country by country. As well, the authors trace the growth of non-Canadian funding for Canadian research. In this way, we can easily measure how important globalization has been in the area of research and development.

Chapter 5 is by Howard Clark, who, as a university president, has had to personally grapple with thorny management issues. In this chapter, he addresses questions related to the changing structure of universities. The overview he provides allows us to grasp the significance not only of the organizational changes that reflect transformations in the basic university missions but also of those related to basic decision-making processes. The author presents the key elements of a strategic plan of internationalization, including international training for students and the creation of research consortia. Within this perspective, organizational change has less to do with correcting the past than with the way leadership is involved in paving the way to the future.

It will be seen that the process of internationalization in Canadian universities has gone through four distinct periods. The first, between 1950 and 1968, was a time of individual initiatives on the part of a few people, who, on the basis of their own experience abroad, began to work within the university to encourage greater international involvement. The second period, from 1968 to about 1980, saw the development of universities in a context in which governments were introducing policies, mechanisms, and financing to help universities develop international relations in the areas of teaching, research, and community service. This time was marked above all by support for the individual efforts of members of the teaching body. The third period, which extends to the early 1990s, may be regarded as that of the institutionalization of development assistance programs in the university context. During this time, the universities were called on to get involved in development assistance on an institutional basis. Finally, since the beginning of 1990s, Canadian universities, like those abroad, have entered into a phase of internationalization that affects potentially all university missions and the entire university community. This phase is witnessing both the generalization of international activities and programs and a virtual explosion in the diversity of such activities, which is opening up a new range of issues, discussed in the second part of this publication.

9

This part is intended to highlight current activities that offer the best pointers for the major changes yet to come. We have not tried to cover all the possibilities but to discern what at present appears to be an underlying trend in the restructuring of the higher education system.

In Chapter 6, Catherine Vertesi sheds some light on areas of consideration and action with which our universities are currently preoccupied, namely, mobility for our own students and the recruitment of foreign students. These efforts, which will become even more important in the future, will come to little, however, unless a number of practical conditions are met. The highly operational approach taken by Vertesi has the significant advantage of letting us measure the gap between discourse and day-to-day practice and highlights the challenge of creating convergence between university service and the interests of academic stakeholders.

Chapter 7 is devoted to new forms of internationalization. Fernand Caron and Jacques Tousignant offer a fairly comprehensive picture of current initiatives for the internationalization of universities. These are astonishing in their profusion, variety, and complexity. It is clear that, in addition to traditional bilateral initiatives, a whole new range of multilateral forms is emerging. Moreover, in increasing numbers of projects, we find the most significant feature of the initiatives is the impact on the structure of the universities themselves. From thesis cosupervision, to the creation of international training consortia, to the offer of Canadian programs abroad, certain forms of internationalization seem sure to have a permanent impact on our future. In this respect, the panorama of initiatives and perspectives presented here will help us identify more clearly the challenges we face.

In Chapter 8, Jon Baggaley addresses a question of increasing concern to the university community, namely, the impact of information technologies on national and international education. On the basis of his analysis of the effects of conventional distance-education technologies, the author urges us to be realistic in our expectations of the new possibilities opening up in international instruction. Technical limitations, the language factor, the importance of appropriate teaching methods, and national cultural and political traits are among the elements that make the Internet — this supermedium — not merely a new tool of dissemination but, more importantly, an instrument for the promotion of true dialogue and interchange.

Because we can only know ourselves through comparison with others, we have left to Jane Knight the daunting task of comparing the status of internationalization in the Canadian higher education system with that of other countries, particularly those examined in OECD studies. Knight, who is very familiar with the situation both in Canada and abroad, is the ideal choice to identify the issues in various countries and highlight the unique features of our own system. It will be seen that internationalization is a worldwide phenomenon that everywhere suggests the same basic questions and concepts, although the dynamics may vary from region to region and the ways of responding to those questions are intimately linked to differing conceptions of the role of higher education within society. Knight thus brings us back to the objectives that each of us can pursue in this vast and multifaceted world of internationalized higher education.

The conclusion to the book points to the major characteristics of the state of internationalization in Canadian universities by examining how disciplines have become internationalized and partnerships have become institutionalized. Partnerships are an increasingly common form of collaboration on a worldwide stage, where universities are constantly cooperating and competing with each other, showing solidarity in one case and fierce rivalry in another. Internationalization thrusts us into a situation in which the laws governing the production and dissemination of knowledge are more and more clearly stamped by the financial interests of universities. Governments are pushing universities to seek independent sources of funding and forcing them to enter increasingly into commercial relationships. This raises questions about the fundamental role of universities in the new economy.

A portrait of Canadian universities

As background to help the reader in understanding the process of internationalization, I offer below a snapshot of Canadian universities, focusing on a few essential elements needed to place in perspective the ideas put forth by the authors of this book.

I have restricted the discussion to a few broad indicators and a summary presentation of a limited number of issues that can help explain certain subsequent phenomena. For readers who would like a more detailed and descriptive panorama, I would refer them to a presentation of the Council of Ministries of Education, Canada, on the Canadian postsecondary-education system (CMEC 1996–97) on the Internet, also found in *Orientations 1996* (AUCC 1996b), and to Robitaille and Gingras (CIRST–ENVEX 1998), in the *Bulletin CIRST/ENVEX*, on the restructuring of the universities. As well, the Canadian university web sites listed in Appendix 1 can be visited for more focused research. Readers seeking a more analytical or historical background on Canadian universities can also turn to the numerous publications in this area (see, for example, Harris 1973; Jones 1997) and to the situation reports that provincial governments have commissioned to guide policymaking (see particularly Roblin Commission [Manitoba] 1994; Quebec 1998).

Thus, it goes without saying that Canada has not 1 but 10 university systems, one for each province. In fact, however, those systems are based on philosophies that are so similar in terms of autonomy, financing, human-resource management, etc., that we can place these institutions together in a common framework, even though provincial variations are real and each university has its own unique history and characteristics.

One important difference between Quebec and the other provinces is the presence there of the CEGEPs (collèges d'enseignement général et professionnel [colleges for general and professional education]). These institutions, situated between the secondary and university levels, enable Quebec students to enter university at what would be considered the second year of studies in the English Canadian system.

We have steered away from attempting to compare the universities, either at the provincial or the national level. The merit of such an exercise is always open to question. We have even more pointedly refrained from offering any broad-brush judgments because the qualities of any one institution will vary considerably from one sector to

Table 1. Number of universities, by province.

British Columbia	9
Alberta	7
Saskatchewan	5
Manitoba	4
Ontario	29
Quebec	19
New Brunswick	4
Nova Scotia	10
Prince Edward Island	1
Newfoundland	1

Source: AUCC web site (see Appendix 1).

another. With these caveats in place, what then are the broad typical characteristics of Canadian universities?

In 1998, Canada had 89 universities. The oldest of these, with
roots in the Seminaire du Québec, is Université Laval, founded in
1663. Other universities were created throughout the 19th and 20th
centuries. Although they were originally tied to religious denomina-
tions, we may say that today nearly all are lay establishments. The
most recent wave of university expansion occurred in the 1960s and
1970s, with the creation, for example, of York University in Toronto,
Simon Fraser University in Burnaby, British Columbia, and the
Université du Québec network. Table 1 shows the number of universities by province.

The most populous universities are those located in the major
urban centres of Toronto, Montréal, Vancouver, Ottawa, Québec
City, Calgary, etc. Table 2 ranks the largest universities by the size of
their overall student body. In fact, 43 institutions, or nearly half of
the total, had fewer than 5 000 full-time students in 1994/95
(CIRST–ENVEX 1998). These institutions offer for the most part only
undergraduate or highly specialized programs.

Canadian universities, because of their origin, generally have private legal status. In practice, however, they are public institutions, in
the sense that provincial-government funding for universities takes
no account of their legal status. Thus, a private institution like McGill
University is funded on exactly the same basis as Université du
Québec à Montréal, which, as a member of the Université du Québec
network, is a publicly chartered institution.

Most Canadian universities are English speaking. Francophone
universities are concentrated in Quebec but are also found in
Manitoba (Collège universitaire de Saint-Boniface), New Brunswick
(Université de Moncton), and Nova Scotia (Université Sainte-Anne).
Some universities, notably the University of Ottawa and Laurentian

Table 2. Canadian universities ranked by total number of students, 1997.

Students (*n*)	Universities (*n*)	
>50 000	3	Université de Montréal and associated schools Université de Québec network University of Toronto and associated institutions
40 000–50 000	0	—
30 000–40 000	3	University of British Columbia Université Laval York University
20 000–30 000	8	University of Alberta University of Calgary Concordia University University of Manitoba McGill University University of Ottawa Ryerson Polytechnic University University of Western Ontario
10 000–20 000	15	Carleton University Dalhousie University University of Guelph University of Lethbridge McMaster University Memorial University of Newfoundland University of New Brunswick Queen's University at Kingston University of Regina University of Saskatchewan Université de Sherbrooke Simon Fraser University University of Victoria University of Waterloo University of Windsor
<10 000	60	

Source: Author, using a list source from AUCC.

13

University, offer programs in the two official languages. Quebec also has exclusively anglophone institutions, such as Concordia University. Francophones represent about 25% of the entire Canadian student body.

In 1995/96, there were 846 409 students enrolled in Canadian universities, and these students were distributed by province and status as shown in Table 3. Following World War II, the student body grew steadily, almost without interruption, but in 1992 the number of full-time students began to reach a plateau and the number of part-time students declined. Since then we have seen stagnating enrollments of full-time students and a continuing decline in the number

Table 3. Full-time and part-time university students, 1993/94 to 1997/98.

	1993/94	1994/95	1995/96	1996/97	1997/98
Full-time students					
Canada	574 314	575 704	573 194	573 635	573 099
Newfoundland	13 029	13 144	13 472	13 193	13 115
Prince Edward Island	2 691	2 544	2 425	2 313	2 452
Nova Scotia	29 996	29 922	29 723	29 941	30 077
New Brunswick	19 493	19 551	19 401	18 931	18 503
Quebec	137 750	135 603	132 927	132 054	131 074
Ontario	231 156	230 306	228 158	226 998	227 153
Manitoba	20 296	22 962	21 459	22 024	21 024
Saskatchewan	23 018	23 173	23 637	23 571	23 864
Alberta	51 083	50 803	52 399	53 044	52 824
British Columbia	45 802	47 696	49 593	51 566	53 013
Part-time students					
Canada	300 290	283 252	273 215	256 133	249 673
Newfoundland	4 368	4 025	2 745	2 861	2 683
Prince Edward Island	776	587	476	424	482
Nova Scotia	7 989	7 323	6 917	6 894	7 006
New Brunswick	5 566	5 233	5 398	4 698	4 181
Quebec	117 804	112 818	109 106	103 639	101 021
Ontario	99 567	94 081	91 256	79 835	76 255
Manitoba	16 758	12 806	11 950	10 031	9 796
Saskatchewan	8 689	8 060	7 939	7 748	7 364
Alberta	17 685	16 632	15 519	16 990	18 594
British Columbia	21 088	21 687	21 909	23 013	22 291

Source: Statistics Canada (1998).

of those studying part time. Rising tuition fees, as noted below, have no doubt had an impact on enrollments.

In 1995, the number of postgraduate students was at 113 435, representing 13.4% of the total student body. Robitaille and Gingras (CIRST–ENVEX 1998) showed that the proportion of master's and doctoral degrees granted in Canada was lower than that in the United States, although Canada was more active in certain disciplines.

In 1994, the number of degrees awarded totaled 170 074, of which 14% were at the master's (21 292) and doctoral (3 556) levels. Generally speaking, the numbers of degrees granted have considerably increased, mainly at the postgraduate level. Table 4 shows the trend in doctorates awarded, by discipline.

The full-time teaching body stood at 36 007 in 1995/96 (Table 5), and more than 80% had their doctorates (CREPUQ 1998). There are no data on the numbers of part-time teaching staff or on their qualifications. After rising steadily since 1955, the teaching body began to decline in 1993/94. Thus, in the wake of budget cuts, 1 055 teaching posts were eliminated in Ontario (COU 1997), and an estimated 900 were eliminated in Quebec (Lacroix et al. 1998).

Table 4. Doctorates: number of graduates, by year and discipline, 1983/84 to 1993/94.

	1983/84	1987/88	1991/92	1993/94
By year (*n*)	1 878	2 415	3 186	3 552
By discipline (% of total)				
Engineering	9.64	13.91	15.18	15.96
Physical sciences	15.55	15.11	13.65	13.54
Health professions	9.42	9.61	10.71	11.51
Education	11.13	9.57	10.01	10.36
Social sciences and history	13.15	12.17	11.03	10.16
Biological sciences	8.15	7.91	7.05	7.55
Psychology	9.11	7.95	7.11	6.25
Art and literature	7.77	6.05	5.58	5.66
Agriculture and natural resources	4.31	5.34	4.91	5.10
Mathematics	2.93	2.61	3.48	3.18
Informatics	1.38	1.53	1.69	2.56
Philosophy and religious studies	3.09	2.94	2.10	2.11
Administration	1.12	1.61	2.33	1.46
Visual and performing arts	0.69	0.54	0.86	0.84
General arts and science	0.48	0.70	1.12	0.62
Theological studies	0.53	0.62	0.73	0.56
Communication and journalism	0.16	0.21	0.10	0.45
Law and jurisprudence	0.37	0.37	0.38	0.42
Social work and social welfare	0.21	0.29	0.35	0.39
Ethnic, cultural, and area studies	0.16	0.17	0.38	0.34
Household and related science	0.48	0.58	0.67	0.31
Architecture	0.00	0.08	0.10	0.08
Library science	0.16	0.08	0.16	0.08
Translation and interpretation	0.00	0.00	0.00	0.00
Military studies	0.00	0.00	0.00	0.00
Other	0.00	0.04	0.32	0.48

Source: AUCC (1996b).

15

Table 5. Number of full-time professors, by province, 1992/93 to 1995/96.

	1992/93	1993/94	1994/95	1995/96
Canada	37 266	36 957	36 361	36 007
Newfoundland	1 049	959	943	962
Prince Edward Island	178	199	196	183
Nova Scotia	2 062	2 067	1 998	2 004
New Brunswick	1 208	1 189	1 181	1 183
Quebec	8 924	9 013	9 019	8 919
Ontario	14 050	13 854	13 456	13 362
Manitoba	1 784	1 740	1 717	1 637
Saskatchewan	1 509	1 480	1 422	1 433
Alberta	3 233	3 198	3 080	2 981
British Columbia	3 269	3 258	3 349	3 343
Yukon	0	0	0	0
Northwest Territories	0	0	0	0

Source: Statistics Canada (1995–96).

16

In 1990/91, total government funding — as shown in Table 6 — was $1.133 million, and nearly the same 6 years later, in current dollars; in fact, in constant dollars, the cut was significant. However, universities were successful in securing more funds, especially from the nongovernmental sector (foreign governments, gifts, donations, etc.). University revenues from all sources amounted to more than $10 billion in 1995/96, with a distribution as shown in Table 7, from which it is possible to appreciate the relative weight of the various levels of government in providing funding for higher education. As can be seen, the share of tuition as a portion of overall revenues rose steadily between 1980/81 and 1995/96 as did the total of funding from private sources. In contrast, provincial funding declined continuously, to the point at which it accounted for only 55.6% of university financing in 1995/96. Table 8 shows the growth, in nominal terms, of average tuition fees in Canada, which has contributed directly to the impoverishment of students. To remedy this situation, the Millennium Foundation was established by the Canadian government to grant scholarships in great numbers. As well, a number of other provisions are now being made in an effort to reduce the economic burden on students. Note also that tuition fees are lowest in Quebec.

Table 6. Funded research, by source, 1980/81 to 1996/97.

Source	Funding (thousand $)[a]		
	1980/81	1990/91	1996/97
Total from governments	386 172	1 133 276	1 170 607
Total from federal government	290 058	822 470	828 989
Health and Welfare; Health Canada	8 943	35 626	31 220
NSERC	137 440	367 853	366 831
MRC	69 308	200 652	213 227
SSHRC	14 459	51 625	55 248
Other federal government grants and contributions	59 908	166 714	162 463
Provincial government grants and contributions	87 556	287 075	294 711
Municipal government grants and contributions	293	2 878	4 617
Foreign-government grants and contributions	8 265	20 853	42 290
Nongovernment gifts and grants	89 108	336 512	623 398
Investment income	5 025	15 671	27 217
Miscellaneous income	17 481	16 210	39 346

Source: AUCC.
Note: MRC, Medical Research Council of Canada; NSERC, Natural Sciences and Engineering Research Council of Canada; SSHRC, Social Sciences and Humanities Research Council of Canada.
[a] In current dollars.

Table 7. Distribution of university revenues, by source, 1973/74 to 1995/96.

	1973/74	1975/76	1979/80	1984/85	1989/90	1994/95	1995/96
Source (% of total)							
Fees	14.4	12.2	10.6	12.5	12.7	18.0	18.9
Total from governments	75.9	78.5	78.5	75.3	74.0	67.1	64.9
Federal government	6.5	5.9	7.4	10.2	9.7	9.8	9.2
Provincial and municipal governments	69.4	72.7	71.1	65.1	64.4	57.3	55.6
Total nongovernment	6.1	5.7	7.3	8.5	9.7	11.0	11.8
Nongovernment gifts and grants	3.7	3.5	4.5	5.4	6.5	8.2	8.1
Investment income	2.3	2.1	2.8	3.1	3.2	2.8	3.7
Other	3.7	3.6	3.6	3.7	3.6	4.0	4.5
Total (thousand $)[a]	1 532 044	2 201 992	3 283 363	5 441 134	7 862 208	10 033 090	10 150 018

Source: ACPAU–CAUBO (1998).
[a] In current dollars.

Table 8. Tuition fees, by year, 1971–98.

	1971	1975	1980	1985	1990	1995	1998
Tuition (current $)	516	558	705	1 030	1 483	2 414	3 067
Tuition (constant $)[a]	1 618	1 263	1 049	1 072	1 241	1 808	2 183

Source: AUCC. 1998. Tuition fees. AUCC, Ottawa, ON, Canada. Unpublished document obtained by special request.
[a] 1986 = 100 for tuition constant.

18

The fact is, government funding has been reduced considerably, and the recent cuts have brought the universities to the point of crisis. These cuts, together with the need to respect collective labour agreements, have led the universities to trim their operating budgets by reducing the number of full-time teaching staff, spending less on maintenance of infrastructure (which is beginning to deteriorate or even to become dysfunctional, as in the case of libraries), and going into debt. Thus, in Ontario, only 3 of the 29 universities escaped deficits in 1996/97, and Quebec's universities all had deficits in 1998/99, to the tune of some $300 million. Universities are fully engaged in the race for revenues.

In short, the universities expanded rapidly until the 1970s. Their growth thereafter became more moderate, and the oil crisis of 1979 made itself felt for the first time. Since then funding has failed to keep pace with the increase in activities (a growing clientele, etc.). Since 1989 provincial budgets have been reduced to a greater or lesser extent in nominal terms, with some provinces retrenching faster or earlier than others. In 1991/92, the real cuts started and the universities and their students started to feel the impacts described above.

This overview provides the context in which to examine the importance of development-assistance activities and the rapid emergence of certain kinds of commercial activity in recent years. But this context cannot by itself provide an understanding of all the new forms of internationalization now arising, as other phenomena come into play, such as technological development, the accelerating pace of globalization, and a more institutional approach to scientific cooperation.

It is important to note as well that, depending on their geographic location, different regions of the country have different sensitivities to international realities. It is clear, for example, that British Columbia has shown far more interest than the rest of Canada in relations with Asia and the Pacific basin, whereas Quebec has a closer relationship with Europe, particularly with France.

This institutional variety also explains why the manner and degree of internationalization of university activities can cover such a broad range of possibilities. I cannot attempt here to provide a fully representative view of the situation. It is changing too quickly for any description to remain valid for long; nor would a static view necessarily identify the elements of greatest portent for the future. This variety represents a wealth that may be difficult to analyze but is bound to prove very valuable in practice.

Final notes

A conscious decision was made to limit this book to some 300 pages. Thus, each author set forth his or her ideas within the space of 20–25 pages. As would be expected, then, we have had to leave out a number of specific aspects. This is the case, for example, with the internationalization of postgraduate studies. To compensate for these gaps, to the extent possible, with available data, we have inserted boxes to call attention to a given statistic, commentary, analysis, or alternative viewpoint. These boxes are the responsibility of the editors and do not necessarily reflect the views of the authors.

19

The editors wish to thank the authors for the efforts they made in all cases to summarize and present their arguments as clearly as possible. It will be noted that they come from different provinces, fulfill diverse functions in their universities, and represent a broad spectrum of international experience in cooperation with both industrialized and developing countries. In this way, we have attempted to give a voice to a range of sensitivities that, although they are not necessarily representative, offer differing points of view on the complex process of internationalization.

The Editorial Board included representatives of various professional and geographic viewpoints. Its members are listed in the Acknowledgments. They made a major contribution in identifying the authors and in undertaking a critical read of the first version of the book.

Finally, we hope that this work will help everyone to better understand the various features of the internationalization now under way in Canadian universities and join us in thinking about the shape and role of our universities as we enter the third millennium.

Chapter 2

From Here to There and Back Again: International Outreach in the Canadian University

James Shute

The outreach tradition

Outreach is the interactive extension of university teaching and learning resources to individuals, groups, and communities beyond the campus. "It benefits both the educational institution and the society which it serves by providing a more direct interactive link between the two" (Fuller and Waldron 1989, p. 101). This definition of outreach adds a layer of exchange and dialogue to the conventional one-way service-oriented relationship. Fuller and Waldron go on to argue that such interaction with society generates knowledge founded directly on real-life situations and needs, which in turn strengthens university functions. It is this conception of outreach that provides the framework for this chapter and inspires its title. What Canadian universities have extended through their international partnerships has come back to benefit them directly and, indeed, to affect them deeply.

Outreach and public service have a long and honourable history in Canada's universities. Queen's University offered the first university distance course in Canada in 1888, with the universities of

21

Toronto and McGill following shortly after. Soon after the turn of the century, the universities of Alberta, Saskatchewan, British Columbia (UBC), Western Ontario (UWO), McMaster, Montréal, Acadia, Mount Allison, New Brunswick (UNB), and Bishop's had organized summer schools and extension departments offering both credit and noncredit courses, public lectures, night classes, and specialized training programs. Following World War I, Khaki College provided for the educational needs of demobilized soldiers; it was established under the leadership of President H.M. Tory, the first president of the University of Alberta, a university initially established to serve rural Alberta (Wilson et al. 1970; Campbell 1978). Institutions like the University of Saskatchewan were animated by sentiments such as those expressed in 1908 by the university's first president, W.C. Murray:

> The University's watchword must be service to the state in the things that make for happiness and virtue as well as in the things that make for wealth. ... It is fitting for the university to place within the reach of the solitary student, the distant townsman, the farmer in his hours of leisure, or the mothers and daughters in the home, the opportunities for adding to their stores of knowledge and enjoyment. ... Whether the work be conducted within the boundaries of the campus or throughout the length and breadth of the province, there should be ever present the consequences that this is the university of the people, established by the people, and devoted by the people to the advancement of learning and the promotion of happiness and virtue.
>
> Quoted in Campbell (1978, p. 147)

In 1928, St Francis Xavier University established its extension department, under Moses Coady, to promote the social goals of the Antigonish Movement in Nova Scotia.

As a time of social experiment and creativity in Canada, the 1930s saw the formation, with university leadership, of the Canadian Association for Adult Education, Frontier College, the New Canada Movement, Farmers' University of the Air, and the Banff School of Fine Arts. Between the wars, Workers Education Association programs benefited from tutorial, library, and financial support of universities like Queen's, McMaster, Toronto, and UWO. University staff also contributed to the formation of the CBC, National Farm Radio Forum, National Citizens Forum, and a raft of nongovernmental organizations (NGOs) set up to serve Canada and, subsequently, the global community (Crowley 1988). After World War II, university extension departments grew; new forms of distance learning appeared, using radio, correspondence, television, video, and computers; large noncredit university programs became available to the public; and university programs entirely devoted to open learning — Athabasca and Télé–université — were established (Faris 1975). And, following the Parent Commission's recommendations in the mid-1960s, the Université du Québec was set up in 1969, to be innovative and to serve part-time students (Whitelaw 1978).

This picture is hardly the image of stuffy, elitist, remote universities. I suggest that it is precisely this long tradition of community connection and outreach that led many Canadian universities quite naturally to look beyond provincial and national boundaries and to assume an international role in the late 1960s and the 1970s. This explicit early adoption of international roles by some Canadian universities evolved directly from an orientation and commitment to the larger communities of which they were — and are — a part. It might even be suggested that many of those very institutions with the longest and deepest domestic outreach experience are those that have been most active in international outreach. And so, although the earliest university international office in Canada dates back to only 1967 (McAllister 1998), which means that internationalization is a fairly recent phenomenon in Canadian higher education, this development is heir to a long tradition of domestic community engagement. It is not the result of the types of policy formulation (based largely on geopolitical considerations) that pointed universities in the United Kingdom and the United States in the direction of international work even earlier than Canada. To understand the internationalization of Canadian higher education, it is, therefore, essential to grasp the long-standing sense of responsibility that many Canadian universities have expressed in relations with their surrounding communities. This tradition also explains, at least in part, the emergence of the two major formative strands of internationalization in Canadian universities — development cooperation and international students.

Parenthetically, it should be noted that there is a contrasting perspective on this issue, which also deserves attention. Simply put, it is that "international activities at Canadian universities have not generally been seen, in the past, as central to the university's main functions of teaching and research in the context of the Canadian community" (AUCC 1977, p. 4[1]). This observation was made by a 1977 committee of the Association of Universities and Colleges of Canada (AUCC)–Royal Society of Canada, which added that Canadian universities had taken a somewhat parochial attitude,

---

[1] AUCC (Association of Universities and Colleges of Canada). 1997. Scotia Bank–AUCC Awards for Excellence in Internationalization. AUCC, Ottawa, ON, Canada. Unpublished document.

23

which had made international involvement the exception, rather than the rule. In the late 1970s, however, a more positive attitude toward international development was growing on Canadian campuses as universities became more aware of their international responsibilities, particularly those toward the Third World (AUCC 1977[2]).

This view has been common in critiques of Canadian university internationalization, particularly in the 1960s and 1970s. At the same time, it implies a moral imperative for universities to develop international relationships, primarily if not exclusively, in the context of official development assistance (ODA). In this critique, it is argued that rapid changes in global relationships in the post-Suez period left Canadian universities out of touch with world realities and that Canadian academics, in Walmsley's words, "found themselves involved internationally more or less in spite of themselves" (Walmsley 1970, p. 3). Indeed, throughout the 1960s, a series of recommendations emerged to promote university internationalization, related largely to ODA links. Walmsley herself recommended, inter alia, the establishment of a University Council on International Development, special grants from the Canadian International Development Agency (CIDA) to strengthen university development resources, an AUCC conference on development, and an international office on each campus (Walmsley 1970). Few of her recommendations were implemented at the time (although some certainly were implemented later), which left a distinct impression of uncoordinated, uncommitted, and marginalized internationalism in parochial and Euro-centric Canadian universities (Walmsley 1970). Although this view has some merit historically, it does not explain the rapidly growing internationalization evident across Canadian universities in the 1980s and 1990s.

Development cooperation

In 1961, the first university contract funded by the External Aid Office (CIDA's precursor) linked UBC and the University of Malaya in a project designed to initiate new academic programs in accounting and business administration. By the end of the 1960s, a significant number of such "twinning" projects were established, linking UBC, again, with the University of Rajasthan; the University of Alberta with

---

[2] AUCC (Association of Universities and Colleges of Canada). 1997. Scotia Bank–AUCC Awards for Excellence in Internationalization. AUCC, Ottawa, ON, Canada. Unpublished document.

Nairobi and Thailand's Ministry of Education; Université Laval with Rwanda and Tunis; the University of Saskatchewan with Makerere; the University of Guelph with the University of the West Indies (UWI) and Ghana; the University of Manitoba with Khon Kaen; UWO with Ghana and UWI; the University of Toronto with UWI and Lagos; and McGill University with Nairobi. There were other projects with nonuniversity partners. Although they were all fundamentally technical-assistance projects (in a way foreshadowing the later emphasis on technology transfer) designed to upgrade partner universities in the developing world to international standards, the twinning concept implied partnership, joint planning and decision-making, peer-based academic relationships, and mutual benefits, and this concept permeated many of these early university-based technical-cooperation projects (Shute 1972).

25

Barnard drew a helpful distinction between technical assistance and cooperation. The former is the provision of a service "time-limited, task-specific, and typically a-contextual in its relative lack of attention to the social, organizational, or theoretical factors obtaining in the project." Cooperation "is based explicitly on the assumption of equity and on the mutual respect for and acknowledgement of each side's particular strengths and limitations, socio-organizational context, research interests, and the rights and abilities of each to contribute substantially to the work" (Barnard 1988, pp. 166–167). The senior–junior, we–they, advanced–backward dichotomies were not always the norm, even in the early aid-oriented relationships (Shute 1980, 1995). Most projects were in applied, technical, and professional fields that were then (and are still) in demand abroad, like health, management, business, agriculture, education, law, and engineering. This level of international activity, which was new to Canadian universities, would have been impossible without the financial support of the External Aid Office and later CIDA. The partnership between CIDA and the universities has endured for almost four decades and, although the procedures and guidelines have evolved (and the budgets have declined), the partnership persists in support of South–North cooperation. It should be added that aside from general Canadian foreign- and aid-policy guidelines, political considerations have rarely dictated the content or conduct of university-based partnerships between Canadian and developing-country universities. Moreover, in Canada, the universities took on international initiatives entirely independently, without any provincial or national encouragement, in contrast to those in countries like Sweden, where governments enunciated national policy goals for internationalization that assigned universities a central role. A brief review of the shifts in Canada's development assistance from the 1960s to the 1990s should serve to illuminate some critical influences on CIDA–university relations.

26   Up to 1962, 95% of Canadian aid went to Ceylon, India, and Pakistan, the initial expression of which was the 1950 Colombo Plan, which brought the first wave of international students to Canadian universities. The Commonwealth was the focus, with 27 Commonwealth-aid recipients by 1970, reflecting rapid postwar decolonization (Morrison 1994). Simultaneously, and coincident with the Quiet Revolution in Quebec, a francophone program was initiated in 1961; by 1970, 21 francophone African countries were recipients of Canadian aid (Morrison 1994). Since university overseas projects depended exclusively on the aid budget, they mirrored this geographic distribution, with most project partners located in Commonwealth and francophone countries. Of the top 10 aid recipients in 1970, 6 were Commonwealth countries, and 3 were francophone. By 1990, two of those Commonwealth countries, Ghana and Pakistan, and one of the francophone countries were still on the list, together with three additional Commonwealth countries or regions (Bangladesh, Jamaica, Southern Africa Development Coordination Conference, and Tanzania), but by then, Cameroon and Indonesia had joined this top-10 group. By 1970, the Trudeau government had been elected, and Maurice Strong had assumed the presidency of what had in 1968 become CIDA. Under his leadership, "Canada became a major player in francophone Africa, developed the new bilateral program in Latin America, and increased considerably the number of recipient countries" (Morrison 1994, p. 126).

In the 1960s, establishing contracts with the External Aid Office was a trying process for universities. First, there was no precedent in Canada for such contracts. Second, the External Aid Office had little experience with universities, and the negotiators on both sides were often wary, if not somewhat adversarial. Third, the universities themselves had no corporate international experience, although in many universities the interest was strong, prompted by the personal overseas experience of individual faculty members, the hopeful and energized ethos of the time, a growing Canadian awareness of global realities, and a Pearsonian enthusiasm for Canada's modest but growing importance on the world stage. In one memorable Ottawa meeting, in which a group of university internationalists pushed senior CIDA officials to support their entrance into the international arena, it was apparent that the university community was more ready than CIDA to launch university-based efforts. Impatience and mutual scepticism have, ever since the 1960s, continued to characterize CIDA–university relations to some degree.

By the early 1970s, the list of CIDA recipients had grown to comprise 67 countries, rather than being condensed, as had been proposed (and promised) for several years (Morrison 1994). This apparent inability to concentrate the eligibility list for Canadian ODA has persisted: in 1998, 118 countries were eligible for university Tier-1 (program) and Tier-2 (project) partnerships. During this period, the Canadian aid budget tripled. India's pride of place was taken up by the new Bangladesh; Uganda dropped off the bilateral list; and Tanzania became the most prominent African aid partner. The education sector deployed the largest number of technical-assistance personnel throughout the 1970s and beyond. In 1973, for example, of 970 Canadian educators working abroad, 493 were in postsecondary positions; about half of them were in universities in the South (MacKinnon 1975). These numbers grew to more than 1 500 by 1990 (Pratt 1994a, b).

27

In 1979, Michel Dupuy, then president of CIDA, announced at an AUCC-sponsored workshop at the University of Guelph that 37 Canadian universities were participating in CIDA-funded projects (Dupuy 1980). During Dupuy's tenure, CIDA was brought more closely into line with foreign-policy objectives. Since then aid as a percentage of Canada's gross national project (GNP) has dropped steadily from roughly 0.5% to 0.27% in 1998, its lowest proportion in 30 years. It was during Dupuy's time that CIDA set up its Institutional Cooperation and Development Services (ICDS) division, within the Special Programmes Branch, to administer grants to nongovernmental institutions, which included universities and other NGOs. Much greater CIDA support, however, was channeled to the private sector, largely through the Business and Industry Program (later the Business Development Branch), introduced in 1971. This initiative was the result of what Pratt called "intimate access of Canadian business lobbies to government decision-makers and the responsiveness in general of Canadian public policy to the interests of the corporate sector" (Pratt 1994a, p. 18); it would have long-term and probably irreversible consequences for university-based development cooperation. It marked a pronounced shift away from responsiveness in CIDA programing, which was characteristic of an approach more compatible with university-based linkages than with the more directive commercially oriented programing that began to dominate aid programing in the late 1970s and particularly in the 1980s, with the appearance of the Conservative government in Ottawa.

As Morrison pointed out, the early fears that the right-wing Mulroney government, elected in 1984, would shift the aid program to its ideological perspective were somewhat mollified, both by the appointment of Joe Clark as foreign minister and by the Winegard Committee report (*For Whose Benefit?*) (HCSCEAIT 1987) on development assistance, which ultimately reaffirmed the traditional humane development objectives of poverty alleviation, human development and education, and less aid tying and recommended a stable aid budget at the level of 0.5% of GNP (Pratt 1994a, b). Unfortunately, the government (and CIDA) did little to implement the Winegard recommendations. Indeed, the Conservative government instead cut CIDA's budget severely, endorsed the structional-adjustment programs (SAPs) imposed by the International Monetary Fund and the World Bank on many client countries, and accelerated the shift away from humanitarian-aid goals begun in the Dupuy years. By the time the Liberals returned to office and introduced further budget cuts to ODA, the commitment to political and commercial priorities in aid programing was unapologetic and widespread.

Throughout the 1980s, university contracts were primarily in the ICDS envelope and focused on human-resource development. By 1990, this effort constituted only 13% of CIDA's bilateral spending (Pratt 1994a, b). Also by 1990, despite repeated efforts to concentrate on fewer recipient–partner countries, there were 110 national and regional recipients of Canadian ODA (Morrison 1994). It is probably not coincidental that in 1989/90 university projects reached their highest number, more than 200 (Lemasson 1993).

Few studies conducted during this period documented specific university experience by sector. One exception is Tossell's (1980) analysis for the Science Council of Canada of the participation of universities in the world food system. He found that from 1968 to 1978, Canadian faculty members participated in 364 separate food-system projects, with the highest number (93) participating in 1977. In 1974, academics began to be active in projects funded by agencies other than CIDA or the International Development Research Centre (IDRC), probably because of declining opportunities for involvement in CIDA and IDRC projects. Tossell estimated that from 1968 to 1978 Canadian universities provided 314 person–years (an average of 28 person–years annually) to food-system assistance, largely through CIDA and IDRC. He identified a number of difficulties in CIDA–university cooperation and observed that university experience "is a valuable resource that has not been fully utilized" (Tossell 1980,

p. 102), a view that a great many Canadian university personnel would echo now, 19 years after Tossell made this remark.

The 1990s have seen consistent budget cuts, by both Liberal and Conservative governments; the dominance of strategic considerations in aid planning, including interests in Eastern Europe and the former Soviet republics; phasing out of East and Central Africa; the removal of Ethiopia and Tanzania, two of the very poorest nations, from the aid list; and a continuing shift to private-sector and commercial interests (Morrison 1994). For Pratt, 1993 was the year in which "an era of Canadian aid policies is rather painfully and chaotically coming to an end" (Pratt 1994a, p. 20). For Rawkins, processes of change at CIDA have been "difficult and confused" (Rawkins 1994, p. 82). For Brodhead and Pratt (and doubtless for many people in Canadian universities), "dealing with CIDA clearly has become progressively more complex for Canadian NGO's since the early days of the responsive program" (Brodhead and Pratt 1994, p. 102). Many observers, given this chequered tale of ODA, might be tempted to concur with Therien, who remarked that "Canada has lost leadership in the field of aid" and that "it is unlikely that Canadian aid could again assume the importance it once had" (Therien 1994, p. 330).

29

Yet, many universities have continued to hitch their international fortunes to CIDA budgets and programs and have counted, quite understandably, on CIDA Partnership Branch funding to finance their developing-country linkages. Only a small proportion of their proposals ever receive funding, and rarely have the projects that do receive funding ever obtained support for more than 5 years, a very short time indeed for institutional- and human-development goals to be achieved. Still, universities have few other sources of program and project funding for their partnerships in the South. An impressive array of such partnerships exists: some 2 326 development cooperation projects have been implemented between universities in Canada and the South since the mid-1970s, according to AUCC's CUPID (Canadian University Projects in International Development) 1998 database, not to mention 2 781 linkage agreements with universities and research institutions around the world. Most Canadian universities now have partners in the South; many have international offices; and the great majority have given some priority to internationalization (Knight 1995). Paradoxically, these successes in university internationalism are most evident at a time of decreased funding for universities from all sources and fully one-third less from CIDA than in 1979, when Michel Dupuy, speaking at Guelph, proudly announced that 37 universities (fewer than half of today's number) were receiving CIDA funds for projects.

Box 1
CIDA's support for university cooperation: an overview

Aside from involving universities in bilateral projects, CIDA established an important mechanism specifically to support institutional linkages involving Canadian universities and colleges, the Educational Institutions Program (EIP).

Founded in 1978, as a special section of the Non-Governmental Organization Division, EIP was incorporated into the newly established Institutional Cooperation and Development Services Division in 1980. EIP's objectives were to share the expertise and resources of Canadian educational institutions with those of their developing-country counterparts, enable those countries to contribute more effectively to their own development needs, and expand the knowledge and experience of Canadian institutions. EIP's mission evolved over the years, but supporting the capacity-strengthening of developing-country institutions has remained the priority.

Like other sections of the Canadian Partnership Branch, EIP is "responsive," that is, it responds to project proposals developed and submitted by Canadian institutions. EIP's main programs from the late 1970s to early 1990s have been the University Cooperation Program, the College Cooperation Program, the University Initiated Scholarship Program (UISP), and the Centres of Excellence program. These first two programs funded linkages between universities and colleges in Canada and the developing world. UISP was started in 1988, to further the education of students from developing countries. CIDA and Canadian universities cofinanced scholarships. The universities were responsible for selecting students and for their stay in Canada. CIDA covered the costs of travel, tuition, accommodation, and books. At least 25% of the students were to be women in the first year, rising to 50% by the third year of the program. A second phase of UISP was launched in 1991, this time with the criteria that students coming to Canada be from developing-country institutions already working with Canadian universities and that the field of study be related to an ongoing project of the Canadian and developing-country institutions. This program bolstered international development activities at many Canadian universities and furthered their internationalization. The Centres of Excellence were launched in the late 1980s. Only two were funded in 1989, but four were funded in 1990. Budget cuts meant that no further centres were established.

EIP was the first CIDA section to support cooperation between Chinese and Canadian universities in the 1970s. In 1984, AUCC began managing the China–Canada Management Education Project. Other China programs administered by AUCC succeeded this one, namely the Canada–China University Linkage Program in 1988 and the Special University Linkage Consolidation Program in 1996. This scenario repeated itself with CIDA's support for university cooperation between Canada and Thailand. In 1986, AUCC began administering the Institutional Linkage Program for Thailand and the Microfunds program. Microfunds, which provide universities with travel funds to develop proposals with Southern partners, were later rolled into the University Partnerships in Cooperation and Development (UPCD) Tier-2 program (described below).

By 1992, CIDA's EIP budget had reached some $30 million, and consultants were hired to conduct a review of EIP. This included looking at the effectiveness of university and college projects carried out through EIP. Following this report and consultations with AUCC, the Association of Canadian Community Colleges (ACCC), and their partners, CIDA decided to launch new university and college programs to replace those of EIP. Part of these programs would be administered by AUCC and ACCC, given their close relationship with their members. In 1994, EIP therefore launched the UPCD program and the Canadian College Partnership Program. UPCD has two tiers: Tier 1 provides funds for large programs of up to $5 million over 5 years and is administered by CIDA; Tier 2 supports 5-year projects of up to $750 000, along with the Microfunds, and is administered by AUCC. In 1998, CIDA conducted a review of the university and college programs and is expected to work with AUCC and ACCC to refine the programs and continue them.

Since 1978 EIP has also provided funds to AUCC to support its international division. The division has facilitated the involvement of AUCC members in international development. In the late 1980s this focus expanded to include support for the internationalization of Canadian universities.

31

Because university international interests continue to grow in the face of discouraging CIDA funding prospects, two new and related trends have appeared. One is the search for new funding partners, notably in the private sector and in the system of international financial institutions (IFIs). The other is a shift from broad-based development cooperation to more narrowly focused project activities, like marketing educational services to countries able to purchase them. Knight's (1996) finding, that commercial motivations rank low for universities, is encouraging, but I suspect that given the continued financial squeeze on universities, this commercial motivation will rapidly rise up in the rankings.

Links with IDRC in the 1970s constituted the first diversification of financing for international work in Canadian universities. Although in its early years IDRC appeared reluctant to cultivate research links involving Canada's universities, the situation evolved to one in which clearly focused and productive research collaboration between Canadian university researchers and researchers in the South was supported by IDRC. Many of those research linkages have persisted since the completion of their IDRC-supported research agenda, and this has been of considerable benefit to Canadian university researchers, as well as to their research partners in the South, not to mention the many thousands of ultimate beneficiaries of IDRC-sponsored research around the world.

Of course, other forms of international outreach and collaboration have developed, like training programs initiated abroad for specialized audiences, offshore courses for Canadian degree students, student and faculty exchanges, conferences, workshops, research projects, distance-learning offerings, projects organized jointly with other Canadian universities and private consulting firms, and, more recently, the marketing of educational services abroad. In short, outreach has many faces. But the focus of this chapter is on university-based development cooperation projects, which frequently combine many of these forms.

Assessing the impacts

Strangely, little in the way of formal attention has been given to documenting university development cooperation or assessing its impacts on participating universities and other partners. Commentators tend to examine the general picture, giving less attention to specific institutional impacts (van den Bor and Shute 1991; Berry 1995; Knight 1995; Kerr 1996; McAllister 1996). They all seem to agree that institutional links have progressed from aid to partnership, and they typically offer recommendations on the design and management of more effective partnerships. Few studies have been published, however, with a view to assessing specific impacts or sharing institutional experience. The first such study was Norma Walmsley's groundbreaking report (Walmsley 1970); commissioned by CIDA, it was conducted by Walmsley for AUCC. She examined several elements of international development-related activities in 46 universities, covering all 10 provinces. Her report remains, to my knowledge, the only comprehensive study of its kind and still makes relevant reading, partly as an internationalization benchmark for those 46 institutions.

In 1981, AUCC published the results of a symposium held at the University of Guelph, designed to assess the experience of major university projects funded by CIDA's Bilateral Program Branch. CIDA staff and university representatives from Canada and the South discussed five university projects. Whether the Canadian universities that took part (École polytechnique de Montréal, UNB, McGill, Guelph, and Alberta) benefited from sharing their experiences is unclear (AUCC 1980). Whether CIDA took any real notice of their experiences is also questionable. What is clear is that failing to evaluate both the processes and the results of projects means that many universities are destined to start projects from scratch, without the benefit of learning from others. Unfortunately, this has been the normal pattern. Elsewhere, I have attempted to outline a remedy for this deficiency (Shute 1995). The same university project was the subject of a doctoral thesis, which resulted in two publications (Delage 1987, 1988). My findings challenged the conventional, pessimistic expectations of postproject indifference and decline, as well as pointing to the importance of systematic reflection on partnerships well after the official termination of funded contracts. Funding-agency officials, by contrast, appear to be interested only in short-term results and probably rely more on consultants' reports than on academic analyses (GGA 1991). The paucity of empirical evidence makes it difficult to comment knowledgeably on the extent to which feedback from development projects penetrates Canadian university structures, curricula, exchange programs, research, or even alumni relations. Still, the indicative evidence strongly suggests that broad and deep impacts are widespread and that universities and their Canadian constituencies have benefited substantially at home from their activities abroad. It remains for individual institutions in Canada to document more thoroughly and analytically just how extensive these benefits have been, possibly through systematic application of quality-assurance measures.

33

Development cooperation outcomes

With their focus on specific development objectives, largely those of institutional strengthening and capacity-building, university development cooperation projects have led to a great number of enduring links between Canadian universities and their partners in Africa, Asia, Latin America and the Caribbean, and, to a lesser extent, the Middle East, even when, following the termination of official donor funding, the financial resources to sustain such links are negligible. Such continuing institutional links should be expected. However, a number of unexpected outcomes have also emerged. One has been the growth of an impressive cadre of Canadian academics with first-hand development experience and know-how.

Many have been in demand as consultants and advisers to international agencies like the United Nations, the IFIs, the Consultative Group for International Agricultural Research, and NGOs, as well as CIDA and IDRC themselves. A considerable number have sat on the boards of NGOs like Cansave, Oxfam, World University Service of Canada (WUSC), the Developing Countries Farm Radio Network, Canadian Council for International Co-operation, the Mennonite Central Committee, and many other organizations committed to international economic and social development, including IDRC. Two prominent development NGOs, the Canadian University Service Overseas and WUSC, had for many years an official presence on a number of Canadian campuses. And the internationally experienced faculty members have been the ones who brought their experience (whether in the South or elsewhere abroad) back to their classrooms, labs, and departments, thus fomenting much of the internationalization now evident in universities across Canada. Research and publication on a wide variety of development issues have been impressive, although not initially seen as central to development cooperation (particularly by those with a purely technical-assistance mind-set), and this research has contributed substantially to the output of development knowledge. Although some participating faculty have not translated their development experience into subsequent teaching and research, most have probably done so, with a noticeable internationalizing effect on the campus learning environment.

34

One of the most significant consequences has been the enduring impact on Canadian universities and society of the thousands of international undergraduate and postgraduate students who have studied in Canadian universities, either for short periods or for the length of time needed to complete a degree. Their contribution to the international dimension of Canadian academe is immense; their contribution to university research, indispensable; and their contribution to the Canadian economy, both while here and after returning to prominent positions at home, almost immeasurable. Many such students have come to Canada as participants in university projects, but it should be recalled that international students first came to Canada in significant numbers long before twinning projects were devised, following the establishment of the Colombo Plan in 1950 and the Commonwealth Scholarship and Fellowship Plan in 1960. Therefore, 1950 is probably the most logical choice for the year from which to date the inception of the international dimension of Canada's universities (Shute 1996).

Similarly, Canadian students, both undergraduate and postgraduate, have benefited enormously from research and study opportunities provided by these university projects. Many of these students have gone on to international careers themselves (not to mention contributing to the enlightenment of Canadian citizens), as a result of the stimuli offered by those opportunities for first-hand exposure to the realities of the South and to Canadian responses to those realities.

University curricula in Canada have been affected directly by development projects and particularly by the faculty members who have participated in these projects. Walmsley (1970) could identify a considerable number of these projects and faculty members by 1970. At least 11 Canadian universities now offer international development studies as majors or minors in undergraduate programs, and a considerable number offer postgraduate programs in international development. Chapter 3 contains a detailed discussion of curricula and makes particular reference to undergraduate education.

Still other unpredicted outcomes have been the South–South, North–North, and South–North institutional connections and networks stimulated by university technical-cooperation projects (Shute

> **Box 2**
> **Development assistance and the internationalization of Canadian universities**
>
> Development cooperation projects financed by CIDA have often had a major impact not only on developing countries but also on Canadian universities. For example, when the AUCC gave its latest Award for Excellence in Internationalization to the Université du Québec à Montréal (UQAM), under the category "Contribution of university international development projects to internationalization," the association noted that UQAM's Amazon development initiative with the University of Para had produced a number of beneficial results, including a stronger Amazon content in various advanced-level ecology courses, establishment of two-way student exchanges (involving a total of 55 students), a new introductory course in Portuguese, a master's-degree thesis and two doctoral theses by Quebec students on Brazil's environmental problems, more than $600 000 worth of funding (primarily from IDRC) for research projects on the origin and effects of mercury in the Amazon, several original research articles in international journals, an exhibition on flowers and fruits of the Amazon, and the introduction of Amazonian species into the Montréal Biodome's tropical section.
> If a systematic survey were taken of all project leaders at Canadian universities, the results would likely be a surprise both to university management and to the donors themselves!

35

and van den Bor 1994). Such connections are now frequently designed into Tier-1 and Tier-2 cooperation projects.

Paradoxes and policies

Notwithstanding the argument that development cooperation grew naturally from the domestic outreach tradition, it is equally true that until comparatively recently few Canadian universities explicitly included international outreach objectives in either their mission statements or their operational plans. Aside from the University of Guelph, in 1972, few if any did so until the 1980s and 1990s. One implication of this oversight is that for some universities development cooperation (and by extrapolation, international activity generally) was a low priority. It is certainly true that some university administrators have viewed international development activity as charity, as help for the helpless, as something to do only if outside funding for it is available, and certainly not as central to the institution's priorities. Overcoming this view has taken more time than it should have. By the mid-1990s, however, Knight could report that 72% of universities in her sample had expressly included internationalism in their mission statements and that two-thirds included internationalism in their strategic planning (Knight 1995). Of course, mission statements do not inevitably or consistently guide day-to-day practice. Nevertheless, explicit commitments to internationalize in such statements publicly commit universities to this position, notwithstanding general- and human-resource constraints.

As for policies to guide development cooperation practice, some Canadian universities (but evidently not many) have formulated criteria for good practice. Such policies guide university decisions on ethical questions that frequently arise when projects, partners, and procedures are being considered (McAllister 1996).

A number of policy issues arise from the assumption that Canadian academe is now generally committed to internationalization; among the policy issues most relevant to outreach and its impacts are the following:

36

+ *Faculty renewal* — With extensive early retirements in the 1990s and reduced capacity to hire replacements from the traditional cosmopolitan pool of potential faculty members, universities have lost (at least to direct service) many of their most internationally experienced faculty members. Although many remain available as consultants or continue some form of university affiliation, they are usually no longer involved in mainstream teaching, research, supervision of postgraduate students, project design, or project management. This is a major loss to university-based international projects, unless such early retirees can be convinced to perform some continuing role. The implications are clear for faculty renewal. When new faculty are recruited (where this is possible), the international mission of the university should be one of the selection criteria in assessing both a candidate's experience and his or her potential (as well as subsequent performance). Moreover, there should be continuing opportunities for faculty members of whatever vintage to gain experience beyond Canada, particularly in development cooperation in the South. Without this "maintenance dose" of continuing international experience and exposure for faculty members through various forms of university international outreach, it will be impossible for internationalization of curricula, research, student mobility, sensitivity to international students, and so on to flourish, and the long-term impacts of developing-country experience on Canadian academe and society will diminish.

+ *Administrative support* — As has been frequently observed (Shute 1970, 1980, 1996; Knight 1994, 1995), top-level and genuine administrative support (preferably within a published policy framework) is a sine qua non of internationalization. Not enough senior university administrators have had sustained overseas experience themselves, and thus they may not always see the clear need to incorporate international objectives and policies into mainstream university missions and budget decisions. Fewer still have development-related experience or even a clear view of the rich contributions development cooperation projects can make to broad-gauged internationalization. For some such university managers, development may seem irrelevant to internationalization. Without a vision and robust involvement at the top, faculty members and students have a tough slog to get international activity moved from the margins to the mainstream. And the lack of institutional appreciation of development cooperation may well be eroding the strong contribution to both university and society made by the North–South experience of Canadian universities during the past 20–30 years.

37

+ *Memory* — The ability to learn from recorded and analyzed experience distinguishes universities from consulting firms. Financial and staff pressures, even space limitations, can inhibit the systemic accumulation of a university's memory bank of international development experience. New projects should benefit from the design, implementation, evaluation, and analysis of completed ones. All too rarely is this commonsense rule of thumb honoured. Extrapolating this principle to interuniversity sharing of experience also makes sense, although it would seem to be every bit as rare.

At the national level, the memory of key actors on the university stage should be tapped. Many energetic and far-sighted academics have contributed to the international life of Canadian universities. Examples are Douglas Anglin, Ralph Campbell, Gerald Helleiner, Michael Oliver, Cranford Pratt, Leonard Siemens, Thomas Symons, Fraser Taylor, Norma Walmsley, and William Winegard. Their individual and collective memories need to be recorded. How much was recorded of King Gordon's and Francis Leddy's experience, one wonders.

+ *Integration* — Too few universities have integrated development cooperation experience into the home campus, despite the obvious benefits. Capitalizing on faculty experience overseas in teaching, research and publication programs, and

38

community service requires systematic effort. Too few depart-ment chairs and faculty deans value international, particularly development-related, activity when undertaking faculty-performance reviews. Too few senior administrators view development cooperation as an integral part of internation-alization, despite the fact that so much internationalization (which they virtually unanimously support in general) has arisen directly from university relationships with the South. The additional danger is that financial pressures on universi-ties may delink even more severely the natural connection between development cooperation projects and the broader internationalization agenda as university managers detach income-generating international activity from the traditional mandate of teaching, research, and domestic community service.

✦ *Progress evaluation* — Once an institution has made the com-mitment to internationalize, it probably needs to find mech-anisms to evaluate its progress. If "little by little grow the bananas," then a set of criteria or benchmarks is probably needed to assess that growth. Canadian universities can ben-efit from some of the work on internationalization quality-assessment benchmarking now going on around the world (Vroeijenstijn 1995; OECD 1996a; Fielden 1997; Fogelberg and Pajala 1997; Irvine 1998). But that evaluation effort, in many cases, ignores the fact that development cooperation is a crit-ical element in internationalization. Analyses of the impact of development cooperation on Canadian and international stu-dents are also urgently needed. Tracer and impact studies of international and Canadian students participating in devel-opment cooperation projects are all too uncommon, as are follow-up studies of the impact that development content in undergraduate curricula has on graduates (Shute et al. 1985).

✦ *Financial considerations* — With the inexorable and lamenta-ble reduction in Canada's ODA and its negative effects on uni-versity capacity for international development cooperation, combined with public disinvestment in higher education in several provinces, it is necessary to confront the temptation to seek private-sector alliances in international bidding, increase income by recruiting full fee-paying international stu-dents, or reduce services and programs. It is within this model that development cooperation is transformed into the marketing of educational products and services (Knight 1996). How universities use partnerships, alliances, and resource-allocation mechanisms to cope with funding stress will probably be the major test of their commitment to internationalization. What seems clear from this analysis is that universities should plan on the continuing diminution of Canadian sources of ODA funding and either diversify their financial sources for North–South links or adapt the limited ODA funds they obtain to their own humane academic objectives, or both. It would be naive to assume that universities enjoy more than marginal support from CIDA or that they figure importantly in Canada's ODA.

39

To conclude

Internationalization in Canadian universities is much more than a reaction to the forces of globalization. In large measure, it predates the present preoccupation with international competitiveness and "preparing graduates for the 21st century." For those institutions that adopted various forms of international outreach in the 1960s, 1970s, and 1980s, the motivation (although mixed) turned on a recognition that internationalization is an integral element of a university's mission and mandate. Others undoubtedly got the gospel of internationalization as a response to market forces and the financial squeeze. Whatever the motivation, Canadian universities have put together an imaginative and impressive repertoire of international activities, frequently with inadequate resources, usually without encouragement, mostly on the margins of national policies, and occasionally in the face of indifferent interest within the universities themselves (AUCC 1977[3]).

For some universities, international commitments came early and naturally from domestic experience. Memorial's creative program in international film and video (now moved to Guelph) began on Fogo Island. The essence of the Antigonish Movement at St. Francis Xavier went around the world with the Coady International Institute. Saskatchewan's experience with its extension division lent itself neatly to the international scene. Guelph's rural outreach in Canada evolved into distance learning, rural development, and agricultural and veterinary science applications in many countries. More recently,

---

[3] AUCC (Association of Universities and Colleges of Canada). 1997. Scotia Bank–AUCC Awards for Excellence in Internationalization. AUCC, Ottawa, ON, Canada. Unpublished document.

Box 3
On the importance of creativity and innovation

Interview with Lewis Perinbam, OC, March 1999

You have played a major role in involving Canada's universities and colleges in international development. Why did you commit so much of yourself to the education sector?

Because I recognized the valuable contribution and the unique role our universities and colleges could make to development and especially in building relationships between them and their counterparts in the developing world. Until the early 1970s, CIDA contracted universities to undertake specific tasks conceived by CIDA, for which the university contracted was simply the implementing agency. Decisions about the project remained exclusively in CIDA's hands; the university did the bidding of CIDA and was paid for doing so.

I wanted to create a way for universities and colleges to take the initiative to develop their own programs in cooperation with their overseas partners and to implement it under their own direction. CIDA, through the then Special Programmes Branch (now the Canadian Partnership Branch), provided funds to match the in-kind contribution of the university–college, which was accountable for the use of these funds. The project itself did not fall under CIDA's control or direction. The financial package was generous and included 10 to 15% overheads. It was a practical and effective way for CIDA to tap the experience, expertise, and resources that reside in universities and colleges. CIDA did not interfere in the execution of their programs, as it did in the case of bilateral projects that it contracted out. CIDA, Canada, and developing countries benefited enormously from the enterprise, imagination, and creativity of universities and colleges in this way.

What were the main obstacles you encountered in creating this program?

The first derived from CIDA's established procedures, whereby it was always in the drivers' seat. Governments are usually driven by a desire to direct, control, and make others comply with procedures and criteria they establish. The notion of giving universities and colleges control over their program was anathema to many bureaucrats.

Second, many officials failed to understand and appreciate how universities and colleges functioned. One of the cardinal principles of the NGO programs was for CIDA to respect the independence, integrity, and personality of NGOs; we followed the same policy for universities and colleges, and it became accepted slowly by all concerned.

As the program grew, however, other players, notably the AUCC and ACCC [Association of Canadian Community Colleges], entered the picture. As a result, the procedure for processing projects, which now includes seeking ministerial approval for CIDA contributions, has become Byzantine. When it takes 2 years to get a decision on a university proposal, you can forget about creativity and innovation. You are working with bureaucrats, be they in CIDA or the AUCC or ACCC. While CIDA plays the dominant role in establishing procedures, the AUCC and ACCC must share responsibility for acquiescing to them.

The third issue emerged after the program was well under way and involving an increasing number of universities. Some of the universities made a major mistake by demanding that the Special Programmes Branch (SPB) provide the same percentage for overhead costs as they received from the Bilateral Branch when they were contracted for their services. But the two CIDA programs operated on entirely different principles. While universities had full control over their projects when they dealt with the SPB, they enjoyed no such freedom when they accepted contracts from the Bilateral Branch to implement CIDA projects. This demand for the same overhead reduced the number of projects that CIDA could fund from the same amount of money and denied the opportunity for many universities to participate in this program. More importantly, it led to greater CIDA control over this program and compromised the independence, freedom, and flexibility that universities had enjoyed. It also resulted in more bureaucratic interference and reporting requirements.

What does your experience tell us about the increasing bureaucratization of international development?

Bureaucratization, although it is inevitable to some extent as programs have expanded and budgets have grown, hobbles international development. It creates frustration among those who regard it as a human enterprise and are trying to liberate people from poverty and despair. More importantly, it has contributed to the rise of a new development industry. Although development programs are usually run by idealistic and well-intentioned people, they are often caught, like other industries, in a system that is self-righteous, self-protective, and geared to perpetuate itself. Forces beyond their control have conspired to undermine or even at times to eclipse the idealism and voluntary spirit that normally characterizes them.

41

Yet, despite their frailties, development agencies and programs are accomplishing much and are our best hope for the future. They manifest at their highest and best the values that are at the heart of our open democratic society — values that inspire people to care about and to help each other.

The challenge that universities face is to recognize what is happening to them as a part of this development industry. They have to realize that the price exacted by the government as a condition of funding may be excessive, unreasonable, and detrimental to its own (i.e., the government's) interest because it creates subservience instead of mutual respect and healthy cooperation. The primary task of universities is to persuade the government of its stake in respecting their independence and their personality and of the benefits of doing so. They must demonstrate that by focusing on their programs, instead of satisfying the often endless petty, niggling, and control-driven demands of junior bureaucrats, they will deliver better programs that enhance Canada's name and are a source of pride to the government and hopefully to the bureaucrats. To be fair, bureaucrats often have to work within strict guidelines, face constraints, and are accountable for the use of public funds, but this should not be used as a shield for treating universities in unreasonable ways. If universities have the courage, imagination, and vision to show leadership, they will find an influential and worthy place in Canada's development effort and enrich it in ways that attract widespread respect and admiration.

Have our graduates changed? Are they seeking something different from the student volunteers of the 1960s and 1970s?

Yes, there are many more opportunities for students to travel abroad. One of the most enterprising organizations that offer students work exchanges in other countries is AIESEC [Association for International Exchanges of Students in Economics and Commerce]. It attracts some of the brightest young men and women, and its membership reflects Canada's changing multicultural personality. These young people manifest a new dynamism and a new spirit. They represent a broader spectrum of interests than before, ranging from development to human rights, governance, and the private sector. Today's young people challenge the status quo and are not the captives of out-dated traditions and conventions based on cultural superiority. They are well informed, culturally sensitive, and hospitable to ideas. They are more willing than previous generations to establish cross cultural relationships, to travel to parts of the world other than the USA and Europe, and to establish enduring ties with their counterparts in other countries. Young people no longer need organizations to move around the world. They are doing it on their own, as well as through internship and co-op programs that many universities have initiated with financial help from CIDA, Foreign Affairs, and Human Resources Canada. I am optimistic that this new generation will chart an exciting course for our country and for the world.

university outreach projects have reflected the domestic strengths and traditions of Dalhousie, Saint Mary's, and Memorial in fisheries; McMaster, Montréal, and Queen's in health; Brandon in education; Saskatchewan and Manitoba in dryland agriculture; Sherbrooke in cooperatives; Lakehead in forestry; Ottawa in public administration; York in economics and transportation; Carleton in cartography; Waterloo in hydrology; Simon Fraser in distance learning; and Trent, UNB, and Guelph in watershed rehabilitation, to name but a representative handful. Models, approaches, policies, and procedures are as diverse as the universities themselves.

Although uneven in consistency, mixed in motivation, and occasionally delayed in development, the internationalization of Canadian universities has been impressive by world standards and possibly the most comprehensive and balanced to be found anywhere. Throughout its evolution, individual faculty contacts have sparked international connections, as well as being the source of substantial institutional change here at home. The faculty members, with their international experience and know-how, have been the ones who make the successful connections between outreach, research, and teaching. And much of their experience was acquired in relationships with the South.

More recently, affiliations have emerged between universities and private-sector firms in the competition for international development contracts, largely to diversify the funding base for continuing overseas work. With a tumultuous financial climate and the erosion of the traditional reliance on CIDA, AUCC itself is considering entering this comparatively new field of Canadian university activity on behalf of its members. Even as the landscape rumbles under Canadian universities' feet, the universities are adapting creatively to the stresses on internationalization in a time of financial constraint, early retirement of seasoned faculty, and competing demands of all kinds. They have acted well internationally. With luck and good management, they may do even better in cultivating the rich opportunities arising from development cooperation: student mobility, curriculum development, research collaboration, private-sector links, international-student reception, scholarships, publications, consulting, and problem-solving.

Although vexing issues continue to confront Canadian universities in their efforts to become more cosmopolitan, the changes observable over the past three decades have been quite dramatic and largely unpredictable. Plenty of lessons have been learned (McAllister 1993; Knight 1995; Shute 1996), such as that outreach and development cooperation must remain central to a balanced internationalization process because of their potentially powerful contributions to other processes. The dangers that threaten this balance, however, are that some universities may abandon their partners in the South for lack of resources to sustain the links and that others may simply see such links as commercial opportunities in an era of continuing financial stress. Although a good deal more remains to be done, the consequences of university international outreach, in all its forms and expressions, will probably continue to influence the international character of Canada's universities for some time.

43

From Reluctant Acceptance to Modest Embrace: Internationalization of Undergraduate Education

Sheryl Bond and Jacquelyn Thayer Scott

Background

This chapter focuses on Canadian universities and their involvement in international relations and relationships, with a view to understanding the impact of these forces on education at primarily the undergraduate level. It looks at trends. It does not touch on particular accomplishments outside these trends. This does not mean that those accomplishments are insubstantial or undeserving of scholarly attention, but they are not within the scope of this chapter.

We have adopted a perspective in which education is more about learning than about teaching, in particular, a perspective that recognizes education is also nurtured by the ideas, passions, values, and relationships that are likely to occur independently of the traditional discipline-based curriculum. If we had not chosen to take this approach, this chapter would have been considerably shorter because there is meagre evidence that university thinking has evolved much in this area.

It is our contention that context matters. Education implicitly embodies ways of thinking about knowledge and of seeing ourselves.

Therefore, we have tried to identify the educational, political, and philosophical strands that have made it possible to develop a Canadian sense of self within the international community. This development has been centred more in the universities than would have been typical in other developed countries, and in turn it has changed our universities. To bring some clarity to the challenges

46

inherent to the internationalization of education, we look briefly at the national context and the changing fashion in concepts of development and internationalization. However, we do not wish to imply that the relationships between internationalization, universities, professors, and the education of students resulted from an orderly planning process. They did not. Essentially, they have resulted from many independent choices occurring within a shared context that gives them a loose connection.

The Canadian way: early antecedents and powerful ideas

The university first took root on Canadian soil nearly 300 years ago and has educated by disseminating values and beliefs, along with knowledge. Although values and beliefs have been much more implicit than explicit in universities since the early 1950s, they have played as important a role as the subjects studied, be they physics, languages, medicine, or even marketing. Immigrants from the British Isles and Europe came seeking a place where they could begin new lives anchored in their traditional religious beliefs and where educational institutions, particularly local schools, would protect those beliefs and communicate them to future generations. They felt so strongly about the importance of schools to the perpetuation of their culture that they fought, sometimes bitterly, to ensure that schools remained entirely under the jurisdiction of provincial and local interests. The vehemence with which the different cultural groups fought threatened the emerging Confederation itself. In 1867, the colonies supported the *British North America Act*, which, among other things, acknowledged the right of the provinces to control schools. The decentralization that characterizes government control over education has affected the university as well; there is no system of higher education, and within each university there is no systematic control.

From the late 1600s until World War II, universities were relatively few in number, small in size, parochial in origin and tradition, male dominated, relatively isolated from each other, and the home of the privileged upper middle class. The sense of mission, arising from religious values and class mores, was to prepare educated people who might better serve the lay community and the professions. This vision, albeit parochial and narrow, was powerful. It is not surprising, then, that members of the university community have historically had a deeply embedded sense of service.

The involvement of members of the academic community in the many phases and facets of international cooperation has been varied and diverse. Despite, or most probably because of, the lack of national political will to give direction to institutional decision-making, the academic community has over the last 50 years enjoyed a vast array of associations and partnerships with government that have conferred influence and power on academe. This diversity of experience and an allegiance to historic ties among colleagues and institutions in other developing countries have become the hallmark of the "Canadian way." This same pluralism has contributed to a growing reticence to adopt a centralized university policy that might be perceived as undermining the right of faculty or academic departments, or both, to exercise primary control over the curriculum. In addition, new and different kinds of knowledge and cultural awareness that may have accrued to Canadian academics from their international experiences have, for the most part, failed to enter deeply into the heart of academic programs. Although there has been little systematic attempt to document the impact of these experiences on the changing nature of knowledge or on the undergraduate curriculum, a substantial body of anecdotal evidence strongly suggests that the impact of international cooperation on education at home and abroad far exceeds the very meager institutional resources available to support it.

The relationship between universities and development

Before World War II, the relationship between higher education and the emerging identity of Canada was quite limited, despite the occasional influence of prominent individuals, including lay missionaries. This was all about to change quickly. At the end of the war, the government of Prime Minister Mackenzie King, driven by a liberal social conscience and a desire to avoid dislocations and economic downturn following demobilization after World War I, legislated the right of returning soldiers to pursue higher education. Rising public expectations and the availability of financial support placed enormous pressures on universities to admit large numbers of people, mostly veterans, whose expectations of education were different and more varied than those of their predecessors. These veterans saw higher education as the door to good careers and upward social mobility. Not only had the "how" of higher education changed, so had the "why." Canada's view of its role in the world was changing. Driven by a belief in the values of multilateral organizations, Canada was looking for a special role to play in international affairs. The idea of Canada as a middle power resonated with political leaders and the public during this period of great optimism. As a former colony and a white nation acceptable in certain roles to the neutral, nonaligned, and nonwhite nations, Canada was strong enough to influence world events as an "honest broker," an intermediary in world affairs that posed no new imperialist threat (Bruneau et al. 1978). Canada's first aid efforts began in the late 1940s, at a time when Canadian universities were struggling to remake themselves to fit larger social and political realities at home.

By the late 1950s, Canada and her Western allies had begun to realize that development assistance, once thought of as a short-term "leg up" for developing economies and peoples, was in fact going to involve longer term efforts. Although there were some disagreements about the ethics of aid at the time, it was generally agreed that aid was the best approach to redressing social and economic inequalities, at home and abroad. This should not be surprising, given that national priorities and programs — such as Mothers' Allowances, the Canada Assistance Program, and, later, Medicare — arose from the same philosophical beliefs as those underpinning our values and initiatives in international development. Educated people were needed to build a country and to help others to build their nations abroad. Because in the minds of most Canadians the university defined what it means to be educated, education in general and universities in particular were at the heart of development. Given that education and development were synonymous in the minds of Canadians, it seemed like the natural thing to appoint Paul Gérin-Lajoie, then Minister of Education for the Province of Quebec, as the first head of the Canadian International Development Agency (CIDA).

Early pioneers

As the children of returning veterans entered the universities in the 1960s, student numbers increased significantly. Although the federal government was moving to a "Canadians first" approach to trade and immigration issues, there was a dearth of postgraduate programs in Canada to supply new faculty members. An increased investment of government funds allowed Canadian universities to begin to build their own postgraduate programs in a wide range of disciplines. Nonetheless, by the late 1960s and into the 1970s, the rapidly rising demand for postgraduate education made it necessary for Canadian universities to recruit reasonably large numbers of young faculty members from abroad. To some extent, hiring foreign academics afforded Canadian universities the opportunity to become more cosmopolitan and open to cultural diversity.

But, not long after this large intake of highly educated immigrants, spending on universities began to show real signs of slowing down. It became much more difficult to get a university job. Operating budgets continued to grow, but at a much slower pace. Student enrollment, coupled with a rapid increase in specialization of knowledge and degrees, put enormous stress on the universities to respond to changing external and internal expectations. Such factors may have played a significant role in dampening the enthusiasm of the newly hired foreign faculty, whose diverse backgrounds and disciplinary perspectives might have played a significant role in the internationalization of the institutions nearly 30 years ago.

The faculty's having to do a lot more with a lot less funding drove calls for unionization and, invariably, a reconsideration of the university's mission. It also produced a certain narrowness of thinking and a circling of the wagons around the primacy of the academic department. Despite the contraction of generosity felt across campuses (most academics felt overburdened just teaching and carrying out disciplinary-based research), some professors continued to work to broaden the educational experiences available to themselves and to their students. It wasn't easy.

Resources to enrich teaching were increasingly difficult to acquire. Unlike researchers, who could be expected to apply to the granting councils for external support, teachers had their work funded through institutional budgets, and the amount of funding dispersed in real dollar terms was decreasing. Flexibility in the assignment of duties for faculty also dramatically decreased, and those academics with a continuing commitment to international work were hard pressed to justify this to their overburdened colleagues. But the passions of individual faculty members to pursue their ideas and work abroad, as well as at home, once again resonated with the federal government's belief that education still had to play a central role in development. In 1968, the Canadian government established CIDA,

---

Box 1
A very Canadian attitude

Interview with Norma Walmsley, OC, March 1999

Why do you think universities have failed to document the many facets of international activities carried out by their academic staff?

If the universities have failed to document international activities of academic staff, it must be because they have not established policies to make this a priority. I find it puzzling that at a time when the gathering and compiling of information has been so facilitated by computers, the information you seek does not appear to be readily available. There seems, too, to be an inherent fear at administrative levels that by joining in a national effort, institutions may forfeit some of their own decision-making powers — a very Canadian attitude!

What was the most important message you wanted to convey to the readers of your 1970 study, Canadian Universities and International Development?

You have to picture the mood of optimism that prevailed in educational circles at the time my report was written. My main message was that educational and government leaders should seize the moment at a time when postsecondary education in Canada was receiving strong support and when many of the developing countries were in the process of establishing their own policies, following their achievement of noncolonial status.

Do universities have a special role to play in internationalization?

I have always maintained that if universities are to fulfill the universal role implied in their name, the encouragement of a global vision should be presumed to be part of their mandate. How this plays out in practical terms today, when multinationals have become such a dominant factor and government (i.e., CIDA) support has decreased so significantly, is anyone's guess.

What should universities be doing to encourage internationalization?

Again, it comes down to priorities and effective application of the tremendous changes that have taken place in technology — communication technology, to mention just one.
    I am sure you will have found some outstanding examples of individuals and departments that are making amazing use of the means at hand. And they should be examples of what can be done. In the 1970s, for example, the University of Guelph was a leader in integrating an international approach in all aspects of curriculum. This was the result of a calculated policy decision at the right level. I would think that universities specializing in distance education will now have the edge in encouraging internationalization.

What are the lessons we should have learned from your study?

While the influence of my report cannot be measured, I have reason to believe individuals did learn many lessons from the information that I was able to gather and the recommendations that flowed from that information. I had recommended that a University Council on International Development ... [be established], and comprised of representatives from the universities and professional institutes, but also some members nominated by university-oriented organizations, plus those appointed by government.

> The International Development Office at the AUCC, established belatedly in 1978, in response to my study, did not have the authority that might have resided in an inter-disciplinary organization dedicated to international development.
> The mechanisms for cooperation that were proposed in my report and the recommendations specifically outlined at the end of each chapter were relevant at the time. Your book, I trust, will reveal just how many universities chose to make the necessary commitments. But the truth is that universities probably let financial conditions, instead of goal-directed priorities, drive their actions. I feel strongly that had collective action been taken by the university community as a whole, agreeing on specific centres of excellence, for example (whereby scare resources could be maximized instead of dissipated by spreading among individual universities, etc.), much more real internationalization could have been achieved.

51

in an effort to settle the ongoing debate about the importance of having an "arm's-length" organization for the distribution of development aid. Seen as an integral part of the Canadian government, rather than as an autonomous champion of development activities, CIDA sponsored work by university faculties, as well as by private and public-sector nongovernmental organizations (NGOs) and community colleges.

As the fraction of the gross national product invested by the government in development began to rise CIDA program budgets increased and the variety of fields of study and disciplines broadened (moving beyond the original focus on infrastructure programs to issues of the environment, sustainable development, and gender). The government was committed to broadening citizen participation, including support for volunteer student organizations. The number of new proposals submitted to various CIDA programs by university faculty members grew rapidly (Morrison 1998). CIDA established the International Programmes Division and, later, other branches that focus on building institutional linkages.

> A new program in "institutional cooperation" represented the culmination of a lengthy and often frustrating process to find both an appropriate responsive mechanism for funding initiatives from universities and a means of strengthening the Agency's liason with them.
> (Morrisson 1998, p. 170)

Monies flowed in many different ways. First, student NGOs received support. Second, funding was given for proposals received directly from individual faculty members. Third, academic units, particularly those in the social sciences with a concentration of scholarly expertise in specific areas of postwar interest to the Canadian government, were beneficiaries of CIDA funding.

The international experience for students, professors, and departments not only benefited peoples and institutions abroad but also increased the potential of ideas and experience to change how we see ourselves and how we think about what it means to be an educated person.

52

Leading the way: student volunteers

The university may have provided a forum for debate on postwar issues, but as an educational institution it was unable to harness the talents and enthusiasm of Canadian students to learn by doing. Student outreach began to take shape, not within the lecture theatres or academic structures of the university, but in relatively small groups of students meeting at the universities of Toronto, Laval, and British Columbia (UBC), where they were working on such matters on their own, often with visions of education and development quite different from those of the government.

When student volunteers began work in a variety of technical capacities abroad, it became clear that volunteers in the field needed a coordinating body at home. With rare exception, university presidents were overwhelmingly reluctant to commit their institutions or their community, aligned through the Association of Universities and Colleges of Canada (AUCC), to any involvement in such activities. Many warned that "such a project was Utopian, likely to prove troublesome and expensive to manage" (Smillie, interview, 1998[1]).

This view was successfully challenged by Lewis Perinbam (formerly General Secretary of the World University Service of Canada [WUSC]) with force of persuasion and by Dr Francis Leddy (then Dean of Arts and Science at the University of Saskatchewan) with force of character, and in a meeting of the AUCC, the members agreed to debate the issues. The records and recollections of the meeting would show that not all interested parties thought alike. The debate centred on two key issues. The first issue was philosophical: Were Canadian students going abroad to become better educated and hence more able to assume leadership in a changing world or were they exporters of Canadian expertise to developing countries? The second issue was strategic: Who, if anyone, should assume responsibility for coordinating and meeting the needs of university student volunteers in the field, so far from home? Among those participating in the debate, consensus was never reached on which worldview best fits the

---

[1] I. Smillie, development consultant and author, interwiew with SB, November 1998.

emerging Canadian sense of self, a divergence that has plagued our thinking and policies ever since. To the student volunteers, the debate may have been academic. When the volunteers went off to do "good works," it was they who, on returning to Canada, attested to having a fundamentally different world vision and a sense of themselves that changed their lives and the lives of many others (McWhinney and Godfrey 1968; Smillie 1985).

53

Over the years, alumni of the Canadian University Service Overseas (CUSO) went on to establish the first international development offices on Canadian campuses; others went into senior-level ministerial and ambassadorial posts; a large number chose to devote their life's work to development and were absorbed into the growing number of government and nongovernmental agencies, including CIDA, the International Development Research Centre, Crossroads, and WUSC (Walmsley 1970). By the early 1970s, most Canadian universities reported that members of their faculties were to some extent involved in the CUSO program (Walmsley 1970). Although CUSO alumni distinguished themselves in the many public aspects of nation-building, regrettably (with all the knowledge, experience, and talent that they possessed), they were not made welcome within the university itself:

> Each year a group of approximately 500 CUSO volunteers returns from overseas to Canada but the training and experience of these young people does not appear to have been taken into consideration by very many of the universities: a) when planning for their graduate study needs (university graduate courses with interdisciplinary, international and developing country emphases could be established, perhaps by giving credit for research conducted overseas), and b) for utilization of the invaluable assistance which they could contribute in many ways.
>
> Walmsley (1970)

When members and alumni of student volunteer organizations such as CUSO had the potential to enlarge and enrich the educational arena for undergraduate students, they did so. But the university was mostly disinterested in aspects of learning that were student motivated and occurred outside the traditional boundaries of the classroom. This stance made it easy for the institutions to overlook how CUSO and other similar initiatives may enrich the universities' work and the ways of knowing that such initiatives embrace.

In the 1980s, when university budgets became tight and institutional officers were looking for ways to save or to make money, many CUSO offices, which had been centres of activity for Canadian students seeking a more internationalized educational experience, were offered a choice: either pay rent or go off campus! Eventually, CUSO offices moved off campus, and the university experienced more than a loss of revenue. The absence of CUSO offices on campuses left a vacuum that has only partially been filled by new, independent student organizations such as the Association for International Exchanges of Students in Economics and Commerce (AIESEC) and smaller institutionally based independent groups, such as the Queen's Project in Development.

54

The invisible champions: faculty members

> The rationale for the internationalization of undergraduate education must of necessity take us back to the meaning we give to liberal education and liberation of the mind. Whatever our definition might be, it is clear that acquiring global awareness and an understanding of the diversity of cultures and societies on our planet has to be considered an integral part of education.
>
> Harari (1992)

Most universities in the period 1960–80 did not share this view. More commonly, administrators assessed international projects in terms of their economic potential for their universities, rather than on intellectual or curricular merit. This reflected some degree of financial opportunism, built on a comfortable sense of self-satisfaction that Canadian universities had little to learn from colleagues and contexts in other, "less developed" countries, a stance that enabled universities to abstain from genuine self-reflection about the changing nature of a liberal education and make only the most minimal investment of institutional funds in such endeavours.

This lack of understanding may have been compounded by the fact that few faculty members and even fewer administrators had themselves engaged in international development activities. Whatever the cause, the failure of informed and thoughtful consideration on the part of many administrators and their departmental colleagues held consequences for undergraduate programs. The enrichment that should have naturally occurred from the exposure of Canadian faculty members to different cultural contexts and different ways of knowing was most often thwarted, even at the departmental level. An "institutional voice" could often be heard to declare that educational projects carried out in partnership with colleagues from other developing countries were clearly secondary to teaching and other departmentally based activities at home, although they were interesting to the faculty member(s) involved. The reflections of Dr John Burton of Guelph delineate the kinds of tensions that arose in the latter part of the 1970s:

> What happens to the career of a person who participates in an international development project? Dr. John Burton, who spent two-and-a-half years in animal science, related his personal experience ... there were problems upon his return. At first it was difficult to utilize fully the experience gained overseas because other faculty did not understand what he had been doing ... the problem then was of reconciling two interests: making a contribution to Canadian agriculture and putting to use the experience gained in Ghana.
>
> Quoted in Shute (1979, p. 61)

55

These same tensions remain a frustrating reality for faculties 25 years later. Knight, in her 1996 study, *Internationalizing Higher Education: A Shared Vision?* (Knight 1996), reported that 84% of university administrators believed that faculty involvement in international activities is still receiving little recognition in faculty-assessment procedures. One might expect that in the changing contemporary context, recognition of this effort would be the easiest reward to bestow. Curiously, the trend between 1993 and 1996 was in the opposite direction (Knight 1995).

Living and working in cultures other than one's own is a powerful learning experience for those ready to take up the challenge. Many faculty members did. However, in general, the university has failed to embrace, or even formally recognize, international experience as a source of educational reform.

The heart of the problem

At the heart of the problem is an ethnocentric assumption that the university, with its current veneration of disciplinary based paradigms, is the holder of truth. This leads to a simplification of the complex relationship between knowledge and context (Teichman, interview, 1999[2]). Although allowing for complexity is more exciting and relevant to students and faculty alike, it requires a willingness on the part of faculty members to retool themselves to acquire new knowledge and a deeper understanding of culture; and a reorganization of the protocols and structures that have served universities for

---

[2] J. Teichman, President, Canadian Council for Area Studies Learned Societies, Toronto, Ontario, Canada, interview with SB, 14 Feb 1999.

centuries. Student volunteers and members of the faculty engaged in international work have known about complexity and context. So have their hosts and partners. Such experiences have the potential to change the ways in which life and truth are understood.

A more reflective appraisal of such experiences allows one to see the potential they have for transforming all parties. For a very long time, internationalization was a project or consultancy carried out separately from teaching. This separateness may have provided a sense of comfort in that the right of individuals to pursue their own interests was assured without any real substantive change in what it meant to be "educated" at home. But internationalization, as it is coming to be understood, encompasses a change in the ways we think and the ways we educate others and ourselves, a change that has yet to yield fundamentally different courses of action. Mestenhauser (1996), writing about his colleagues at the University of Minnesota and in other American universties, suggested that many faculty members cannot draw on their own repertoire of international experiences when they redesign their courses. Other instructors oppose curricular restructuring on the grounds that it impedes academic freedom, and many regard international or comparative additions to their own disciplines as an intrusion into the purity of their own field or the tight calendar in which they have already so much to include.

It is possible to close one's eyes and to hear the same scenario described in Canada as Mestenhauser described in Minnesota. We are rich in largely untapped resources (volunteer student organizations, faculty members with extensive international experience, fields of study, and institutes) to inform current discussions on internationalization. The marginalization of this type of academic activity has created an environment in which the time and effort that faculty members are prepared to spend on redesigning curricula to catch the spirit of their new knowledge and understanding depend on individual strength of character and the exigencies of the moment. International work has often been seen as an "add on," a further expenditure of departmental resources in times of restraint, and an expensive activity for the institution. Faculty members could be heard referring to their colleagues engaged in international activities as being "away on junkets." Although some projects may have been of dubious value, the fact was that unless the institution had a special international mandate, the choice of faculty to be away when they were needed at home to help departments cope with the large numbers of students and the decreasing amounts of resources was an unwelcome choice to have to make. With some notable exceptions, departmental tenure and promotion committees tended to minimize or flatly refuse to recognize the academic importance of international work. Although this lack of collegial and institutional recognition kept the international experiences of faculty on the margins of academic life, it failed to curtail enthusiasm for being a part of such work.

This may be explained in several ways. Most professors who had the opportunity to live and work abroad had likely reached a stage in their career at which they were insulated from peer criticism. In addition, the satisfaction derived from doing something worthwhile and building (institutions, departments, and relationships) at a time when Canadian universities were losing their sense of excitement and purpose was and remains compelling. The personal or professional need for recognition often paled beside the prospect for meaningful, good-natured relationships and good works abroad. It was also a testing ground, a place where one found extraordinary challenges and opportunities to clarify one's ideas and beliefs.

Institutional champions of internationalization

The first major disciplinary program specifically focused on international study appeared at UBC as early as 1947 (Hamlin 1964), but growth in the numbers of academic programs directed to understanding different places and different cultures was slow to emerge. Political scientists, sociologists, geographers, and others working in the social sciences built academic programs at the undergraduate as well as the postgraduate levels that focused on specific regions and languages. Beginning in the early 1950s, these programs continued to spread through the 1960s into the 1970s. Area-studies programs enlarged their scope to include European, Soviet, and East European studies, as well as Asian, Latin American, and African studies (Shute 1996). Such programs work toward building a comprehensive understanding of geographic regions and languages, especially regions in which postwar governments saw either a threat or an arena for trade and political influence (O'Neil 1998). In Canada, area studies appear to have other origins as well. Some missionaries, after having spent much of their lives in developing countries, return to Canada to take up faculty posts.

For a variety of reasons, some related to defence and some related to deep-felt moral convictions and intellectual perspectives, area-studies programs grew across the country. Students who enrolled in these programs were exposed not only to knowledge of different

> **Box 2**
> **The "mish-kid"**
>
> According to a sociological survey done several years ago, the children of former missionaries have acquired a high level of academic achievement and a significant number concerned went into service occupations, with education being high on the list. York University has gained much from that small but talented group. Vice President Bill Small provides an example representative of the scope of influence which this group has exerted. In addition to holding a senior administrative post, over many difficult years and several presidents, he found time to serve as a founding member and long-time President of the Canada–China Friendship Association and for several years voluntarily taught a college tutorial for Founders College on the rise and nature of the Chinese Revolution. The "mish-kid's" course was joined by several others of similar inspiration, all of which helped greatly in the emergence of the East Asian Studies Programme, now approaching its 30th year of service to the students of Ontario.
>
> Source: Interview with Maria Cioni, Director, York International, York University, November 1998.

places but also to multidisciplinary teaching methodologies. The "what" was taught differently than in disciplinary programs, and differences could also be found in the preferred methodology of teaching. On many campuses, area-studies programs were the centre of an internationalized education. Sometime in the mid- to late 1980s, as a result of differing intellectual perspectives and the withdrawal of federal funding and the failure of institutions to fully fund programs coming off "soft" money, area-studies programs ran into difficulties. The number of programs declined, and those that survived had to be reconceptualized. Despite their rather rocky road over the years, a current scan of the universities that continue to have departments for area studies, international studies, development studies, or comparative studies reveals that the number of programs is substantial. For example, 15 Asian-studies programs are offered in universities from the University of Victoria on the west coast to Saint Mary's on the eastern seaboard. Although there are only a few African-studies programs, Slavonic studies is offered by at least 14 institutions, including the universities of Alberta, Manitoba, Waterloo, Wildfred Laurier, and McGill. International and cultural studies each have more than 10 programs for undergraduate students at the University College of Cape Breton, King's College, Université Laval, Université du Québec à Trois-Rivières, and the University of Northern British Columbia.

In addition to offering academic programs with a multidisciplinary approach to the study of regions, a few institutions changed the nature of the undergraduate education experienced by larger numbers of students. In these special places, such as the University of Guelph,

Université de Montréal, and the Coady International Institute, an internationalized sense of education began much earlier than elsewhere. Over time, aided no doubt to some extent by the Canadian government's changing international priorities and those of the business sector, the collective experience within the universities (including that of student volunteers, faculty, and institutional champions) produced a grass-roots movement that succeeded in prodding the universities to think more broadly about their educational mission and what it means to be "educated."

 59

Slow metamorphosis of the institutional mission

> Canada possesses resources of expertise and experience that we wish to share more fully with the developing countries. The universities have an unusual opportunity to demonstrate the practical role they can play, their ability to harness ideas and knowledge to the needs of an emerging world, and to take initiatives of the sort that governments are usually incapable of taking. What will be the quality and the direction of your response?
>
> Dupuy (1980)

Nudged along by the volunteer experiences of students overseas, the accumulated impacts of international experiences of faculty, and the efforts of a small number of disciplines and institutions to champion internationalization, the level and diversity of international activity were by the late 1960s clearly on a rapid rise. At the national level, the AUCC was taking notice of the increasing interest and effort made in these areas. But having taken the position that the participation of students and faculty in international activities was something best left to the discretion of member institutions, the AUCC maintained no records of these activities. Without reliable information about the largely uncoordinated activities of students and faculty, discussing internationalization was nearly pointless. To remedy this, in 1970, the AUCC commissioned Norma Walmsley to carry out the first national survey on internationalization.

Although the universities in Walmsley's (1970) study reported becoming more thoughtful about international development, the AUCC's CUPID database (Canadian University Projects in International Development), which it began to keep after the Walmsley study, shows that the number of institutions acknowledging receipt of international cooperation contracts was in reality very small. In

1979, the first year the database was kept, only five universities (UBC, Laval, Guelph, Ottawa, and Manitoba) reported receiving outside funding to support the work of their academic staff abroad. It seems likely that the actual number of institutions receiving such outside funding was larger than reported to the AUCC, but such work was clearly not widespread. The potential for international exposure to basically change the nature of the undergraduate education of students was further circumscribed because not all disciplines were likely to be beneficiaries of external support. The CUPID database illustrates this point, subject to the caveat that it is only as good as the information it receives. From 1979 to 1998, the 10 fields or disciplines receiving the most external funding in support of international cooperation tended to be professional faculties (Table 1).

In most universities, with some notable exceptions, development activity was not something the "institution" set out to do. Development activities, other than those directly and independently engaged in by students, depended heavily on the energy, enthusiasm, and commitment of individual professors, who sought support, not through the university, but directly through CIDA (and others), as when they agreed to work as consultants and project coordinators. Arising in large measure from a vigorous intellectual curiosity and built on relationships with colleagues in other countries, faculty involvement increased significantly through the middle of the 1980s.

Given that the original collection of data presented in Table 2 was limited to PhD theses that specifically named countries or regions in the title in selected years, it is possible that more effort at the postgraduate level is being directed to research questions pertinent to the international domain than is reflected in the data. Nonetheless, it is

Table 1. Ten fields or disciplines receiving the most external funding for international cooperation, 1978–98.

Field or discipline	Number of projects
Higher education teacher training	356
Business administration and management	175
Development studies	130
Educational administration	101
Higher education	95
Agriculture	83
Curriculum and instruction	80
Distance education	68
Soil and water science	64

Source: CUPID database, 1999.

Box 3

Table 2. Canadian PhD theses with an explicit international focus in selected fields, compared with total number of PhD theses in the subject area, 1988, 1992, and 1997.

Subject	International total (total in subject)		
	1988	1992	1997
Agriculture	3 (26)	4 (118)	1 (32)
Biology	1 (83)	1 (300)	1 (70)
Business	1 (8)	9 (55)	1 (8)
Economics	4 (18)	8 (73)	0 (16)
Education	6 (50)	5 (161)	2 (14)
Engineering	0 (88)	2 (289)	0 (36)
Geography	2 (11)	10 (29)	2 (3)
Political science	8 (14)	4 (54)	4 (9)

Source: Dissertation abstracts (UMI 1997).

The data in Table 2 suggest that in the disciplines surveyed the number of PhD theses is small. It is clear, however, that the interest varies significantly by discipline. Given that education (higher education teacher training, administration, curriculum, and instruction) received more external funding in support of international cooperation efforts than other fields, it might reasonably follow that the number of PhD theses in education would reflect such depth of faculty involvement. The findings do not support this hypothesis. Only 5% of PhD theses completed in education fall into the "international" category (as it was defined by the survey), far below the level of PhD theses completed in business (15%), economics (11%), geography (30%), or political science (22%). It is not surprising to find that geography and political science, with their historic associations with area studies and international issues, should produce more international theses than any of the other disciplines. Source: CUPID database.

surprising that, with the exeption of political studies, the overall work appears to represent so little of the postgraduate effort.

Unlike postgraduate students who, in some fields, were able to work on international projects or write theses based on international collaboration, undergraduates were rarely made aware of the international activities of their professors. Except in the case of area, cultural, and development studies, there is little evidence that the educational programs of students or the graduates themselves were in any significant way changed by the international experiences of faculty. Students were, and most likely still are, only tangentially exposed to that aspect of the life and work of their professors. For undergraduate students, the benefits of having their professors working on international projects could be said to "trickle down" into the curriculum and into informal discussions when they occur in the halls or in cafeterias on campus.

A continuing lack of documentation, noted first by Walmsley (1970) and subsequently by other researchers and practitioners who have looked at such questions, makes it difficult to assess not only the success of the projects but also the degree to which our own Canadian institutions have been changed by the experience. It also reveals a systemic institutional bias. In institutions that stress the importance of communicating knowledge, documentation of valued work is essential. The lack of institutional self-knowledge concerning international activities is a silent scream; no one cares because it is not really seen to be important to the institutional or scholarly mission.

62

Retrenchment and reexamination: 1975–95

In times when both human and financial resources are in short supply, people and institutions reexamine at least some of the assumptions on which they organize their lives and work. As with most such challenges, the one facing Canada's universities during the late 1980s was affected by a rich mix of environmental variables. First, the country was changing. The period 1945–75 saw the growth of the social-welfare state in Canada. But by 1975, all that began to change. During a national review of social-welfare policy, federal and provincial governments could reach no consensus about future directions. Some felt the social-welfare state was the appropriate model but that it needed some tinkering; others argued for a more fundamental restructuring of how services were accessed and delivered. And, for the first time, some voices were raised in favour of pulling back the outer boundaries of the welfare state, with a much more restricted view of the state's roles and responsibilities. By the mid-1980s, Canada and several of its provinces had fully joined New Zealand, the United Kingdom, and the United States in implementing public policies designed to drastically reduce public expenditures.

At the same time, the global economy continued to be in great flux. Canada was already beginning what would later become a full-scale commitment to freer trading partnerships in North America and globally. As the 1990s neared, there were signs of cracks in an overheated domestic economy (which varied dramatically among and within regions), and the government braced for severe recessionary changes. For universities, once collaborators in defining and building nationhood, the market-economy mind-set of the government produced tensions between itself and the academy community and within academe itself. The public language of education changed, further promoting the idea of education as a commodity to be traded and sold at home and abroad. Although academics have embraced their role as educators, they have not been so prepared to be seen as producers of goods and services. The changing external environment for universities meant tighter budgets, rumblings about accountability, but continued growth in enrollments (bringing students of many more varied cultural and experiential backgrounds) and government emphasis on accessibility.

63

Faculty members who could do so continued their international work, but it was increasingly difficult to get CIDA support, and the continuing real-dollar cuts to faculty budgets increased the likelihood that time spent away from the campus would be seen as an unacceptable "drain" on institutional resources in tight times. Up until the mid-1990s, no major new activity or philosophical development took place regarding Canadian universities and their global involvement. New creative impulses for educational change only arose outside the traditional structures, and they operated on the margins of the academy.

This continuing transition period heralded even greater environmental changes in the 1990s, during which it became clear that the entire knowledge paradigm was changing in the latter half of the 20th century. New ideas began to take shape, and the language of the academy began to become much more diversified. Paradigms of learning and knowledge started to catch up with what the faculty and the students were learning about the natural and physical world. Increasingly, knowledge was seen as less hierarchical and linear and more interconnected and relational. The fiercest academic debates of the day were often about the unity of knowledge versus its diversity. Words like *rhythms, cycles, networks, readiness, collaboration, problem-centred multidisciplinary perspectives,* and *participation* were entering the curriculum-development discussion, undermining canons, prerequisites, arbitrary definitions and rules for access, and single-discipline perspectives in course syllabi. In universities, where changes appear to occur slowly, an idea is powerful and can generate not only academic debates but also educational change.

The growing interconnectedness of the world and the rapid interconnection of knowledge would most likely present very different career patterns, requiring change, refocus, and reeducation. The standard approaches to knowledge generation and dissemination began to diversify. A comparison of mission statements from 1995 to 1996 (Knight 1996) would show that more than 80% made reference to the importance of the international dimension in their teaching and that the language used began to include such words as *transnational, interdisciplinary,* and *experiential learning.*

It is, however, important not to confuse the appearance of change with the real thing. Knight, in her studies (1995, 1996), sought to clarify how perceptions and policies were changing across the country. Her data indicate that 35% of the senior institutional representatives responding to her survey gave internationalization of their institution a "high priority"; 47% ranked it as a medium priority; and only 4% indicated that no priority was given to internationalization. The 82% of the respondents who ranked internationalization as a medium-to-high priority indicate a sense of optimism about real change, at least at the level of institutional commitment.

A general consensus among university presidents and their representatives emerged by the mid-1990s. While envisaging the diverse ways in which it might be accomplished those at the senior level increasingly accepted that the purpose of higher education was to prepare university graduates for the 21st century and that internationalization would require internationally and interculturally competent graduates (Knight 1996).

The extent to which the language of mission statements and policies has been translated into changed educational practices can be looked at from different vantage points. Universitas 21 (UBC 1998) suggested that the degree to which a university is internationalized depends on several factors, including who is admitted; how ideas, values, and paradigms are embraced; and how the curriculum is designed and delivered. If we accept these as valid indicators, then it becomes critically important that faculty be committed to change. This makes a piece of data in Knight's study worrisome (Knight 1995). Senior administrators reported that only 11% of faculty were increasingly interested in internationalization. If this portrayal of faculty is accurate, then either (1) the faculty have always been more convinced about the merits of internationalization or (2) the degree of commitment to an internationalized education may be too low on many campuses to support substantive change.

Whereas Knight's work and that of others point to the importance of having the support of presidents and vice presidents, the faculty members are the ones who hold the key to change. The faculty members are the ones whose perspectives on knowledge generate the design and structure of the curriculum, and it is the curriculum that still shapes the educational experience of students. Judgments about knowledge are often the subject of debate and are not immune to the effects of the broader social context within and external to the university, but the most powerful features of the arguments will be found in their intellectual merit, rather than in the political will for their acceptance.

From cooperation to reconceptualization: a cognitive shift

Universities in Canada have a long tradition of international collaboration. Today, however, internationalization of the University
means far more than inter-personal or even inter-institutional
cooperation across borders. It is a necessary, vital and deliberate
transformation of how we teach and learn and it is essential to the
future quality of higher education in Canada, indeed to the future
of Canada.

65

AUCC (1995a)

The cognitive shift implied in this AUCC statement comes more easily to some than to others. No longer to be seen solely as a set of unre-
lated and uncoordinated activities added to the menu of learning
opportunities for students, internationalization is moving deep into
the heart of the academy, affecting the nature of knowledge, defining, for example, what it is, how it is structured, and how it is
expressed in the curriculum. This is the domain most fiercely protected by faculty. Nonetheless, if we look at what internationalizing
the curriculum might entail (see below) and the experience of academic groups such as those at the Institute of International Studies
and Programs at the University of Minnesota (Ellingboe 1996; Morris
1996) and the British Columbia Council on International Education
(Whalley et al. 1997), it becomes clear that a shared understanding
of the concept and the process is beginning to take shape:

+ Infusing an international dimension throughout the curriculum;

+ Using an interdisciplinary approach to explore a field of study;

+ Emphasizing experiential and active learning;

+ Integrating and coordinating with other international activities;

+ Enriching readings with material that promotes comparative
  thinking;

+ Broadening knowledge of at least one other country or culture
  (at home or abroad); and

+ Encouraging self-reflection on our own culture and the way
  it influences our cognition.

Internationalization requires an openness to different cultures, values,
and ways of knowing. Teaching and learning strategies, particularly
those for undergraduate students, would necessarily become more

contextualized and more interdisciplinary. One would think that internationalization would open up the disciplines to new ways of knowing. Unfortunately, there is early evidence to the contrary. A strong tendency is apparent in some disciplines for the nearly internationalized faculties to promote "intellectual tourism," applying traditional knowledge and practice to new cultures without a thorough understanding of those cultures, an understanding that comes over time by living and working in a culture (Teichman, interview 1999[3]). The potential danger of the belief that all faculty can easily become "internationalized" is that it oversimplifies the process by which teachers becoming learners. The implications for faculty, therefore, are wide ranging; we will need to reexamine accepted structures of knowledge, course curricula, program requirements, duties, and the process for recognition of merit for the purposes of promotion and tenure.

66

While attitudes and practices are changing unevenly across the country the vision statement proposed by the President of UBC may become a beacon for others:

> The trend of "internationalization" reflects the increasing awareness that we are entering a truly global environment. Hence, universities are charged with the preparation of the future citizens of the world ... individuals who will live and work in an international environment, rather than a regional or even national milieu. The creation of an optimal undergraduate learning environment should incorporate the three "I's" (internationalization, interdisciplinary and information technology).
>
> UBC (1997)

It is clear that some Canadian universities are more prepared than others to embrace internationalization, together with all of its demands for diversity, and we can get a sense of what is happening from studies that look at the issues nationally. Such studies are relatively few. Knight's work in *Internationalizing Higher Education: A Shared Vision* (Knight 1996) suggested that senior university administrators are increasingly seeing a potential link between internationalization and the nature of the undergraduate experience. The data in her 1996 study give a new sense of value to the following strategies, although these strategies have all been around the university for quite some time. Ordered by degree of their perceived importance they are as follows: the presence of international students

---

[3] J. Teichman, President, Canadian Council for Area Studies Learned Societies, Toronto, Ontario, Canada, interview with SB, 14 Feb 1999.

or scholars (75%), participation of students in overseas international development activities (68%), faculty exchanges (62%), Canadian students with diverse cultural or ethnic backgrounds (56%), international development education activities (53%), Canadian students with international experience (54%), and research policy analysis or area-studies initiatives (48%).

Knight's study (1996) also points to the ways in which institutions have sought to enrich the educational experiences of students through student mobility (exchange), curricular changes, international students, faculty exchange, and international development projects and research. However, what institutional representatives say and what people at the institutions actually do may differ. In fact, the process of reconceptualizing education is barely beginning. Given the diverse histories and contexts of Canadian universities, it is not surprising that change is not everywhere occurring in the same way or at the same speed. UBC, one of the first universities to send student volunteers overseas and the first to offer a program focused on international studies, is one of the very small number of institutions approaching internationalization as a process of institution-wide renewal. Most of the recent initiatives have originated within a faculty, such as the following two:

+ *The Faculty of Education, University of Prince Edward Island —* Undergoing a change in programmatic structure and curriculum renewal provided members of the Faculty of Education, University of Prince Edward Island (UPEI), the opportunity to define and embrace a concept of internationalization that generates faculty renewal through the provision of an enriched educational experience for students. It began when the faculty decided to offer a specialization in international education. Its purpose was twofold: to prepare UPEI students to be internationally knowledgeable and interculturally competent; and to understand, through study, the increasingly interdependent nature of the world. While preparing the new specialization the faculty also developed a new core course, "Culture and Society in Education," which introduces all students in education to the ways cultural, moral, and social issues impact on education and offers strategies for dealing with these issues in the classroom. To help with the important curricular changes, a research assistant was hired to work for 1 month with each faculty member. To enrich the experience of the faculty members, travel grants have been made available for every faculty member to go abroad and work in their field. The faculty of education takes the view that its members thereby acquire the information needed to infuse courses with an international perspective and that this perspective is most effectively derived from direct experience with other cultures and educational systems. It also established a hiring policy, according to which any new member should be able to contribute through his or her experience or research in this specialization (Timmons, interview, 1999[4]).

+ *School of Architecture (Rome Programme), University of Waterloo* — Building on its strengths in design, culture, and cooperative education, the School of Architecture, University of Waterloo, established a program of studies in Rome, Italy, for fourth-year students. Founded in 1979, it has been a cornerstone of the curriculum in architecture ever since. The initiative is intended to provide students the opportunity to live and design in one of the richest cultural and architectural environments on Earth. More than an experience in cultural tourism, this program has, from the onset, been intended to constitute a piece of the fabric of architectural and intellectual culture in Italy and a bridge between Canadian and Italian students, academics, and practitioners of architecture. More than 800 Canadian architectural students have spent 4 months in what, by their own accounts, was their most valued educational experience. The program has spawned a series of academic, cultural, and professional collaborations and exchanges, including an exchange with the University of Chieti–Pescara, which offers the only formal opportunity for Italian architectural students to gain experience in a North American school of architecture (Knight 1999[5]).

In these examples, the move to internationalize undergraduate education (as reflected in the curriculum and field-based learning) was part of a strategy to reconceptualize an entire program of study. Other conclusions can be drawn as well. It appears that successful strategies embody important elements, such as (1) the preparedness of faculty and students to think differently about program content and approach; (2) the willingness of faculty and students to be open to

---

[4] V. Timmons, University of Prince Edward Island, Bachelor of Education with a Specialization in International Education, interview with SB, 5 Feb 1999.
    [5] Knight, D. 1999. The Rome Programme of the School of Architecture, Faculty of Environmental Studies, University of Waterloo, Waterloo, ON, Canada. Personal communique, 19 Jan. 9 pp.

(and live or work in) other cultures and societies; (3) the availability of resources to support the development of new curricular materials and travel; and (4) a clear understanding of how such work enriches the educational experience of students and faculty.

It is clear that there are exemplars in increasing numbers (such as those mentioned above) but that there is also work to be done. The challenges of internationalizing undergraduate education reflect the state of the academy and the professorate. When politicians and employers become frustrated by the seeming inability of universities to see the merits of education as a trade commodity or as a way to prepare graduates for jobs in an interconnected society, it is because this argument often fails to excite academics in the way desired. Internationalization, when expressed in terms that excite the mind, must challenge faculty members to open themselves up to more diverse ways of thinking and educating. Such magnitude of change comes slowly.

69

A modest embrace: internationalization of undergraduate education in the 21st century

Canadian universities have demonstrated a varied, if somewhat subdued, enthusiasm for the many aspects of internationalization. This is in part due to widely varying interpretations of what the term itself means, but equally important is the vantage point from which one views the assumptions and implications of the concept. Not surprisingly, a rather pluralistic approach to internationalization is reflected in the various sectors' values and priorities. The NGO community has stressed social and economic processes; business has emphasized the importance of entrepreneurship and trade; and Canadian universities have focused on the special role they can play in human-resource development, both at home and abroad: "Canadian universities are important players in this field, and regardless of Canada's future abroad, they will remain a permanent feature of the landscape" (Strong 1996).

Maurice Strong's statement appears to give Canadian universities the benefit of the doubt when it comes to the various ways in which they may choose to engage in a process of internationalization. Such engagement, it would appear, is only warranted insofar as these efforts are integrated into the university fabric. Despite our history of student volunteerism and the continuing presence of faculty and institutional champions, it remains true that many faculty members ignore internationalization completely; some embrace it as a welcome friend; and others are sceptical and ask where the new money is to achieve it. Even on a single campus, one can expect a varied reception to both the ideas embedded in the language of internationalization and the actual institutional transformations needed to achieve it.

70

The lack of documentation continues to hinder our ability to understand ourselves and think critically about the changes, if any, needed in what and how we teach and in what and where learning can occur. Such research, where it exists, is ad hoc and not widely read. We have very limited ways of knowing the extent to which the education of students today is more internationalized than it was 5 years ago. And we are nearly at the point of losing the opportunity to document, through first-hand accounts, the impacts of the international experiences of the early pioneers on themselves as people and on their students. There is no systematic body of knowledge to draw on. This lack of documentation does not, however, mean a lack of experience to build on.

And, for a host of reasons, some Canadian universities are beginning to tackle the fundamental issues involved in internationalizing education. Some of these institutions are affiliated with the older, "established" institutions, such as Dalhousie, Université de Montréal, and UBC. Others have a special connection to their communities at home and abroad (the University of Calgary, the Coady International Institute, and the University of Waterloo). Still others were, from their inception, fundamentally different (Open Learning Institute, Athabasca University). Some are still shaping the types of teaching and learning relationships needed to enable them to pursue their ideas and shared interests (University of the Arctic, College of the Americas).

The challenge of internationalizing undergraduate education is complex. Consider one of many possible scenarios as an example. To begin with, the volunteer student movements that played such a critical role in the early internationalization of education have for a variety of reasons moved off campus and assumed responsibility and control of their own efforts. Although this is understandable, given the course of events over the last 25 years, the absence of their leadership is a loss, notwithstanding the outstanding efforts of AIESEC and other independent student volunteer groups. Particularly in their formative years, they provided an energetic and optimistic balance to the conservativism of university senates and faculty councils. So, how do students today engage in international activities?

Box 4
New voices, new perspectives

David Hughes, President and founder of the Impact Group, and Darin Rovere, President and founder of the Centre for Innovation in Corporate Responsibility, were chosen to address a range of questions raised in this book, because they saw themselves as aligning their future with these important issues and because they had had some contact, during their years as students, with international development. Both David and Darin had completed university degrees within the previous 7 years at Canadian universities. Both had held top leadership positions within the Association for International Exchanges of Students in Economics and Commerce (AIESEC), provincially, nationally, and internationally. Both had worked with NGOs in Africa, Canada, Europe, and more than 50 countries around the world. Their work as student leaders and as young entrepreneurs had taken them throughout the world. Both saw themselves as committed to working on important world issues as members of the rising third sector. Their views are expressed below.

Do you think the career you have chosen falls into the field of international development?

In this day and age, the conventional wisdom is that most individuals from the baby-boomer generation and beyond will go through several distinct careers in the course of their lifetime. Both agreeed that their first careers had indeed been in international development. Now on their second careers, as young entrepreneurs, they focused on promoting the interests of the third sector. More specifically, they concentrated their efforts on an emerging field referred to sometimes as "compassionate commerce," "social entrepreneurship," "venture philanthropy," or "corporate social responsibility." "While this career is not exclusively within the field of international development, it does overlap into this field and is most certainly founded on the skills and principles inherited from prior involvement in international development." Although they acknowledged that their careers might lead them again into quite different fields, both had been driven by one common motivation — "to have a positive impact on those who, through circumstances beyond their control, are disadvantaged, disabled, and disenfranchised." Given the increasing scope of Canadian companies with operations in developing countries, they perceived this involvement in international cooperation as a huge opportunity to give others the benefit of our mistakes. "We simply can't do what we did here, and ... new technologies not only allow us to do it better but to do it quite differently." A leap-frog effect in the developing countries would lead to a big payoff for Canada and Canadian companies. "What we see is a transfer of new knowledge and infrastructures back to North America to enable us to work on where the real problems are."

What are the big issues you think the world has to deal with over the next decade?

Although everyone has their own perspective, area of specialization, and vested interest, for David and Darin the "top-of-the-pops" in the big issues category were the environment (global legislation, consumerism, corporate production practices, food production, eating habits, global warming), military arms, technological innovation, human rights, the imbalance of wealth and power, humanity's use and abuse of all these, and more. Whereas all these are important issues, "they are all symptoms and bi-products of a much larger problem related to how individuals, organizations, and nations govern themselves — locally, nationally, and internationally." They each felt that fundamental questions demanded their attention and that they needed to spend more time addressing issues such as as the following: How do we set priorities and make decisions within our families, our communities, our public institutions? How do we divide up the boundaries and territories over which we are able and willing to be responsible

71

72

and accountable? Who should make which decisions? How do we share our resources and finance our common initiatives, and how do we ensure the safety, security, development, education, health, and well-being for all in our community — rich and poor, young and old, sick and healthy?

What factors (people and circumstances) either help you engage in the issues that concern you or hold you back?

Critical success factors for making a difference — making an impact — on any range of issues would have to include the following:

+ *Knowledge—expertise in a given area* — Ignorance is the greatest hindrance.

+ *Trust, lack of biases, and a willingness to cooperate* — Successful involvement in any issue requires open and honest communication between people.

+ *Information and communications technology* — Developments in this area are profoundly improving and facilitating the knowledge, expertise, trust, and cooperation, mentioned above. Failure to embrace such technology will lead to growing ignorance and breakdowns in communication that will ultimately be detrimental to the discussion and resolution of "the big issues."

+ *Clear lines of authority and accountability* — The hierarchical organization is a thing of the past, and today we are surrounded by "teams-based management," "virtual organizations," partnerships, and alliances. These models bring with them many great benefits, but an effort must be made to retain clear lines of authority and accountability.

How does the phenomenon of globalization or internationalization impinge on your life and aspirations?

In no way! Both of these men believed that they had become global citizens in every sense of the phrase — with regard to career, education, friendships, recreation, interests, daily communication, financial transactions, and entertainment. "It is precisely the phenomenon of globalization and internationalization that has enriched our past and will continue to influence our future."

Did the university prepare you for the world you have to live in?

Overall, the university experience prepared them well for what they encountered in business, both in Canada and abroad. However, both acknowledged that only a small portion of this preparation was due to lectures or class assignments. For Darin, not much critical thinking was taught at university and not enough time was devoted to world issues beyond those of his discipline. They learned much more, each agreed, through their involvement in AIESEC and through ancillary discussions on many issues with fellow students outside the official curriculum.

What really matters to your generation when it thinks about the world in which it has to live and work? What really matters to you?

Acknowledging the risk of making an unfair generalization, David and Darin felt that what really mattered most to their generation, sadly, was social status and material wealth: the house, car, summer cottage, and position. "All too many of my contemporaries have set this as their life target and only now are beginning to reassess whether this pursuit has ultimately made them happy, secure, and fulfilled." Both reported that they, as founders and presidents of their own companies, and their colleagues at work "have been concerned much less about such issues and placed emphasis on other issues related to public service, concern for our communities, and the need for stimulating and rewarding careers." They found it had not been easy to stick to their principles. "In the end, we will probably obtain the same level of wealth and prominence as our contemporaries but will have taken quite a different path to getting there." When asked to comment on the reasons for their values, both young men saw their earlier work in international development as a strong influence on their choices.

Do you feel that the new information and communications technologies really do make your generation very different from your parents' generation? If yes, what is the evidence?

We are hardly friends with our neighbours, yet we have daily conversations with people around the world, and that has changed both our neighbourhoods and our perspectives. In addition, the information and communications revolution has forced this generation to respond more quickly to more information and to a seemingly faster changing world. Response times are quicker, and less time is available to reflect on issues and circumstances. This has had its advantages with regard to productivity and efficiency, but it may have had its disadvantages in terms of the quality of those responses.

According to the senior university administrators in Knight's study (1996), overseas student exchanges rate high on their list of strategies to change the institution. But for university students at the beginning of the 21st century, who are more likely older, female, and employed in at least one part-time job (Bond 1998), the current economic context makes it difficult to pursue the type of experiential learning offered by overseas exchange programs. The pressing concerns of a great many students will continue to be the cost of tuition, the cost of living, and for some (men and women) the responsibilities of supporting a family. In reality, unless funding is made available to help students pay for the higher than average costs of international study, universities will be unable to rely on overseas exchange programs to make a significant difference in the educational experience of most students. It also means that the responsibility for providing an enriched and diverse educational experience for the majority of students will reside with the faculty members who remain at home.

If this scenario is representative, then we need to ask an important question: How knowledgeable and informed are faculty about cross-cultural and interdisciplinary issues in their own field or discipline and in the university context? Although we have only anecdotal evidence to answer that question, it is not unreasonable to expect institutional centres with the responsibility for faculty development to think carefully about designing programs to help faculty acquire new types of knowledge and integrate it into their educational practice. If, as some instructional-development professionals contend, the already "converted" attend such continuing professional education courses, how, one might ask, do universities reach faculty who are clearly sceptical? A good starting point would be for universities to publicly recognize and reward the efforts of those who try to internationalize their courses. UPEI, Saskatchewan, and Calgary have already, or will shortly, include in their collective agreements with the faculty associations specific wording to recognize international activities for the purpose of tenure (Timmons, interview, 1999[6]). In addition, it should be possible to acquire special funding to support research programs to identify the dilemmas, document the outcomes, and widely communicate the results.

Arguably, the most important decision a university can make is the one about who to hire for a tenure-track position. It is, therefore, important that the criteria for appointment reflect the changing needs of the university. At the beginning of the 21st century, as the result of large numbers of retirements (in selected fields), the exercise of clarifying the desired qualities of candidates will be enacted many times over as universities find themselves in the position of having to make a substantial number of new appointments. Not since the late 1960s has such an opportunity to diversify the body of knowledge and experience in the academy been encountered. Is it unreasonable for a university to recognize the special merit of candidates who have studied or even just lived overseas or who have otherwise demonstrated their ability to enhance the internationalization of the academy? Recent notices in *University Affairs* would suggest that this opportunity is not being overlooked, at least not by some.

Canadian universities are about to be in a unique position. Many of the early pioneers are still among the ranks or still living close by. At the same time (or very nearly so), the opportunity will become available to appoint fairly large numbers of new staff. The argument that the continuing underfunding of the university would make all these efforts to change more difficult, as valid as it may be, cannot in and of itself mask the potential for most institutions to deliberately reshape themselves, if they wish to do so. Although some institutions and some areas of specialization may be seized by the "idea" of internationalization because of its potential economic benefit to students and to Canada, it is unlikely that members of the academy will fully embrace internationalization and call it their own until they see that the driving force behind it is not jobs, or the economy, but

---

[6] V. Timmons, University of Prince Edward Island, Bachelor of Education with a Specialization in International Education, interview with SB, 5 Feb 1999.

an invigorating intellectual opportunity to enrich their own lives and those of their students. When and where that happens, the universities will in much greater numbers provide the intellectual leadership that is rumoured to be missing from the current dynamic of the universities.

Chapter 4

The Internationalization of University Research in Canada

Yves Gingras, Benoît Godin, and Martine Foisy

Introduction

The issue of the internationalization of universities has recently sur-
faced in the context of discussions of the globalization of trade and
markets. The last few years have seen a number of studies devoted to
this question. Several deal with the attitudes of senior administrators
and professors to this phenomenon (AUCC 1995a; Welch 1997;
Altbach and Lewis 1998) or with the growing presence of foreign students in the educational system (Umakoshi 1997). Yet, because no one
is against virtue, the opinions offered on international exchanges
have for the most part been confined to pious wishes. Other studies,
taking a more quantitative approach, have looked at the actual practice of international cooperation through formal channels, as revealed
in joint publications and programs offered by granting agencies
(Miquel et al. 1989; Leclerc et al. 1991; Luukkonen et al. 1993). There
are of course informal exchanges as well, which means that the
literature-based measure of exchanges used here will underestimate
the full extent of such activities. The advantage of formal exchanges,

however, is that they are easier to measure than informal ones, and they therefore provide a more accurate basis for assessing trends.

Because science is by its very nature international, we should begin by noting that international exchanges in the area of scientific research have been going on for a long time. Without looking as far back as the scientific revolution, we need only consider the 19th century, when many international societies were founded to promote various disciplines in both the physical and the social sciences (Rasmussen 1990; Schroeder-Güdehus 1990). International scientific collaboration is also evident in the publications of the late 19th century (Beaver and Rosen 1978a, b). That said, it is true, as we shall see further on, that international scientific exchanges have grown impressively.

The internationalization of university research is evident in both of its principal components, namely, the training of researchers and the production of knowledge. After looking briefly at the evolution of Canadian programs for promoting such exchanges, we shall devote the rest of this chapter to an analysis of the changes apparent in scientific publications, which are giving an increasingly important place to articles written in collaboration with foreign partners. Although the data here are more fragmentary, we shall also say a few words about the internationalization of sources of research funding available to Canadian researchers.

Internationalizing the training of researchers

The Canadian university community has long been open to international exchanges. The attraction of prestigious institutions, whether American or European, or of famous professors and the absence in Canada of certain specialized skills in some areas of study have encouraged many individuals to look abroad. Among the teaching staff at universities, it has been found that those engaged in research are more likely to participate in international exchanges than those who are primarily oriented toward teaching (Altbach and Lewis 1998). This openness to the outside world is also encouraged by various financial programs that support projects of this kind.

Since the end of the 19th century, young Canadian scientists have been able to benefit from a British funding program, the 1851 Exhibition Scholarship, to go to the United Kingdom for study (Gingras 1991). We may also point to the Rhodes scholarships, granted by the foundation of that name to allow young Commonwealth students to continue their education at Oxford, and other funding for advanced studies offered by the major American universities. These scholarships, however "colonial" they may seem, did in fact help to train generations of Canadian scientists before the creation of the National Research Council of Canada (NRC) in 1916 led to the establishment of a Canadian scholarship system. Francophone students from Quebec were also eligible, after 1920, for European scholarships provided by the provincial government. Originally, these grants were intended solely for use at universities in Paris, reflecting the militant francophilia of that time, but this rule was abolished in due course, allowing recipients to attend the institution of their choice (Chartrand et al. 1987).

In 1948, NRC established a program of postdoctoral fellowships accessible not only to Canadians but also, with few exceptions, to young researchers from the entire international community (Tickner 1991). Making its appearance at the end of World War II, this initiative helped to reestablish the kind of international scientific exchanges that had always been a feature of academic life apart from wartime (Schroeder-Güdehus 1978).

In addition to the higher education fellowships offered by federal and provincial funding agencies to help Canadian recipients study abroad, there are also a great many exchange programs — too numerous to list here — introduced since the 1960s by various agencies, such as provincial and federal ministries, paragovernmental organizations, embassies, university associations, and international organizations for education and youth.

The major agencies that have followed NRC in providing funding for university research in Canada (the Social Sciences and Humanities Research Council of Canada [SSHRC], the Natural Sciences and Engineering Research Council of Canada [NSERC], and the Medical Research Council of Canada [MRC]) also earmark a portion of their budgets for international-collaboration programs (Table 1).

Within SSHRC, these programs can be grouped into two broad categories. On one hand, there are representational activities, such as grants to international associations and conferences and individual funding to participate in conferences abroad. On the other hand, there are cooperative activities that include grants provided in the context of exchanges or bilateral agreements (with the Soviet Union until 1980, with China, Japan, France, etc.) and grants for guest researchers.

Generally speaking, the representational programs account for the major part of SSHRC funding for international relations. Since

Table 1. Allocation of grants by federal funding agencies to international exchange programs, 1978–95.

	MRC			SSHRC			NSERC		
	Total budget, T (thousand $)	Grants for international programs (thousand $)	(% of T)	Total budget, T (thousand $)	Grants for international programs (thousand $)	(% of T)	Total budget, T (thousand $)	Grants for international programs (thousand $)	(% of T)
1978	64 216	73	0.11	30 351	179	0.59	109 706	171	0.16
1979	70 115	107	0.15	32 760	458	1.40	118 400	185	0.16
1980	80 475	128	0.16	37 757	615	1.63	158 950	190	0.12
1981	100 239	146	0.15	42 162	815	1.93	196 944	367	0.19
1982	110 908	847	0.76	51 348	994	1.94	238 702	336	0.14
1983	137 313	542	0.40	54 429	1 100	2.02	274 621	694	0.25
1984	153 191	444	0.29	57 009	1 174	2.06	300 528	854	0.28
1985	157 700	382	0.24	57 234	1 230	2.15	298 976	880	0.29
1986	163 990	546	0.33	64 424	1 543	2.40	308 065	870	0.28
1987	170 467	412	0.24	64 279	1 564	2.43	326 258	862	0.26
1988	183 860	505	0.27	69 260	1 243	1.79	350 246	913	0.26
1989	197 339	576	0.29	74 580	1 275	1.71	375 350	1 188	0.32
1990	235 421	625	0.27	82 048	475	0.58	448 832	1 230	0.27
1991	240 797	1 477	0.61	89 455	475	0.53	465 820	1 233	0.26
1992	249 325	949	0.38	94 887	770	0.81	482 687	1 429	0.30
1993	251 288	356	0.14	93 825	476	0.51	476 725	1 391	0.29
1994	257 634	415	0.16	94 027	415	0.44	474 995	1 154	0.24
1995	243 187	228	0.09	92 119	150	0.16	451 856	511	0.11

Source: Presidents' reports.

Note: MRC, Medical Research Council of Canada; NSERC, Natural Sciences and Engineering Research Council of Canada; SSHRC, Social Sciences and Humanities Research Council of Canada.

they were established, the number of grants for these programs has risen constantly. In 1983/84, for example, 215 individual grants were awarded, allowing Canadians to deliver presentations at 140 international congresses abroad, for a total cost of $382 000; this represented more than a third of the international-relations budget (SSHRC 1984), which amounted to only 2% of the agency's total budget. According to SSHRC's president at that time, if the budget devoted to this program seemed rather modest, "the interest, the results and the prestige" flowing from these grants "are beyond measure." After reaching 2.5% of the budget in 1987, the proportion of grants devoted explicitly to international programs dropped swiftly to less than 0.2% in 1995 (Figure 1). This decline is attributable to the fact that SSHRC cut back considerably on the number of its granting programs and dropped the small peripheral programs, which were felt to be too costly, considering the budget and the number of participants. Since the early 1990s internationalization has been supported through the permanent research funding programs, and this has diminished its visibility.

Within NSERC, cooperation programs take the form of study travel for periods of several weeks. NSERC supports the same formal cooperation agreements as SSHRC. Although this type of exchange program may seem rigid, it is invaluable in some parts of the world where experience has demonstrated that the difficulties facing Canadian researchers can only be resolved with the help of local authorities, which such agreements are intended to ensure (SSHRC 1979). NSERC is also engaged in cooperation research with a broad range of partner countries on all five continents. In 1987, exchange

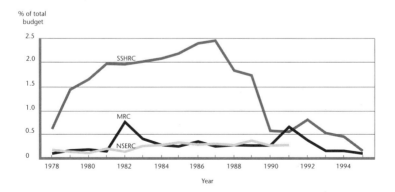

Figure 1. Proportion of federal funding-agency budgets devoted to international programs, 1978–95.

programs with Austria, Brazil, Bulgaria, Czechoslovakia, Japan, Switzerland, and the United Kingdom accounted for nearly $200 000, or about one-quarter of the budget for international programs, a budget that represented only 0.26% of NSERC's resources.

Like SSHRC, NSERC was forced by budget cutbacks in 1996 to terminate the peripheral activities such as the international programs. International activities are now financed through the usual research grants provided to researchers. One of the few surviving programs is the fellowship program, which allows exceptional young foreign researchers to spend a period of study in Canadian universities. This program, which has been in effect since the early 1990s, has the two objectives of creating a network of contacts and attracting foreign researchers to our universities.

At MRC, there has been to date only one international exchange program; it links MRC with the Institute of Health and Medical Research in France. Other exchanges are undertaken under the guest-researchers program, which is aimed at both foreign and Canadian researchers. In the mid-1980s, a program was instituted to provide travel subsidies and support for workshops and conferences. However,

---

Box 1
Scientific cooperation programs in Quebec, 1998

Quebec has always felt the need to have its own science policy. Quebec is the source of the most advanced thinking in Canada about science and technology policy, and it is the only province that has set up a funding agency like the Fonds FCAR. Moreover, Quebec has signed international cooperation agreements in science and technology with several countries or foreign legal jurisdictions. From this viewpoint, Quebec researchers are often envied by their peers in other provinces. These cooperation programs can be divided into two broad categories:

- There are science and technology cooperation programs that allow Quebec and foreign researchers to work together in certain predefined areas of collaboration involving postgraduate students. The program pays their travel and per diem costs. Major programs in operation in 1998 were science and technology cooperation programs with France, Flanders, Italy, Wallonia, other Canadian provinces, and the French-speaking community of Belgium.

- Quebec also has scholarship programs, which can be subdivided into several categories. The postdoctoral fellowship program targets candidates from 16 countries active in scientific research. The Bourses d'excellence program is reserved for master's- or doctoral-degree students from certain developing countries. Shorter term bursaries are offered to foreign partners to pursue their studies here.

Grants are also available for Quebec postgraduate students to study in China, Tunisia, and the French-speaking community of Belgium, and there are postdoctoral fellowships tenable in Catalonia. Finally, students and professors can obtain grants under the doctoral thesis coadviser program between France and Quebec.

it is not possible to identify the portion of that program devoted to international activities.

Provincial governments also offer various exchange programs for researchers, whether they are professors or postgraduate students. These programs are typically designed to reflect the regional affinities and specialties of each province. For example, many of Quebec's programs give preference to France and Belgium for exchanges and scientific collaboration. Alberta, on the other hand, has put great stress on cooperation programs with the Third World, under the aegis of the Canadian International Development Agency (CIDA), in recognition of that province's special research expertise in agriculture. The presence of a sizable Ukrainian community in Alberta has also led to the development of collaboration with Ukraine. Finally, British Columbia has a natural proclivity toward Asia.

83

International scientific exchanges, North–South cooperation in particular, receive significant support under specific programs of the International Development Research Centre and CIDA. Canadian researchers are also active under programs of the World Bank, which promotes international collaboration as well. The nature of these programs and their targets change, depending on the needs of the partners, and it is impossible to list them here.

Generally speaking, the effects of these local initiatives on the internationalization of universities are real but difficult to measure, and the best way to assess the situation is still to examine the evolution of the formal-collaboration programs. As we shall see, the level of collaboration rose sharply in the period 1981–95, but its intensity varied greatly from one discipline to the next.

The growth of international scientific collaboration

As noted, the development of international scientific collaboration has not waited for the introduction of formal cooperation programs. Collaborative links between researchers are often formed at conferences or during postgraduate study abroad and are then kept up over the years. Thus, the fact that foreign students come to Canada and, after completing their studies, return to take up posts in their home country often helps to ensure continuity and further exchanges between professors and students.

We can trace the evolution of this international scientific collaboration by Canadian researchers with the help of data that allow

Box 2
IDRC and the internationalization of Canadian research

Founded in 1970 by an Act of Parliament, the International Development Research Centre (IDRC) receives an annual grant from the Parliament of Canada. It maintains an arm's-length relationship with the government through a Board of Governors, which comprises 11 Canadian and 10 non-Canadian members, including 6 nationals of developing countries.

IDRC's 1993 mission statement, *Empowerment through Knowledge*, states that "research provides the means for the acquisition of appropriate knowledge and, by extension, for development ... . IDRC is dedicated to creating, maintaining and enhancing research capacity in developing regions in response to needs that are determined by the people of those regions in the interest of equity and social justice" (IDRC 1993, p. 7). Although after 1980 IDRC began to provide support for Canadian collaboration through a cooperative-project mechanism, the researchers of developing countries have, as the following shows, received the bulk of funding:

	Researchers (n)	
	1980s	1990s
Total, developing-country researchers	3 655	3 546
Total, Canadian researchers involved	369	359

Although the number of Canadian researchers is modest (10%), the fact that IDRC has supported the creation of networks with researchers in developing countries has undoubtedly contributed to the internationalization of Canadian research, especially in those applied fields of research that have been IDRC's priorities.

A survey of project leaders of the last 25 years (Salewicz and Dwivedi 1996) shows that 53% had PhDs and 57% had studied in Australia, Europe, or North America. These researchers were consequently already "internationalized." Some 69% of all project leaders continued to work either in universities or in research institutions.

IDRC funding, around $60 million a year, represents less (on average) than 10% of the total funding from other Canadian agencies (SSHRC, NSERC, MRC, etc.) but much more than the $2.5 million on average spent on the international programs of those agencies during 1988–95. On balance, IDRC has probably had a much more important impact on internationalizing Canadian university research than the international programs of the other Canadian agencies have had; it is especially important in the fields mentioned below and perhaps contributes most to the growing collaboration with what Gingras et al. (this volume) call "other countries."

The most important fields of IDRC spending during the 1990s were, in order of level of support, health ($108 million), agriculture ($82 million), institutional support ($80 million), economics ($48 million), and education ($43 million):

	Funding (million $)	
	1980s	1990s
Total, IDRC project funds	669.5	614.8
Total, Canadian cooperative projects	96.1	101.7

Given the highly innovative nature of many IDRC projects and their high international visibility, they have not only contributed to international development but also helped developing-country researchers establish their credibility.

With the new joint IDRC–SSHRC program — Canada in the World — which pays for the extra cost of Canadian researchers doing research work in Third World countries, the internationalization of Canadian research is entering a new phase.

Publications

IDRC's database does not permit ready identification of the number of scientific articles, research communications, etc., published in reviews indexed in the Science Citation Index. Nevertheless, it is interesting to note the number of research-based documents produced during the decades 1979–88 and 1989–98: 6 894 and 5 348 documents, respectively (some 540 documents a year for the last 10 years).

Even without the tools to measure IDRC's relative impact on the internationalization of Canadian research, it is clear that it has been important, perhaps most significantly through the creation and internationalization of development research (and the creation and support of national scientific communities in developing countries).

For more complete information, consult IDRC's website: http://www.idrc.ca

us to identify the addresses of authors of scientific articles. As scientific publications are a typical output of university research, this source gives us a very good idea of the degree of internationalization of research. This measure understates the real degree of internationalization of exchanges, but the conclusions to be drawn from it remain, a fortiori, valid.

It must be recalled at the outset that Canada produced nearly 26 000 publications in the natural sciences, engineering, and biomedical sciences in 1995, or 4.2% of all scientific publications in these areas worldwide. (As is usual in bibliometric studies, we retain for analysis only three types of documents covered by the Science Citation Index: articles, notes, and review articles.) This level of output puts Canada in sixth place among member countries of the Organisation for Economic Co-operation and Development in terms of the output of scientific knowledge. Over the period 1981–95, the growth rate of Canadian publications (59%) was higher than the world average (38.4%). In 1995, the universities produced, alone or in collaboration with industry or government laboratories, 82% of all publications. The proportion was 75% in 1980. Universities thus essentially define the tendencies observed in our bibliomtric analysis.

In the humanities and social sciences, in 1995, Canada produced some 5 500 articles in the journals surveyed by the Social Sciences Citation Index. Although this database is less complete than the comparable database in the natural sciences, it still allows us to form a good idea of the trends at play. Thus, the output of articles in the social sciences and humanities rose by 22% over the period 1981–95. International collaboration, as measured by the coauthorship of articles by researchers from different countries, has grown much more

Table 2. Canadian and world publications, by year, 1981–95.

	Canadian publications						World publications		
	Humanities and social sciences			Pure sciences and engineering			Pure sciences and engineering		
		With international collaboration			With international collaboration			With international collaboration	
	N	n	% of N	N	n	% of N	N	n	% of N
1981	4 478	493	11.0	16 273	2 761	17.0	389 301	22 440	5.8
1982	4 659	527	11.3	17 062	3 017	17.1	402 105	24 666	6.1
1983	4 808	534	11.1	18 235	3 135	17.2	417 267	26 902	6.4
1984	4 845	539	11.1	19 205	3 588	18.7	425 054	28 958	6.8
1985	5 099	545	10.7	20 113	3 742	18.6	434 144	30 888	7.1
1986	5 144	629	12.2	20 274	3 973	19.6	428 027	33 441	7.8
1987	5 155	619	12.0	21 360	4 332	20.3	438 061	35 742	8.2
1988	5 060	624	12.3	21 456	4 530	21.1	449 681	38 982	8.7
1989	5 296	663	12.5	22 269	4 942	22.2	463 707	42 351	9.1
1990	5 304	786	14.8	22 979	5 613	24.4	477 816	47 221	9.9
1991	5 446	791	14.5	23 662	5 956	25.2	489 709	54 010	11.0
1992	5 506	796	14.5	24 872	6 737	27.1	498 290	60 556	12.2
1993	5 685	905	15.9	25 303	7 259	28.7	514 379	66 435	12.9
1994	5 573	955	17.1	26 043	7 660	29.4	534 525	73 309	13.7
1995	5 467	967	17.7	25 882	7 955	30.7	539 157	78 255	14.5

rapidly than the total output of articles. In fact, we note over the same period a growth in Canadian international collaboration of 188%, or three times the general publication growth rate. Yet, this was less than the average world growth rate, which was 248%. As shown in Table 2, the growth of international cooperation in Canada has been regular. In sciences and engineering, it rose from 17% of total publications in 1981 to 30.7% in 1995, whereas in the social sciences and humanities it grew by 7%, from 11% to 17.7%, over the same period. In these areas, objects of research are generally more regional, and this is reflected in a lower potential for international collaboration.

The trend to internationalization in research is more clearly pronounced in the pure sciences and engineering, and the databases are also more complete for these disciplines: we shall therefore concentrate on these latter areas to analyze the phenomenon.

As can be seen from Figure 2, the Canadian rate of international collaboration is twice as high as that for the world as a whole, which stood at 14.5% in 1995. In this respect, Canada's performance is consistent with that of other small countries (measured by gross domestic product), which have a greater tendency to collaborate with foreigners than do the larger countries, as they need to frequently look beyond their own borders in search of the expertise that may be missing at home. The fact that large countries like the United States have more domestic resources at their disposal has meant that their

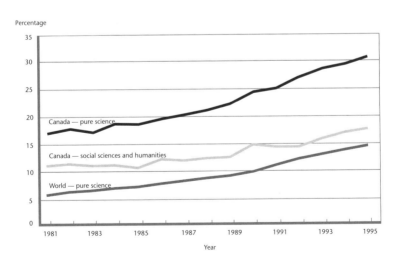

Figure 2. Percentage of Canadian publications written in international collaboration.

researchers have less interest in international exchanges. The surveys conducted by the Carnegie Foundation for the Advancement of Teaching in 1991 and 1992 highlighted the fact that American researchers were much more insular than their colleagues surveyed in 13 other countries (Altbach and Lewis 1998).

The rapid growth in international collaboration since the beginning of the 1990s has been due more to the greater ease of communication (through the Internet, for example) than to the impact of official programs in support of exchanges and collaboration, which, as we have seen, have generally been declining in importance during this same period. However, it is clear that these technical factors are insufficient to explain the whole picture and that other variables must be looked at, including the size of the country and its cultural traditions.

Diversifying international partnerships

In Canada, as elsewhere, the choice of foreign partners seems to be explained essentially by four factors: the size of the collaborating country (and of that country's scientific community), geographic proximity, language, and traditions as they have evolved over history (Luukkonen et al. 1992). Thus, the United States, which is contiguous with Canada and is the world's largest producer of scientific knowledge, is Canada's first partner in collaboration. It is followed, far behind, by the United Kingdom and by France, the former mother countries of Canada.

Over the period 1981–95, we can see, however, that Canada's international scientific collaboration has diversified. In 1981, the United States accounted for 50% of publications written in collaboration with Canadians. In 1995, this proportion stood at only 39.2%. The diversification of collaboration has not necessarily favoured the major countries of Europe, however. Collaboration with Germany has grown, reaching 5.4% in 1995, but collaboration with the United Kingdom has declined, dropping from 11.1% to 7.9%, and that with France has stagnated at around 7.0%. The most significant growth in collaborative work is seen with researchers from the smaller European countries, such as Italy and Spain, and with those from Asian countries, particularly Japan and China. In fact, apart from those from Japan, these new partners were nowhere to be seen in 1980, except for a few publications. Yet, in 1995, they accounted for more than 5% of collaborative undertakings.

In the social sciences and humanities, the data for 1995 suggest that Canadian researchers collaborated mostly with researchers from the United States (56%), the United Kingdom (10%), and France (4%). Figures 3 and 4 show that between 1981 and 1995 the share of the United States declined gradually, whereas that of the other countries remained stable, as was the case for the physical sciences. Thus, a diversification of international collaboration was occurring in both the physical sciences and the humanities and social sciences.

89

International collaboration by the provinces

Overall, provincial rates of international collaboration are roughly comparable to the Canadian average (Table 3). In pure sciences and engineering, only Saskatchewan (24.6%), Newfoundland (25.5%), and Prince Edward Island (20.7%) had rates much below that average in 1995. In the humanities and social sciences that year only Newfoundland and New Brunswick fell significantly short of the Canadian average.

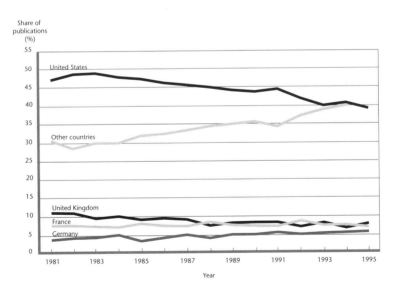

Figure 3. Principal countries for Canadian international collaboration: pure sciences and engineering.

90

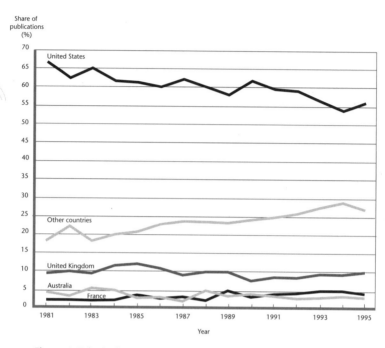

Figure 4. Principal countries for Canadian international collaboration: humanities and social sciences.

Table 3. Publications written in international collaboration, by province and proportion, 1995.

	Pure sciences and engineering		Humanities and social sciences	
	(n)	(%)	(n)	(%)
Prince Edward Island	92	20.7	—	—
Ontario	11 547	31.2	482	18.2
British Columbia	3 363	33.9	140	18.4
Saskatchewan	959	24.6	26	21.1
Nova Scotia	964	31.7	32	14.3
Alberta	2 980	29.2	86	15.7
Newfoundland	364	25.5	4	6.3
Manitoba	1 088	28.2	33	19.9
Quebec	6 471	30.8	211	17.7
New Brunswick	356	28.9	4	6.1
Canada	25 882	30.1	967	17.7

In the pure sciences and engineering, the first partner for all provinces, as for Canada as a whole, is the United States. The second and third partners, however, differ depending on the province. The United Kingdom is the second partner for a great many provinces, but France holds this honour in Quebec and New Brunswick. Similarly, Germany occupies the third rank for more than half the provinces, in fact, for all provinces from Ontario west (Table 4). In the humanities and social sciences, the situation is similar, except that the third partner is no longer Germany but Australia (Table 5).

The internationalization of disciplines

Research exhibits different patterns of international collaboration, depending on the field. In 1995, for example, the greatest degree of international collaboration was to be found in mathematics (46.1%), followed by physics (43.4%), Earth sciences (36.6%), and biomedical research (33.4%). Falling below the general average for all disciplines, we find clinical medicine (28.2%), engineering (26.3%), chemistry (25.2%), and biology (21.6%) (Table 6). The more "applied," and hence localized, nature of many of the specialities linked to these disciplines may explain this lower tendency to engage in international collaboration.

In the humanities and social sciences (Table 7), the variations between the disciplines were much more pronounced, and there was a less systematic growth trend than in the pure sciences and engineering.

The relative propensity for international collaboration is easier to observe if we consider the intensity index of international collaboration. This index is obtained by dividing the share of international collaboration for each discipline by the share of Canadian publications in that same discipline. As Table 8 shows, only four out of eight disciplines have an index greater than unity, which implies that there is a stronger propensity to produce publications through international collaboration in these areas: mathematics (2.0), physics (1.42), Earth sciences (1.19), and biomedical research (1.08). In the humanities and social sciences, it is economics that has the highest index, followed by administrative sciences, archeology, psychiatry, anthropology, and psychology. The areas for which collaboration is virtually nil are literature, philosophy, history, communications, and the fine arts. The local character of studies in these areas explains this performance in part, but it must also be recalled that these are disciplines in which most articles are products of a single author. In the social sciences, for example, 47% of articles published in 1995 had only one author, whereas this proportion for the humanities was 90%. This means that in these areas, international collaboration, when it exists at all, takes

Table 4. International collaborations, by province: pure sciences and engineering, 1995.

	ON	PQ	BC	AB	MB	NS	SK	NB	NF	PE	NT	YT	Total	Canada
United States (n)	1 998	991	640	462	172	161	139	51	38	11	1	1	4 665	4 152
% (row)	42.8	21.2	13.7	9.9	3.7	3.5	3.0	1.1	0.8	0.2	0.0	0.0	36.4	39.2
% (column)	38.8	32.7	37.4	35.5	30.8	44.7	40.9	38.6	35.5	47.8	33.3	100.0		
United Kingdom (n)	468	196	145	114	39	31	19	7	9	3	2	0	1 144	832
% (row)	40.9	17.1	12.7	10.0	3.4	2.7	1.7	0.6	0.8	0.3	0.2	0.0	8.9	7.9
% (column)	9.1	6.5	8.5	8.8	7.0	8.6	5.6	5.3	8.4	13.0	66.7	0.0		
France (n)	269	412	102	75	12	17	8	10	8	0	0	0	913	755
% (row)	29.5	45.1	11.2	8.2	1.3	1.9	0.9	1.1	0.9	0.0	0.0	0.0	7.1	7.1
% (column)	5.2	13.6	6.0	5.8	2.1	4.7	2.4	7.6	7.5	0.0	0.0	0.0		
Germany (n)	297	166	105	99	35	16	17	6	3	1	0	0	745	575
% (row)	39.9	22.3	14.1	13.3	4.7	2.1	2.3	0.8	0.4	0.1	0.0	0.0	5.8	5.4
% (column)	5.8	5.5	6.1	7.6	6.3	4.4	5.0	4.5	2.8	4.3	0.0	0.0		
Other countries (n)	2 123	1 261	719	550	301	135	157	58	49	8	0	0	5 365	6 314
% (row)	39.6	23.5	13.4	10.3	5.6	3.8	2.9	1.2	0.9	0.1	0.0	0.0	41.8	59.6
% (column)	41.2	41.6	42.0	42.3	53.8	37.5	46.2	43.9	45.8	34.8	0.0	0.0		
Total (N)	5 155	3 030	1 711	1 300	559	360	340	132	107	23	3	1	12 832	10 587
% (row)	40.2	23.6	13.3	10.1	4.4	2.8	2.6	1.0	0.8	0.2	0.0	0.0		

Table 5. International collaborations, by province: humanities and social sciences, 1995.

	ON	PQ	BC	AB	MB	NS	SK	NF	NB	Total	Canada
United States (*n*)	307	128	96	60	15	15	13	4	4	642	608
% (row)	47.8	19.9	15.0	9.3	2.3	2.3	2.0	0.6	0.6	56.0	55.5
% (column)	55.3	54.7	60.8	64.5	40.5	42.9	50.5	80.0	100.0		
United Kingdom (*n*)	63	1	16	8	5	7	4	0	0	118	111
% (row)	53.4	12.7	13.6	6.8	4.2	5.9	3.4	0.0	0.0	10.3	10.1
% (column)	11.4	6.4	10.1	8.6	13.5	20.0	15.4	0.0	0.0		
France (*n*)	12	26	4	2	2	1	0	0	0	47	45
% (row)	25.5	55.3	8.5	4.3	4.3	2.1	0.0	0.0	0.0	4.1	4.1
% (column)	2.2	11.1	2.5	2.2	5.4	2.9	0.0	0.0	0.0		
Australia (*n*)	14	4	9	4	1	4	3	0	0	39	37
% (row)	35.9	10.3	23.1	10.3	2.6	10.3	7.7	0.0	0.0	3.4	3.4
% (column)	2.5	1.7	5.7	4.3	2.7	11.4	11.5	0.0	0.0		
Other countries (*n*)	159	61	33	19	14	8	6	1	0	301	294
% (row)	52.8	20.3	11.0	6.3	4.7	2.7	2.0	0.3	0.0	26.2	26.8
% (column)	28.6	26.1	20.9	20.4	37.8	22.9	23.1	20.0	0.0		
Total (*N*)	555	234	158	93	37	35	26	5	4	1 147	1 095
% (row)	48.4	20.4	13.8	8.1	3.2	3.1	2.3	0.4	0.3		

Table 6. Evolution of international collaboration, by discipline: pure sciences and engineering, 1981–95.

	Mathematics	Physics	Earth sciences	Biomedical research	Clinical medicine	Engineering	Chemistry	Biology
				Proportion of international collaboration (%)				
1981	33.6	26.4	21.7	17.8	13.5	16.9	16.0	11.2
1982	33.3	26.1	23.8	18.8	15.0	20.3	16.6	10.3
1983	34.3	23.6	22.6	17.9	14.7	16.9	17.7	11.0
1984	42.4	25.4	26.0	19.5	14.7	20.9	18.0	13.0
1985	38.7	25.5	25.6	21.0	15.6	17.1	19.5	10.8
1986	39.3	27.1	25.2	22.2	16.8	19.7	19.2	12.3
1987	44.3	29.5	27.4	22.0	17.7	18.9	18.2	14.0
1988	42.3	30.2	28.8	22.2	19.3	20.6	18.8	13.5
1989	41.0	34.3	28.0	23.6	20.0	21.4	18.8	13.9
1990	43.8	37.5	32.3	25.2	21.0	21.8	22.7	17.0
1991	44.2	36.7	34.1	25.9	21.4	24.1	23.1	18.6
1992	45.1	38.0	34.8	28.7	24.1	26.6	25.4	18.3
1993	50.0	42.1	35.4	30.1	26.3	23.9	24.6	18.6
1994	49.0	42.7	35.8	31.9	26.7	23.7	24.6	19.5
1995	46.1	43.4	36.6	33.4	28.2	26.3	25.2	21.6

Table 7. Evolution of international collaboration, by discipline: humanities and social sciences, 1981–95.

	Proportion of international collaboration (%)														
	1981	1982	1983	1984	1985	1986	1987	1988	1989	1990	1991	1992	1993	1994	1995
Anthropology	8.7	13.5	7.7	6.7	13.0	6.9	8.8	3.0	22.2	11.4	8.0	14.3	6.8	17.1	23.9
Archeology	14.3	—	5.4	22.6	8.7	23.7	26.3	17.2	28.2	22.0	21.7	22.9	37.5	36.2	28.6
Fine arts	1.6	5.1	3.0	5.0	5.2	—	2.5	0.8	1.1	2.9	5.1	—	3.8	4.9	9.3
Library science	—	5.1	2.7	6.1	4.3	7.7	2.9	1.4	5.1	7.6	11.1	4.3	7.1	4.7	4.5
Communication	18.2	24.1	15.0	9.1	13.0	17.6	15.4	3.7	—	—	15.4	9.5	15.8	8.3	9.8
Law	2.6	15.3	3.4	3.8	6.7	8.6	10.8	13.0	17.0	14.1	18.4	7.5	4.0	4.9	9.8
Economics	25.8	21.6	27.3	24.4	27.7	33.6	30.5	29.0	30.9	31.8	32.3	31.7	36.7	39.3	32.5
Education	12.4	8.5	13.6	12.4	7.8	12.1	10.8	8.9	10.0	13.7	11.6	11.6	14.6	14.5	15.5
Geography	17.9	10.4	10.8	13.8	10.1	8.3	8.8	14.7	9.6	10.8	15.3	11.0	12.4	10.6	14.1
History	1.9	3.8	2.8	2.9	1.8	1.6	3.6	5.4	2.6	4.5	3.5	3.1	6.9	7.4	2.9
Linguistics	6.3	11.8	12.4	19.0	8.0	15.8	7.6	10.1	25.8	20.3	8.6	17.3	11.3	15.9	15.9
Literature	1.3	1.5	0.4	1.1	1.4	0.6	0.6	0.7	1.4	0.7	1.5	0.7	0.6	0.5	1.2
Psychology	15.8	17.3	15.7	13.4	15.8	15.8	15.4	15.4	15.5	18.4	17.8	16.1	18.5	19.6	22.1
Philosophy	5.2	3.8	3.0	3.4	2.7	4.3	4.1	2.1	3.0	4.1	2.6	5.3	2.7	4.1	2.9
Psychiatry	10.0	6.5	14.8	3.0	10.3	8.7	9.9	20.9	15.0	7.8	18.2	18.2	21.2	22.5	25.9
Health	6.6	12.4	7.0	7.3	5.2	9.7	7.5	6.9	7.4	10.7	12.8	11.6	13.7	11.8	13.9
Political science	4.1	6.6	6.7	8.3	9.6	5.4	6.0	8.0	11.5	11.0	7.4	5.8	10.8	12.3	14.2
Administrative science	16.7	17.0	13.5	18.4	20.6	23.5	19.4	22.2	17.5	21.4	22.5	26.1	22.2	28.9	29.8
Sociology	17.4	7.4	13.0	7.4	5.1	17.1	18.9	7.8	12.8	10.6	13.7	9.6	12.0	12.7	13.6
Social work	6.7	7.7	7.1	—	4.0	4.0	4.2	12.0	7.1	18.2	4.0	8.6	28.6	18.2	8.0

Table 8. Internationalization index, by discipline, 1995.

	Share of production (%)	Share of international collaboration (%)	Internationalization index[a]
Pure sciences and engineering			
Clinical medicine	28.0	25.7	0.92
Biomedical research	15.6	16.9	1.08
Biology	11.5	8.1	0.70
Physics	9.5	13.5	1.42
Engineering	8.7	7.5	0.86
Chemistry	8.6	7.1	0.86
Earth sciences	8.5	10.1	1.19
Mathematics	1.5	3.0	2.0
Humanities and social sciences			
Psychology	23.4	31.6	1.35
Literature	11.6	0.9	0.08
Health	9.8	8.3	0.85
Economics	8.4	16.6	1.98
Administrative science	7.5	13.7	1.82
Education	6.3	6.0	0.95
Geography	4.4	3.8	0.86
History	4.1	0.7	0.18
Philosophy	3.2	0.6	0.18
Political science	3.2	2.8	0.87
Sociology	3.0	2.5	0.83
Psychiatry	2.6	4.1	1.58
Fine arts	2.5	0.7	0.30
Linguistics	2.1	2.0	0.97
Law	1.2	0.7	0.60
Social work	1.2	0.6	0.49
Archeology	1.2	2.0	1.75
Anthropology	1.1	1.6	1.46
Library science	1.0	0.6	0.57
Communication	0.5	0.1	0.28

[a] Share of international collaboration for each discipline divided by the share of Canadian publications in that discipline.

the form, not of copublications, but of informal contacts during conferences or of exchanges of professors and students.

Finally, it should be noted that in the pure sciences and engineering, articles written in international collaboration generally enjoy greater visibility than articles written by Canadians alone, as measured by the impact factor of the journals in which those articles appear. In 1995, for example, the average impact factor for all Canadian publications was 3.07, but it was 2.95 for those containing only Canadian addresses and 3.35 for those written in collaboration with foreign researchers.

Box 3
Internationalization and postgraduate programs

In the social sciences and humanities, in which the objects of study are locally and culturally determined, research is very often carried out through comparative studies. Consequently, it is necessary to develop special programs to achieve an international dimension within postgraduate programs in such disciplines. A look at programs in literature, history, and political science gives us a good illustration of the way research is influencing the internationalization of programs. In the natural and applied sciences, in which the objects of research are much more linked to the fundamental laws of nature and, for that reason, are more universal, we find no specific international programs, even though very often the international aspects are literally built into the objects studied. This is clearly the case in mathematics and physics but is also true of fields such as geology and engineering. An analysis of master's and doctoral theses is needed to compare the realities of content independent of the formal structure of programs.

97

Internationalizing sources of funding

The worldwide tendency in scientific collaboration demonstrated by these data on publications is also reflected in the level of funding available to researchers. Historically, governments have tended to allocate their funding to research performed by their own scientists. Access to foreign sources of finance is a more recent phenomenon than international collaboration itself, and it is still at a relatively low level. Nonetheless, it has been growing, and all indications are that this trend will continue in the future. Thus, for example, the European Union recently opened its Framework program to researchers of several countries, including Canada and the United States.

Although no reliable data on this question are available for Canada as a whole, figures gathered for Quebec show that between 1984/85 and 1995/96, the number of contracts and grants of foreign origin received by university researchers increased 8-fold while the value of such transactions increased 10-fold (in constant dollars) (Table 9).

Conclusions

The data presented in this chapter confirm the notion that the internationalization of trade affects not only the world of economics but also that of universities. Both in the area of training — where Canada has from the beginning been very open to, not to say dependent on,

Table 9. Research contracts and grants received by Quebec universities from foreign private-sector sources, 1984/85 to 1995/96.

	Contracts		Grants	
	(*n*)	(thousand $)[a]	(*n*)	(thousand $)[a]
1984/85	12	315	44	1 048
1986/87	34	1 387	59	2 094
1988/89	42	1 558	111	2 946
1989/90	50	1 470	121	3 007
1990/91	79	1 743	135	4 098
1991/92	90	1 904	184	6 649
1992/93	101	2 573	200	7 548
1993/94	222	5 686	207	7 166
1994/95	244	8 054	195	7 045
1995/96	252	7 440	197	7 164

Source: Quebec Ministry of Education. SIRU system. Special request of the Quebec Council of Science and Technology.
[a] In constant 1996 dollars.

foreign expertise — and in that of research practices, we find significant growth in international collaboration in the last 20 years. In the sectors in which these practices are most pronounced, such as in mathematics, we may have approached something of a plateau. In other sectors, however, there may still be room for growth in international exchanges. Finally, the most interesting phenomenon, one that deserves to be monitored closely, is the tendency of funding sources to be international. This suggests that internationalization has yielded to globalization, with its characteristic weakening of national frontiers.

Chapter 5

The Dilemma of Institutional Structures

Howard C. Clark

The context outlined in Chapter 1 describes the many factors presently affecting the institution of the university, an institution that has been preserved and has survived almost uniquely over many centuries. However, survival has only been possible because of a willingness to change, sometimes reluctantly, in response to the pressures of a changing external world. In this chapter, I am concerned with institutional structures and decision-making processes as they relate to internationalization, the ways in which they have developed, and the changes that may be needed to ensure their success. But first, we need to understand how the Canadian university has changed over the last 40 to 50 years and how its present state reflects both internal and external conditions.

As the introductory chapter demonstrates, Canadian universities have much to be proud of; indeed, as a group, they rank among the world's best. However, close examination of these universities reveals a number of features that largely result from their remarkable transformation over the last 40 to 50 years.

Size and coherence

First, the nature of the institution has changed fundamentally, as a result of the growth in size of all Canadian universities. The University of Western Ontario (UWO) today, with a full-time student body of 18 000, bears little structural similarity to the small college it was in 1950, when it had about 2 500 students. The latter rightly considered itself a distinct community, with considerable coherence; people knew each other and shared the successes and problems of the community. With few exceptions, the much larger Canadian university has very little sense of community; faculty members and students know colleagues in their own departments and perhaps in some related departments but know little about the rest of the institution. Instead of a single community that can agree, perhaps with difficulty, on common goals and objectives, each Canadian university is a multiuniversity, comprising a set of separate, isolated minicommunities, whose interests and goals may be quite different and may even conflict.

Diversity

A further contributor to the loss of community in Canadian universities is the much greater diversity found in the institution. The range of subject matter covered by the many departments and schools is enormous, from philosophy, to geology, to women's studies, to engineering, to management, to a wide variety of other professional schools. It is obviously difficult to establish a common intellectual ground across such diversity — a diversity not found in universities in the 1930s. Both the faculty and student bodies are much less homogeneous in terms of ethnic, racial, and socioeconomic backgrounds, reflecting profound changes in Canadian society over the past 50 years. In contrast, a notable feature of Canadian universities in recent years has been the decline in the percentages of international students, to less than 5% in 1995. This contrasts with the experience of other countries, such as Australia and the United States, where the percentages of international students have continued to rise quite sharply.

Financial

Today's university resembles that of the early 1950s in at least one important respect: the lack of adequate financial resources severely restricts the institution. In the early 1950s, finances were still constrained after World War II, despite the considerable influx of veterans into the universities. In the 1990s, the need to balance government budgets and eliminate debt led to severe reductions in funding. However, it should not be forgotten that in the intervening years, both federal and provincial governments poured vast amounts of tax dollars into the universities; and, of course, generous funding in the late 1950s and 1960s contributed significantly to the government's current debt problems! But it remains a fact that, in absolute terms, the Canadian universities have enormous financial resources available to them and are very well endowed relative to those of most other countries.

101

Human resources

A factor seriously affecting Canadian universities, at present, relates to the age distribution of faculty members. Especially during the 1960s and 1970s, when the rate of university expansion was greatest, the universities made large numbers of faculty appointments. This large cohort of faculty dominates the age profile of the total professorate in Canada, as it does in many other countries. But this cohort is now aged between 50 and 65 years, and its members are fast approaching retirement. They are also now struggling with much heavier teaching loads and have less time for research and reflection. Although it may be an overstatement, some would claim that this has resulted in an erosion of intellectual vigour in the universities. As mentioned in Chapter 2, an increasing number in this cohort are opting for early retirement in response to generous early-retirement packages that many universities have introduced to reduce costs. And this significant loss of experienced and skilled faculty members must weaken the university, even if only temporarily.

Although retirements are occurring rapidly, the number of replacement appointments that institutions are able to finance is very small. Nevertheless, the proportion of able, young, and enthusiastic new faculty is now steadily increasing, and their influence on the university, now only just being felt, will become dominant over the next 10 years. Canadian universities are currently undergoing a major transition. At the moment, perhaps, they are somewhat weakened intellectually and less proactive than in the 1970s, but their considerable potential for revitalization is becoming evident.

Governance

The governance of today's Canadian university is also very different from that of 1950. At that time, presidents and deans had considerable authority and, often — in some cases, perhaps, all too often — made decisions with little or no consultation. Today, through intricate committee structures at the departmental and faculty levels, through full control of the academic senate or its equivalent, through membership on boards of governors, faculty members and the students as well, to a lesser extent, have very substantial governing powers. The scope of a university president's authority is limited to a degree that is surprising to the business community and the general public, and this is also the case for the governing powers of boards of governors, which have been substantially eroded. Governance is achieved by consensus, usually formalized in senates and boards in voting procedures. Given the diversity within the institution, along with the many different and often conflicting interests, consensus can be extremely difficult to achieve. Some would argue that this is appropriate for an academic institution, where, without consensus, no action should be taken. But all too often this means that decisions are taken by default; in a rapidly changing world, the university is seen as reactionary and out of touch with reality.

With decision-making thus constrained, the task of leadership is both frustrating and extremely challenging, especially when it comes to setting institutional priorities. This is perhaps best illustrated by the fact that institutions only very rarely concede that they are less than excellent in any subject area or suggest that specific programs be dropped to allow the institution to concentrate on its recognized strengths. Even now, when essentially all universities are vocal about the inadequacy of funding, proposals for new academic programs are still being approved, but consensus is only extremely rarely reached on proposals that an existing program should be terminated. In such a climate, institutional leaders can ensure that internationalization is a strategic objective for the institution, but to put an operational plan in place to achieve this objective is a far greater challenge, as competing vested interests can frustrate leadership and make decision-making almost impossible. Still more important is the fact that a major institutional initiative can only succeed at the grass-roots level if faculty members can see that the reward system recognizes and values participation in that initiative. Nevertheless, smaller initiatives can be, and are, successfully undertaken at the departmental and faculty levels. They do not require institutional approval or support, and they often proceed with little recognition from the institution; indeed, it is not unknown for people at the senior levels of the university to know nothing whatsoever about such a new activity! The structures and decision-making processes of today's Canadian universities thus allow for incremental growth, largely from the grass roots, often unplanned, and certainly not institutionally coordinated. But major changes such as institutional internationalization are extremely difficult to initiate.

External pressures

In addition to having to deal with reduced levels of government funding, Canadian universities have experienced pressures from many other agencies over the past 50 years that have brought about changes in attitudes and policies. Very significant relationships have been those with the Canadian International Development Agency (CIDA) and the International Development Research Centre (IDRC). The former has been the principal source of funding for many of the universities' international involvements. Consequently, changes in Canadian foreign policy and in its development aid programs brought changes within the universities. The increased CIDA emphasis on project management in the 1970s led to the creation of international-program offices in universities, which had significant managerial responsibilities. With the policy change in CIDA's University Partnerships in Cooperation and Development (UPCD) program, it has shifted the emphasis to longer term, multidisciplinary, cooperative projects that are institutionally based and managed. IDRC, on the other hand, has played a very significant role, although with far fewer resources, in encouraging development research within the universities.

Of particular importance in the 1950s, 1960s, and into the 1970s were the relationships between the universities and nongovernmental organizations (NGOs), such as the Canadian University Service Overseas (CUSO) and the World University Service of Canada (WUSC). These were of course initially student organizations, and through students' enthusiastic support for them and students' international participation through them, a great deal of the Canadian universities' commitment to international development emerged. These relationships are still very important. Moreover, although they are usually unofficial, they still provide excellent opportunities for students to gain international experience. Certainly, such relationships have had an enormous influence on attitudes in Canadian universities.

A further influence over the past 50 years has been the Association of Universities and Colleges of Canada (AUCC); this voluntary organization, to which all of the about 90 universities and colleges in Canada belong, went through a major restructuring in the early 1970s and became a very effective voice in Ottawa for the universities. Also, in the 1980s, AUCC formed an international division, owing in part to encouragement from CIDA. This division was developed to undertake international projects funded by CIDA and other international agencies on behalf of the Canadian universities. At first, it was — as some correctly saw — acting as a direct competitor of individual institutions. But the division has come to play a very important role as the policies of CIDA and other agencies have evolved. For example, CIDA has steadily placed more emphasis on country-to-country programs, and the AUCC division has been highly effective in developing the relationships between Canadian and Chinese universities and now manages an extensive China program. It has, in this case, helped to focus Canadian universities' interest on China, which would not have occurred otherwise, and has also encouraged the universities to work together more cooperatively.

With these comments in mind, let us now turn to the central issues of this chapter: How can the university as an institution provide intellectual leadership in the new global society? What changes are needed to internal structures and decision-making processes so that the institution can be genuinely internationalized? I make three major assumptions in addressing these issues. First, the definition of *internationalization* is only intellectually and morally valid if it means that the universities show a greater concern for the entire global society. It is not intellectually or morally valid to define *internationalization* only in terms of linkages with people and institutions in the already developed world; it must also include linkages with, and growing knowledge of, developing societies, such as those in Asia and the underdeveloped areas of Africa and Latin America. Also, it must not be based on the automatic acceptance of the Western capitalistic socioeconomic view of the world. The urge to internationalize must come from the university's basic intellectual mission: to search for truth on a genuinely global basis. Second, resources have to be allocated to achieve internationalization, and this is essentially an internal issue, not just one of the universities' waiting for external bodies to provide additional funds. Third, I assume that the university can successfully address internationalization on an institutional basis and that an uncoordinated, piecemeal approach by faculties and departments can only cause confusion and create problems. However, an institutional approach may not be possible; if it is not, then this raises troubling questions about the future feasibility of any of the universities' institutional initiatives.

The threefold mission of the university consists of education, research, and outreach, or service. In terms of internationalization, the university needs first to consider possible changes to the structures and decision-making processes for each of these functions.

Education

The universities in Canada and elsewhere are under great external pressure, and rightly so, to produce genuinely "internationalized" graduates, ones who are globally knowledgeable and ready to be citizens of the world. This requires internationalization of the entire curriculum for all students. But the institution does not generally control or manage the curriculum. In most Canadian universities, control of the curriculum and its content lies almost entirely in the hands of individual faculty members, or perhaps individual departments. This is at the heart of academic freedom — the right of faculty members to determine what they will teach — but it means that few mechanisms are in place to encourage faculty members to give the curriculum a greater international perspective.

It would be wrong to suggest, however, that very significant changes have not already occurred. In the 1950s, the university curriculum was traditional and Eurocentric and seriously recognized only Western culture. This is no longer the case: new programs now reflect a diversity of cultures; a much increased range of languages is offered; and the content of many courses has become more international, albeit to widely differing degrees. And, in a few instances, there are also structural means to achieving greater internationalization more quickly. At least one Canadian university requires a detailed institutional review of the nature and content of all courses as they are introduced or changed; in this way, it is possible to directly insist on greater international content.

However, Canadian universities have not yet begun to address the issue of evaluation: To what extent has the curriculum been internationalized in recent years? What evidence is there that today's graduates are indeed more internationalized than those of the 1950s? How can the effect of future curricular changes best be evaluated? These issues are much more fully discussed in Chapter 9. It is important to stress here that the lack of interest that is presently shown by Canadian universities in questions of institutional evaluation stands in stark contrast to the situation in other Western countries. In Australia, Europe, New Zealand, and the United Kingdom, universities are undertaking not only discussion on an institutional basis but also substantial action to assess, monitor, and improve the level of internationalization, usually at the insistence of the governments of these countries.

Numerous specifically institutional initiatives can be taken to advance internationalization, including the following:

+ *Area studies* — Programs that focus on a particular country, geographic region, or international theme can now be found in virtually every Canadian university. Although most of these programs certainly produce graduates with genuine international awareness, the numbers of students enrolled in such programs tends to be small and both the program and its students often form nonmainstream enclaves outside the traditional departmental and discipline-oriented boundaries, as in many other small nontraditional programs.

+ *Student exchange programs* — These probably offer the best and most direct approach to the internationalization of undergraduate students, as students actually live and study for a time in another country and culture. Such opportunities are usually an outcome of an exchange agreement between a Canadian university and a sister institution overseas. The number of these agreements is growing so rapidly that some universities now claim to have well more than 100 of them in place. However, for these agreements to be effective over the long term, the university must structure itself to meet its responsibilities to students. Key requirements include the following:

  ◇ Institutional review and approval of all new agreements;

  ◇ An effective monitoring system to determine periodically whether each agreement is operating effectively;

  ◇ A willingness and ability to meet special student needs (special counseling. assistance with housing, adequate language training, etc.); and

  ◇ Genuinely interested and involved faculty members, willing to spend time at both institutions.

To meet such requirements, a specific structure needs to be in place. Although there is further discussion of student exchange programs elsewhere in this book (Chapter 9), I will describe a suitable university structure later in this chapter. At this point, I only need to point out that at present, in many universities, exchange agreements can be the responsibility of separate faculties or departments, with little if any coordination or institutional monitoring. In a minority of cases, however, institutional responsibility for all exchange agreements is in the hands of a single administrative office.

✦ *Common courses and shared degree programs* — The possibilities for Canadian and overseas universities to share courses, particularly at the postgraduate level, and whole degree programs are enormous. Such arrangements do, however, require a well-established relationship between two institutions, to the extent that they each understand the other's academic culture and standards. Again, however, such arrangements should be formalized on an institutional basis and not left to uncoordinated departmental or faculty initiatives.

There is also the possibility of "twinning," whereby two universities (Canadian and overseas) agree that a complete program will be shared, along with the authorization of the final degree. For example, undergraduates might take their first 2 years of an undergraduate degree program at a Malaysian university and the last 2 years at a Canadian institution. The University of Calgary, among others, is much involved in twinning. Again, the institutional requirements are considerable, and special needs must be met for students to succeed in such programs; the institution is responsible for ensuring that all of the necessary arrangements are in place.

✦ *Cooperation with the private sector* — Many consider university cooperation with the private sector to have great potential for establishing connections and internationalizing Canadian universities. Several Canadian business schools, including those at McGill and the University of British Columbia (UBC), are already active in Asia, offering business programs, usually drawing on the support of major Canadian corporations already operating in Asia. Formal cooperation between businesses and universities would be valuable in the case of major Canadian development projects or investments that have significant educational or training components. Such linkages

108

between business and academia require a considerable degree of trust and understanding and, very important, a joint long-term commitment. Additionally, the universities will need to be more entrepreneurial and will require an appropriately structured management unit to link comfortably with business.

✦ *Marketing of education* — The marketing of places in programs, at full cost, especially professional programs, is one proactive method to enhance the international dimension of an institution. As discussed later, however, it can only be one component of an overall strategy for internationalization. Universities in Australia, New Zealand, and the United Kingdom have undertaken such marketing very successfully; in Australia, marketing has raised the proportion of foreign students to more than 8% over a period during which the comparable Canadian figure actually declined to less than 5%. Moreover, although both Australian and Canadian universities have suffered severe reductions in government funding in recent years, in Australia revenues generated from full-cost-paying international students have covered much, if not all, of the shortfall.

The success of the universities in Australia, New Zealand, and the United Kingdom has not come just from the superior marketing skills of individual institutions; rather, the ability to establish a single, national marketing body, with offices in various countries and strong government support, has been the decisive factor. The offices in targeted countries can then provide information about the universities individually and collectively, aggressively market, and encourage and quickly send on applications for admission. The creation of these offices and their continuing work has the support and official encouragement of the national government. Canada has had very much more difficulty creating a coherent policy, as constitutionally the federal government has no direct role to play in education, which is exclusively a provincial responsibility. Until recently, it was assumed that education marketing would therefore have to be done on a provincial basis or that each university would have to do it independently; either approach is difficult, impossibly inefficient, and very unlikely to succeed in competition with the well-organized approach of, say, Australia. Not surprisingly, therefore, Canadian universities have until now been almost inactive in marketing of education.

Very recently, however, the federal government has increasingly come to see education as a trade commodity, and because it is viewed as an export, there is constitutional room for a federal initiative. Accordingly, 14 Canadian Education Centres have been created at Canadian missions around the world, although mainly in Asia, and the intent is to have 25 of these in operation by 2000. Although they provide information on Canadian universities in response to inquiries from prospective students, their actual marketing activities are limited, at present, by their small staff; it will be difficult to overcome the 15-year lead of Australian universities, unless staffing is increased to allow aggressive marketing.

Research

Many in the university community, faced with the strategic objective to make the institution more international, will immediately assert that it is already international. This assertion is based on the fact that the research community is international and that many faculty members regularly and frequently communicate with colleagues in other countries. This is, of course, true, and indeed the movement of graduate students from country to country and faculty exchanges and sabbatical arrangements often occur through such links. There can also be no doubt that the major portion of any university's international involvement stems directly from the research interests of its faculty members and that these can bring greater international recognition to a university.

Although these linkages usually arise from the initiatives of individual faculty members, the institution itself can develop new linkages to enhance its efforts to internationalize. A notable recent trend is the creation of the first multidisciplinary, multi-institutional, and multicountry research programs. Even before the era of modern telecommunications, Canada was a world leader in the creation of such networks; for the past 25 years, IDRC has managed a number of very successful networks of this type. Now, with modern telecommunications, we are developing large research groups scattered over many sites in a number of countries with considerable success. Canada again leads in the creation of such networks, through both the Canadian Institute for Advanced Research and the more recent Networks of Centres of Excellence (NCEs), supported by the three national research councils. As will be seen later, an institution's

110

strategy for internationalization might well include substantial involvement in several such international research networks. However, difficult structural and governance issues for the individual researcher, the university, and the network need to be resolved, not the least of which is the question of ownership of intellectual property.

Most Canadian universities at present handle all such administrative issues relating to research through an office for research, often headed by a dean, although, in more recent appointments, it is headed by a vice president. Little distinction is made between domestic and international research, and some adjustments would be necessary with any increase in the institution's emphasis on internationalization, at least in terms of specific job responsibilities.

Outreach

Outreach is the third aspect of the university's mission, and in terms of internationalization it has been well discussed in Chapter 2. In many Canadian universities, outreach in the form of continuing (or distance) education has been assigned to separate organizational units, usually a faculty or school of continuing education. The central academic faculties have therefore had little involvement, and the function of outreach has not been seen as being as important as teaching and especially not as important as research. Important exceptions are found, however, in universities such as Saskatchewan and Manitoba, which have solid agricultural bases and have traditionally seen outreach to the agricultural community as central to their missions. Even better examples are found in the United States, where outreach was the basis for the creation and continuing mission of the land-grant universities, as well as of the major roles they played in the global green revolution of the 1960s and 1970s. In the 1990s, outreach is regarded as increasingly important in the universities, although it tends to be equated with creating stronger links with the business community and the hope of generating new sources of funding to replace declining government support.

Clearly, the internationalization of universities must affect their attitudes and emphasis on outreach. Canadian universities have abundant international opportunities for outreach, and participation in them would help internationalize our institutions.

Institutional leadership and decision-making

Although, as described earlier, the governance of today's universities is difficult, the challenge must still be faced, and the central key to success will be effective leadership. All Canadian universities have responded in recent years to external pressures for accountability, usually by preparing a mission statement and providing strategic planning. But in an institution with numerous competing interests and factions and with decision-making based on the majority view, mission statements are all too often vague and unspecific. Nearly all such statements emphasize internationalization as a high-priority objective, but few emphasize how it will be achieved or describe the administrative office to be responsible for it. In some cases, it has been an end in itself to prepare a mission statement, with little real follow-up. In view of the short terms of appointment and consequent rapid turnover of senior university administrators, this should not be surprising.

111

There is at present, however, a great need for presidents, vice presidents, and deans to once again become academic leaders and to afford this role an importance ahead of, or at least equal to, that of their other administrative duties. All senior university officers, not just the president, must be key players in ensuring that the mission statement includes specific, explicitly defined institutional objectives and spells out a clear process for achieving these objectives within a realistic time frame. These senior officers must be actively and continually reminding the academic community of the strategic importance of internationalization; they must be actively seeking new international opportunities; and, above all and especially at the dean's level, they must seize every opportunity to persuade faculty members that greater internationalization of the curriculum is both necessary and desirable. For good academic reasons, faculty members cannot be ordered to change what they teach, but they are usually open to persuasion. What is needed is continual and consistent pressure well applied by the academic leaders of the institution; such pressure can achieve substantial curriculum change.

However, the difficulties should not be minimized. As Jane Knight (1995) pointed out from survey data, 72% of respondents stated that their institution's mission statement referred to the international dimension of teaching, research, and service; 67% indicated that strategic planning included internationalization; 51% stated that there had been a recent review of policies and practices to assess the status of internationalization; only 23% indicated their institution

> **Box 1**
> **The University of Calgary**
>
> As a major Canadian university, the University of Calgary has been very active in CIDA-funded projects and other international activities for many years. The president and his predecessor have placed great emphasis on internationalization as an objective, and for some 8 years the University of Calgary has had a university-wide committee to address internationalization. The Faculty of Medicine was recently asked how this objective might be achieved. This faculty has already had extensive involvement in international development projects, and the senior officers of the faculty have fully recognized the importance of internationalization. In fact, this faculty would be viewed by many across Canada as a leader in international activities. Yet, after some considerable discussion with senior officers, it was frankly stated that the real difficulty, one yet to be solved, was to persuade the rank and file faculty members to buy into internationalization. This was fully confirmed by the chair of the university committee. The major barrier to new initiatives such as internationalization is the failure of leaders and mission statements to relate to the academic culture in which the average faculty member is embedded.

had faculty-level policy statements; and only 15% indicated that the departments undertook any action on internationalization. These results suggest that the leadership may be there, but the faculty at the grass-roots level have not yet fully "bought into" the importance of internationalization.

Such buy-in can clearly take considerable time. Although the amount of time can undoubtedly be greatly reduced by strong and consistent leadership, it remains to be seen whether the required change in attitudes and orientation can occur rapidly enough to catch up with global change. Later in this chapter, there will be further discussion of the existing Canadian academic culture; at this point, it is worth leaving the reader with the comment that change has been much more substantial and rapid in New Zealand and the United Kingdom, where it has been brought about by government decree, rather than by the institutions themselves.

Institutional support and structures

Just as the Canadian universities have changed over the last four decades, so have their means of structuring the organization and financing their international activities. Because to a considerable degree these activities have been funded or subsidized by CIDA, the structural changes have also often reflected changes in Canadian foreign policy or CIDA's policies. Many of these changes were fully described in Chapter 1 and will be only briefly summarized here. In the period 1950–80, Canada's foreign policy greatly emphasized foreign aid to Third World countries, with CIDA functioning as the principal delivery arm for that aid. Initially, the universities were heavily involved in projects that originated from the contacts individual faculty members made with colleagues elsewhere. At that time, funding was relatively easily obtained from CIDA, usually with an overhead component to cover what were referred to as the indirect costs of the university. Although the many activities that developed were undoubtedly beneficial to Canadian universities, the fact that the projects were a product of Canadian generosity and fully paid for by CIDA led to the perception in the universities that international development activities represent aid extended by a "donor" to a "recipient," that they are peripheral to the university's mission, and that they should only be undertaken if full funding comes from an external agency. At the present time, this perception still clouds much university thinking about internationalization. The view is widely held that serious internationalization activities will only be possible with additional government funding. Many have not yet realized that if the internationalization of the university is a significant strategic objective, then appropriate resource allocations must be made from the university's own resources.

113

Lest there be academic howls of outrage at some of the above statements, consider the following points. First, universities have often welcomed participation in CIDA-funded projects, not because of their academic relevance, but more because of the financial benefits they bring in the form of funding for overhead or indirect costs. Some current approaches to marketing educational programs are generating enthusiasm because of the prospect for new funding, not because of the role they play in an internationalization strategy. Again, despite the identification of internationalization as an important institutional objective, few universities have modified their budgets to allocate significant resources to it. Second, few Canadian institutions have consistently attempted to integrate the academic outcomes of CIDA-funded projects into their teaching and research programs. They have been seen as "extras" and peripheral to the university's mission. Third, and directly reflecting this latter remark, at almost every Canadian university some faculty members have suffered in their careers because of their participation in international projects. Departmental and faculty tenure and promotion committees have all too often placed little or no value on such involvements; they have not been valued as scholarly contributions; and if they are recognized as outreach, that, in turn, is given less recognition than teaching and research. Even where the university's official policy statements require recognition of international involvements when tenure and promotion are considered, these policy statements have in many cases been totally ignored. For the faculty in general, international activities per se have been regarded as peripheral, even where participation in international research conferences and membership on editorial boards of international research journals, normally seen as part of research, have been valued highly. It is fair, then, to conclude that, in the past, financial or other institutional support for international involvements has been at best lukewarm and in some respects nonexistent.

In the late 1960s and into the 1970s, Canadian universities began to establish separate offices for international activities. Their mandates varied widely; initially, their role was to coordinate, but with the growth of CIDA activities, these offices became the official

---

Box 2
International Cooperation Offices

In 1995, AUCC (1995b) listed the following as the core functions of its International Cooperation Offices: receiving foreign delegations, negotiating contracts, acting as a clearinghouse, providing information about project opportunities, and liaising with national or international institutions on international activities. Some of these offices prepared cooperation agreements and managed at least the policies dealing with student exchanges and community participation in international activities.

In July 1998, a sample of universities responded to a questionnaire about the evolution of their roles and responsibilities with respect to international work on campus (AUCC data). Some of the findings relating to structural arrangements may be highlighted:

♦ The International Cooperation Offices primarily reported to a vice president research or vice president academic, indicating a relatively close relationship with the university's senior management.

♦ Nearly half of the respondents were directly involved in recruitment of foreign students. In 1995, this was a new responsibility, as almost none of the International Cooperation Offices mentioned recruitment as part of their mandate. This aspect of internationalization is assigned to the registrar's office, an office for foreign students, or a special unit with a broad mandate for national and international student recruitment.

♦ Nearly 75% of the respondents indicated they had to generate revenue if the university was funding at least the infrastructural costs of the office. Most offices had a mandate to negotiate contracts and sometimes to manage them. Contractual activities were clearly a strong rationale for the creation of International Cooperation Offices and still represent a very significant part of their activities, although data on the value of contracts year over year were difficult to access.

institutional channels to CIDA and later to IDRC. Although over time such offices played an increasing role as resource centres — for example, in providing library information and materials on international development to both faculty and students — they tended to be regarded as administrative or, at best, as academic-support units; only in rare cases did they acquire an academic mandate. This also meant that such offices usually had little direct authority over faculty activities, except by way of moral suasion, even in matters such as the legal need for compliance with CIDA's contract requirements. After all, the faculty members were the ones who would be designing and delivering the project itself, and to faculty members administrative concerns are secondary. The director of such an international office, therefore, had to act as the go-between for the faculty and CIDA, trying at the same time to ensure that the institution's welfare was safeguarded. He or she might report to a dean of graduate studies or research, but this reporting relationship was often quite tenuous, and the institution showed very little interest in these activities.

In the mid- to late 1970s, it was recognized that changes were necessary. Although many projects had been quite successful, even under such loose management, there had been a sufficient number of problems for CIDA to question the adequacy of that management, especially at a time when the scope of CIDA's programs was growing substantially, along with the number of more specifically oriented projects. Provided the faculty member was seen as a university employee, agencies such as CIDA, IDRC, and the World Bank could not legally contract with the individual faculty member. Contracts were therefore negotiated between the agency and the faculty member's institution. The director of the international office thus had to have increased authority, not only to meet the increasingly bureaucratic requirements of CIDA, but also to ensure that in a period of steadily declining university funding, the interests of the institution were fully protected.

This was the era of project management by the universities; it was not an era warmly welcomed by many faculty members, at least not by comparison with the more laissez-faire period that had preceded it. It was all too easy for faculty members, acting as independent consultants rather than as university employees, to avoid such administrative complexities. University terms of employment usually allow each faculty member to engage in such consulting, so it has been quite permissable for a faculty member to undertake a consulting subcontract with a private-sector company in, for example, a CIDA-funded international development project. Under these circumstances, the university's name and reputation inevitably become associated with that project, either directly or indirectly, but the institution itself receives neither recompense nor recognition. It is on such grounds that many Canadian universities object strongly to current CIDA policy, which prevents them from competing for development projects outside of the programs but allows the private sector to remain free to recruit and financially benefit from the universities' human resources.

116

Project management

The university is not a management company. It is governed by principles of academic freedom, and it reaches decisions by consensus or majority rule. As a result, the university can encounter great difficulty in meeting its legal obligations in a contractual relationship. In practice, the difficulties have been surprisingly few, and the great majority of contracts with CIDA and other agencies have been satisfactorily completed. But, as an example, the quite reasonable CIDA requirement that the final report for a project be provided within a specified time by the project director, who is usually a faculty member, has caused problems. If the project director refuses, or just doesn't bother to provide such a report, the university suffers financially, as CIDA, rightfully, withholds the final contract payment. Such cases have certainly occurred in the universities but would not be tolerated in the private sector. The university's governance structure is not well suited to providing effective project delivery and management

In the 1990s, with further change in CIDA policies, the emphasis on project management has been greatly reduced. As indicated previously, the universities are now involved in only the UPCD program, which has a Tier 1 (long-term thematic partnerships) and a Tier 2 (short-term focused projects). The success of this new program cannot yet be assessed, but, along with the pressure on the university to internationalize, the program represents yet another change in the role of the international office in each university. This office is now often viewed as being responsible for internationalization, not just for international development activities; in some cases, the change in mandate is occurring by a natural evolution, whereas in others it is occurring as a result of a conscious decision to rewrite the mandate. In universities with very strong leadership and a firm commitment to internationalization, moves are under way to appoint a vice president international or perhaps an associate vice president to be responsible not only for the international office but also for the entire range of the institution's internationalization strategies.

Tensions

From the above, it will be clear that significant tensions are at play in the university and that these must be taken into account if the institution is to internationalize.

Leadership

The importance of institutional leadership was stated above, along with the frustration of many senior university officers who have attempted to provide it. The need for leadership in the institution is severe, and leadership is certainly not to be equated with dictatorial management. But real tension exists between the need to provide leadership and the general faculty insistence on independence and academic freedom. A very fine balance is required, and not all institutions are capable of achieving this. It is, however, essential for internationalization.

In the late 1960s, under CIDA's UPCD, partnerships with the University of Ghana were negotiated separately by the University of Guelph in agriculture and home economics and by UWO in economics. Guelph's very first step was to have its president and the two deans of the involved faculties visit the University of Ghana, as a clear indication of Guelph's commitment to the partnership. A very strong relationship developed, which continues today, now without CIDA support, of course, but to the benefit of both institutions. The expression of commitment from UWO was not as strong, and the relationship has been much less productive.

Tensions with external agencies

Although Canadian universities have achieved considerable success in their international activities, they have had to do so despite perceived weaknesses. CIDA, for example, has continued to show scepticism about the ability of the universities to manage projects, although there has been no objective evidence that universities deliver projects any less successfully than the private sector. CIDA has also been sceptical about the extent to which the institution, rather than the project leader, actually "own" the project. Well-justified doubt is also raised regarding the ability of the governance structure of the university to make project decisions expeditiously.

There is indeed a serious mismatch between academic governance and project delivery.

Box 3
University governance and project delivery

Many Canadian universities have required that major CIDA projects receive institutional approval through the senate and perhaps the board of governors, or their equivalents. Some have also required periodic reports on the project. This can mean that a professor of chemistry might be a member of the senate voting on a project but probably has little knowledge of the environmental policies that might be appropriate for Indonesia, for example, and even less understanding of the social, economic, and environmental circumstances of that country. Discussion and voting in the senate, therefore, may bear little relation to either the subject matter or the management of such a development project but have more to do with the internal politics of the university. In the early 1980s, the University of Guelph undertook a CIDA-funded project in rural development in the Indonesian state of Sulawesi. At the outset, full discussion occurred in the senate, which then approved the project. Some 10 years later, when the project was about to enter a third phase of funding, it came before senate again. Fierce opposition to any continuation of the project was voiced through the senate by a relatively small number of faculty members and students, none of whom had taken part in the original debate or had participated in the project. Their opposition was based on human-rights issues in Indonesia, not on specific criticisms of the project itself. Although there may well have been other factors involved in the political decision at the time, the publicity generated by the university's opposition to the presence of the project in Indonesia was a significant factor in the Indonesian government's later decision to expel the Guelph project staff.

There are also significant tensions between AUCC and individual institutions as they work to internationalize. The creation and role of the international division of AUCC were described earlier, but the continuing tension, despite the accomplishments of the division, reflects the fact that AUCC is indeed a voluntary body and can therefore only act when it has the support of a substantive majority of the membership. For example, the Canadian backwardness in marketing university education has already been described, as well as the constitutional problem that causes it. It theoretically would be possible for AUCC to become, or to create, a national marketing agency, but agreement among the universities on such a solution is not possible, as each university has to consider its relationship with its own provincial government.

The academic reward system

The slowness of change in the academic culture, especially in the university reward system, is by far the greatest impediment to internationalization. Examples have already been given of how difficult it is to persuade faculty to buy into such new initiatives, and the difficulty stems in turn from the perception that faculty members have of the internal reward system. Although many disclaimers will be offered, it is just a fact that in all universities in Canada, as well as in those in most other countries, academics believe research and research-related activities are the ones that bring rewards in academia (salary increases, tenure, promotion). This does not mean that teaching is neglected or is inadequate — it is not. It does mean, however, that in most parts of the university outreach is seen as unimportant and that constant, powerful persuasion is certainly required to convince faculty members of the rewards of participating in internationalization initiatives. Some concrete specific examples are needed to help university presidents begin to make the case for a new attitude and culture. At present, there is considerable tension between the university leaders who see the need for globalization and an academic community embedded to a considerable extent in a culture that is outdated and resistant to change.

At this point, let me briefly summarize some of the chief issues before proceeding to discuss some specific steps a university might take to internationalize. First, the structures Canadian universities currently have for dealing with international development activities are not well suited to advancing internationalization. The existing international offices are largely administrative and have no academic mandate; consequently, they can exert little influence on the content or shape of academic programs. Nor are they really structured to function as management units and manage a variety of international activities. Second, there is little sign that the academic culture of Canadian universities has changed from that of the 1950s: the greatest value is still placed on research, and there is, as yet, little willingness to recognize and reward the valuable contributions faculty make in internationalization, outreach, or other new institutional initiatives. Third, the universities need to recognize that if internationalization is one of their primary objectives, then they must devote some of their own financial resources to it. At a time of serious funding reductions, this may seem difficult, if not impossible, but it really calls for the courage to make hard priority decisions that directly reflect the institution's long-term strategy. Without the commitment of institutional resources, strategic plans that assign a priority to internationalization are likely to be little more than paper exercises.

Developing a strategy

Internationalization as an institutional initiative requires, first, that the university thoughtfully develop an integrated and comprehensive plan, which should be uniquely suited to each institution. Some would argue that this plan should be highly decentralized to accommodate the wide diversity of interests within the university; however, this would further weaken the coherence of the institution, and, on this point, I continue to maintain that internationalization must be addressed institutionally and not in a fragmented and decentralized fashion. Regardless of its detailed structure, any plan must have institutional leadership as its essential component. The senior officers' deep commitment to internationalization must be continually evident in both words and actions. In today's global society, the president and his or her senior colleagues need to devote as much time and effort to creating and nurturing international linkages as they do to encouraging research or obtaining external funding.

Strategic elements of the plan might include the following:

✦ *International experiences for undergraduate students* — This is by far the most important and direct route to internationalization, but the university must then accept responsibility for ensuring that such experiences are well managed. This must be done on an institutional basis and should not be left to individual departments or faculties. Even in purely legal terms, it can only be the institution that bears this responsibility. Ideally, the institution should have some specific but realistic targets for such undergraduate participation; for example, one university might have as part of its strategy the goal of having 20% of its undergraduate students gain international experience by 2005. This might be achieved through a number of carefully managed exchange programs and semester-abroad arrangements. These initiatives might also be used to recruit international students to the Canadian home institutions, and the involvement of Canadian faculty members in exchanges may result in substantial further benefit. Their teaching is likely to reflect their enhanced international experience to the benefit of Canadian students remaining at home.

✦ *Marketing of educational programs* — This issue was mentioned previously in this chapter and is discussed elsewhere in this book. The point that needs to be made forcefully here is that well-planned marketing of selected educational programs can be an important and valid component of a university's strategy for internationalization. Through such marketing, a university can significantly increase its international student population and thereby considerably enhance the university's diversity, cosmopolitan atmosphere, global alumni connections, and internal culture. As well, the experience of universities such as Dalhousie shows that there can be other significant benefits. First, by bringing in international students, professional programs, such as medicine or dentistry, can be kept above the minimum critical size and be more cost efficient. Second, international students' payment of the full cost of their studies to the university is a considerable financial benefit to Canada. Third, classes in these programs — which at Dalhousie, for example, would otherwise only have students from Atlantic Canada — are now more heterogeneous, which helps to internationalize Canadian students.

121

+ *International development activities* — A major assumption of this chapter is that an institution's interpretation of internationalization must be intellectually and morally valid and must show concern for the entire global society. It should be part of the university's moral and intellectual responsibility to examine and address the total condition of the human species in all parts of the world. An internationalization strategy without links to less-developed countries would be morally and intellectually lacking. Although CIDA and IDRC have substantially reduced their funding to the universities in recent years, Canadian universities seem certain to continue to be involved in development projects. Indeed, it is difficult to see how Canada can maintain an aid program without drawing on the expertise in the universities. Canadian universities also have considerable potential to be involved in projects funded by the World Bank or by other international agencies.

As independent institutions, however, Canadian universities also need to recognize that in developing countries, many of these international agencies are seen as advocates of the Western economic-growth model and free-market ideology. The universities should not only be committing some of their own resources to creating linkages with sister institutions in developing countries but also be seeking other partners without this ideological stamp. They can probably best be found among the NGOs, with whom partnerships can be particularly effective in areas such as the provision of undergraduate student placements, continuing education, and outreach. In the recent past, CIDA and a small number of other agencies have encouraged such partnerships, but only a few have developed. Yet, many of the Canadian universities' international undertakings over the past 40–50 years stem directly from individual involvements in organizations such as CUSO and WUSC. It is time to rebuild these links more formally as genuine, mutually beneficial, institutionalized partnerships.

✦ *Creation of international research consortia and networks* — At least some research-intensive Canadian universities are well placed to initiate development of international research consortia and networks. One such network already links the faculties of engineering at UBC and the National University of Singapore. However, a particularly suitable model for new networks might be the Canadian NCEs. Under this model, one or perhaps several Canadian universities would identify a well-defined multidisciplinary theme in which the institution or institutions have internationally recognized expertise. Through the identification of similar intellectually outstanding groups or individuals internationally, a consortium or network might be created. Following the NCE model, the network should have specific objectives and should initially be created for a set period. It should have a formal constitution, be managed by an external body, and be subject to periodic evaluation by an independent body of international experts.

An international research program like this can achieve a number of goals. First, it can bring enormous expertise to bear on complex, multifaceted issues: a single university does not have the same intellectual resources, and its rigid disciplinary structure inhibits interdisciplinary research. Second, an international network can provide a "globalized" form of postgraduate education, in which students can benefit from association with leading researchers from several countries, as well as being internationalized themselves through conducting their research and living in a number of countries.

A comprehensive strategy for a specific university might therefore include the following elements: (1) 12–15 student exchange programs providing international experience for 15% of the undergraduate students; (2) marketing of a number of programs, probably professional in nature; (3) participation in a number of international development projects with governments, international agencies, and

NGOs; and (4) creation of, or participation in, several international research consortia or networks. A well-managed strategy with these elements can achieve a significant degree of internationalization of the undergraduate and postgraduate students of a faculty while increasing the number of international students on campus. A strategy may include other elements in areas such as continuing education, but the point to be emphasized is that it is important for a university to have a detailed and carefully prepared strategic plan for its internationalization.

123

New structures

Institutional structures such as the offices for international programs that many Canadian universities have developed over the past 50 years have served their purpose well. They have encouraged, sponsored, and managed a variety of international projects; nurtured international students on campus; and even helped local communities gain a broader international perspective. However, internationalization of the entire university is a much more profound undertaking and will require new and different structures.

Although the need for leadership from all senior officers of the university is absolutely clear, one person must be assigned full responsibility if an internationalization strategy is to be implemented. This person should not be below the level of associate vice president and would preferably be a vice president. This should be a full-time position, but it should not be permanent; at its inception, it should be well understood that it will exist for not more than 10 years. Internationalization involves building a strong international dimension into each of a university's basic functions of teaching, research, and outreach. A senior position is needed in the initial building process, but once implementation is complete, international activities should be subsumed under the more traditional structures and organization of the university. This vice president international should have significant responsibilities, including the following:

+ Further development and implementation of the internationalization strategy;

+ Development of processes for the periodic evaluation of all components of the strategy;

- ✦ Coordination with the management unit (described below) and the development of suitable links between it and the various academic units within the university; and

- ✦ Oversight of the academic integrity of all components of the internationalization strategy.

124

The vice president international would oversee the immediate creation of an international management unit. This would be an arm's-length, wholly owned corporation (not for profit), governed by its own board of directors, with both internal and external appointees. Essentially, all of the suggested elements of an institutional strategy depend for their success on effective management. A student exchange program must of course be based on a good understanding of each institution's academic standards and values, but its real success depends much more on constant monitoring of all arrangements for the participating students: housing, counseling, travel, health care, etc. These are all management issues and should be in the hands of skilled managers. The responsibility for these issues should not be rotated in an ad hoc fashion from faculty member to faculty member, each with a different interest or lack of interest in the exchange program. Similar arguments can be made for all of the other components of the suggested strategy, which all depend on effective management for success. Good reasons can be given for creating a corporation, as an independent entity, to negotiate directly with both the university and individual faculty members on issues such as the precise terms of the latter's involvement in projects. All parties should know the precise details of the contractual arrangements at the outset, particularly in terms of the faculty member's obligation to the university. This corporation would be much more proactive than any university in seeking out new exchange agreements, opportunities for development projects, or associations with NGOs. It would be able to be more open minded than a university in contracting with private-sector individuals or businesses or with faculty members from other universities, if circumstances required.

Funding

The issue of funding for a strategy of internationalization has already been mentioned but needs to be further amplified. The problem is far from being insurmountable; at least three sources of funding can be suggested, and there may well be others.

> **Box 4**
> **Guelph International**
>
> In 1984, the University of Guelph incorporated Guelph International as an arm's-length, not-for-profit corporation. Its mandate was to seek out and bid on contracts for development projects funded by both Canadian and international agencies. It had a full-time president and its own separate board; the hope was that, given the large number of agricultural projects funded by these agencies, Guelph International would be able to compete effectively in the market and ultimately generate revenues for the university. However, in 1989, it was judged to be infeasible and was terminated.
> Several factors contributed to this outcome. One was the difficulty of trying to penetrate the labyrinthine bureaucracies of international aid agencies. Equally important was the fact that the president was only an academic but should have been a person with considerable business experience. Also, at that time, the initiative was not well received by CIDA. It did not consider such direct entry into the private sector appropriate.

125

First, the institution has a source of funding in its existing budget. The allocation of budget resources must reflect the university's priorities; if internationalization is now to be a high-priority objective, essential to the university's fundamental tasks of teaching, research, and outreach, then less important activities must cease, and the resources must be reallocated to internationalization. This is, however, easier said than done, as seen from the fact that as funding levels per student have declined over the past decade or so very few academic programs across Canada have been closed, but many new programs have been introduced! Canadian universities have yet to demonstrate an ability to set hard priorities, close some programs, and reallocate resources to new initiatives.

Second, there is little doubt that the prime beneficiaries of internationalization programs will be the students, especially those participating in exchange programs. The cost per student will be quite high, but it should be unnecessary for the university to meet all of these costs. It needs to be remembered that students at all Canadian universities now pay all of their own accommodation and living costs and that many of these same students are already traveling abroad at their own expense. Many would see considerable benefit in combining travel with study for degree credits. But there will always be a minority of students who lack the necessary financial resources and require assistance if they are to have equal opportunities to participate in international exchange programs. In an era of continuously rising tuition fees, as in Canada now, it is relatively easy to create the necessary funds to provide such student assistance. If, for example, in any one year, undergraduate fees are increased by 10%, then 2.5%

(that is, 25% of the increase) could be placed in a special student-assistance fund. A substantial amount can in fact be quite quickly accumulated to assist students participating in either exchange or development programs operated jointly with NGOs. Dalhousie has followed such a course for almost 10 years and has created a multi-million-dollar general student-assistance fund, an increasing portion of which is now being directed to assist students in undertaking international study.

Third, some of these are obviously revenue-generating initiatives. Education programs will usually be marketed on a full-cost-recovery basis (but will add only marginal additional costs to the institution) and can be an important source of funds for other internationalization activities. Other possible initiatives, such as those based on distance education or on marketing of health-care programs, can also be made to generate significant revenue.

There must, however, be one cardinal rule accepted and adhered to by all in the institution: namely, all such funds need to be segregated in a separate account to be used exclusively for internationalization activities. It should not be possible, for example, to divert these funds to other uses, such as to support faculty research. Clearly, the universities have the means to supply the funds needed for successful internationalization; to make them available, however, will require the willingness to make some hard choices, as well as the leadership and commitment required for such an initiative.

To conclude, the internationalization of Canadian universities should be founded on a clear institutional definition and a solid intellectual base. With vigorous institutional leadership, a strong consensus can be built on the need for internationalization and on its purposes. A coherent, balanced strategy is needed, and new and different structures need to be created to provide effective management. With careful planning, financial resources can be found. At present, Canadian universities have made an excellent start, but the challenge is formidable, and much remains to be done.

There is one major caveat. The discussion in this chapter is based on several assumptions, one of which is that Canadian universities can, as institutions, successfully undertake an initiative such as an institutional initiative. Of course, numerous arguments show that it must be undertaken on such a basis: the definition of internationalization, the supporting policies, the finances, and the need for effective and consistent management all argue to this effect. But today's university, as I have already stated, is highly diverse, and its coherence and sense of common purpose have been greatly weakened over the last 50 years. Some would argue that in recognition of the university's diversity, a much more decentralized approach to internationalization will be necessary, allowing each faculty or department to go its own way, presumably under the umbrella of a set of broad, nonspecific institutional policies. In Canada, this may indeed occur, as the government has shown few signs of being willing to provide directives on internationalization, such as those in New Zealand and the United Kingdom. If the government fails to act, however, it will fragment the institution still further, make leadership even more difficult, and likely leave major components of the university even more reactionary than at present. If an institutional initiative cannot successfully achieve internationalization, what new initiative can?

Chapter 6

Students as Agents of Change

Catherine Vertesi

In the first 30 years after World War II, the emphasis of student-related international activity was on discipline-oriented field studies for Canadians; overseas projects in which Canadians lived and worked in some developing economy, and the education of foreign students in Canadian universities, most receiving financial assistance from some aid agency. However, by the late 1980s, an economic rationale took over, and the rhetoric surrounding the need to produce graduates who could function in an increasingly globalized economy was followed by intense growth and investment in international-liaison offices, student-exchange coordinators, and institutional linkages. Many Canadian colleges and universities added new courses, degrees, or diplomas as the rationale for internationalization shifted to this economic need to increase the international literacy of young Canadians. At each stage, services and expertise were developed to meet the specific requirements of the project or program at hand. This process has been cumulative, giving the Canadian postsecondary community a wide-ranging set of skills to form a strong foundation to broaden international activity in all our institutions.

The vision of an internationalized campus has been present in many of our institutions for years, and the leaders in those institutions should be congratulated for their Herculean efforts to develop exchanges, field schools, and recruitment activities abroad. Yet, many remain disappointed by the cumulative change in what we do and how we do it. Indeed, it does not appear to be a lack of vision or international-program opportunities that has led many to see an underachievement in the internationalization in Canadian post-secondary education; rather, it seems to be inadequate investment in the internationalization process itself. Some institutions are still in the formative and visionary stage, but most are now charged with increasing the impact of the programs currently in place, moving from rhetoric to reality. For this reason, much of this chapter carries a strong focus on the process and the players in student-related international activity. The devil is definitely in the detail, but a better grasp of the detail should help shape the tactics used by determined internationalization planners to increase the benefits of international activity and spread them to all students on our campuses, not just to those who participate directly in international ventures.

Now, in the late 1990s, Canadian government and university administrators have looked to in-coming international students, not only to help internationalize our campuses, but also to provide an additional source of revenue from differential tuition and the overseas sale of Canadian education. The federal government has supported the development of the Canadian Education Centres (CECs) in Asia and South America to promote Canada as a destination for foreign students. The terminology of the marketplace now plays a significant role in the strategic plans to increase international activity on Canadian campuses.

Our current challenges are directly related to the decrease in funding for the postsecondary system, which is felt to a greater or lesser extent in all regions of the country. Can internationalization continue to be a top priority if it has to compete for resources with the more traditional research and teaching functions of our institutions? Do we have the time and money to develop a portfolio of high-quality internationalizing activities for students with differing academic and personal needs? Will we invest in internationalizing the students and faculty who do not travel, thus gaining a greater impact from the international activities currently taking place in our institutions? And can we resist exploiting full fee-paying international students as cash cows, rather than using their revenue to improve services and contribute to the internationalization of the whole campus?

Hence, this chapter will explore two majors themes: the continued internationalization of Canadian students and the new initiatives to recruit international students to Canada. Finally, I look at the ways these streams merge to bring potential benefits to all students attending Canadian universities. Throughout the chapter, anecdotal examples are used to illustrate some of the issues under discussion. Some major differences appear in approaches to students and their international experiences in the francophone universities of Quebec and the anglophone universities in the rest of Canada. These differences will be described and explored throughout the text.

131

Internationalization of Canadian students

> I learned so much about myself and about how the world works that
> I wonder what I knew before.
>
> Canadian exchange student at the
> University of Ausburg, 1995/96.

The student-related factors driving the need to internationalize our universities and colleges are not new, but they have certainly increased in number in the past decade. Canadians have always felt an ethical obligation to contribute to the growth and well-being of developing nations, and the universities' early international work reflected this. French-speaking institutions were also motivated to support connections with francophone centres in other countries to maintain and strengthen their unique culture. But the increased globalization of business, the interdependency of economies, the changing face of the Canadian population, and the environmental, economic, and demographic problems that transcend borders demand an even greater response from our educational institutions. If universities are to continue to play a critical role in preparing leaders to respond effectively to the urgent needs of society, then we have an obligation to enable graduates to

+ Function effectively in an international and highly competitive economic arena;

+ Interact, within their communities, with a Canadian citizenry of increasing racial and religious diversity;

+ Engage in intellectual and scholarly activity that finds synergy and fresh insight from using paradigms and models from cultures different from our own;

+ Supervise, and be supervised by, individuals from diverse nations and cultures at home and overseas;

+ Generate solutions to issues that transcend national boundaries, using sufficient intercultural skill to ensure widespread participation; and

+ Contribute to world peace and stability.

The internationalization of Canadian students immediately brings to mind the major thrusts of special international degree and course development, student exchange and field-study programs, the presence of international students on campus, and work opportunities overseas. Discussion at meetings of the professionals involved in the delivery of international programs and services, such as the Canadian Bureau of International Education, reveals a high level of consciousness on our campuses that these programs and services are all necessary components of a well-rounded international strategy for student development. The number of mobility programs has grown enormously over the past 10 years, and most campuses in Canada now have some opportunity for Canadian students to go abroad on some university-sanctioned program. Without question, the students who choose to go abroad have gained immeasurably from their experiences. Virtually all returnees report that their exchange, field study, or overseas internship was the high point of their educational program, including those with negative experiences in their host country:

> My year ... enabled me to improve my Japanese and gain a deeper understanding of the Japanese culture while studying engineering ... . The first month of classes was pretty difficult because of all the technical Japanese ... . I caught up by memorizing words until ... my technical Japanese was solid ... . It was my most challenging and fulfilling year of university yet!
>
> Canadian exchange student at
> Ritsumeikan University, 1993/94

> I can only promise you one thing. ...You will have some hard times and you will have some great, unforgettable times. You will learn a lot both from your studies and from the experience of living in another country and speaking another language ... . I'm going back to work there. I guess that just about says it all.
>
> Canadian exchange student at the
> Université de Lyon, 1992/93

On a continuum, the Canadian students who have had the most "internationalizing" experience provided by their university are those who study and then perhaps work abroad for a year, immersed in another language and living with nationals from the host country. These programs are swelling in number and should continue to be encouraged. However, even the most ambitious program can only reach a modest percentage of current university and college students. In addition, only the most intrepid and well-prepared students come forward to apply for such opportunities. Although language skills, practical experience, and even expertise related to the host culture can doubtless be gained from these full-immersion periods, different and less comprehensive skills must also be developed to increase the international and intercultural capacity of students who face barriers in dealing with all-encompassing experiences (even when these experiences are self-imposed). We must develop and exploit the indirect effects of having more international students on campus (from exchanges as well as full-degree students), as well as Canadian students returning from international experiences, either studying or in a cooperative-education placement. Returning students have been well used by study-abroad professionals to recruit and orient the next exchange group; yet, resident students and faculty remain relatively unaffected, as exchange students' observations and insights rarely appear in the classroom setting.

Exchanges are high-profile, labour-intensive initiatives (with candidate selection, course planning, credit transfer, reentry counseling, etc.) and therefore costly. In most institutions, the total number of

---

Box 1
Students' mobility

There are no data on the mobility of Canadian students abroad. There are many explanations for this: keeping education in the provincial jurisdiction contributes to the scattering of education-related information; governments exhibit little interest in these issues; and there are methodological difficulties in identifying this population. Evaluations of the number of these students vary according to source. We estimate that less than 1% of Canadian students go abroad for credited training activities. The percentage of postgraduate students is likely to be even lower. Among the reasons for this situation, it is important to mention the lack of academic incentives, the negative impact of the cost of living in Canada, the Canadian dollar's rate of exchange, the almost total absence of a specific financial-support mechanism, the relative impoverishment of students in recent years, and burdens on a good number of students with family responsibilities. Major efforts are required from universities to offer a wide range of opportunities for mobility, but only a few students are able to benefit from the expected academic and cultural gains.

exchange students is still a small proportion of the student body, and for the most part the exchange students contribute in only minor ways to the overall internationalization of the institutions involved. Even institutions where 300–400 students go on exchange remain relatively monocultural in their values, service delivery, and curriculum.

Figure 1 ranks the effects of various international activities on students. Not all students are ready for the extensive enrichment that a full year abroad can bring, but they may still have an internationalizing experience through other less comprehensive, university-generated activities. Note that, for the purposes of the schematic, whether the student studies or works, the effects seem similar. It is the extent of the immersion (language, exposure to host culture, use of public transport, etc.) that has an impact. *Home language* refers to one's usual language of study, whereas *host language* indicates that the student must accommodate to study in another language. *Abroad* is used in the most general sense to indicate any institution away from where the student normally studies.

I will now explore further the efforts to broaden our internationalization initiatives on campuses and examine some key barriers to, and opportunities in, our current and future programs.

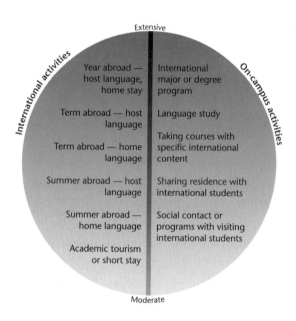

Figure 1. A schematic representation of international effects.

Mobility programs for Canadian students — learning from others

There is a significant difference between the Americans and Europeans when it comes to mobilizing students to travel to other countries for their education. The Americans tend to favour off-site campuses, where the students go abroad to take courses taught in the American style — semesters, midterms, papers, and course credits — and are taught, or at least supervised, by American faculty or staff. With the exception of language programs, they are taught in English. These "island" programs can be as short as 2 weeks or as long as a full year and may be part of the regular tuition structure of an institution or have extra fees attached.

The Europeans, in contrast, have embarked on large-scale mobilization through government-funded mobility programs and institutional partnerships, in which students from home institutions join courses mixed with the normal student population in the host country. The successful European Community Action Scheme for the Mobility of University Students (ERASMUS), now somewhat revised and called SOCRATES, has supported the movement of more than 200 000 students (Teichler 1996b). Intuitively, the immersion experience of ERASMUS would seem to have a more profound internationalizing effect on student participants, but the American approach has the benefit of affecting large numbers of students and taking them to places where study would otherwise be inaccessible because of obstacles such as language, institutional quality, or educational structure.

Inasmuch as Canada shares attributes with both Europe and the United States, internationalization efforts in Canadian institutions are enhanced by providing both types of experience to students. Canadians, like Europeans, are not accustomed to paying high US-style tuition, so families do not save up enough to support an expensive study term abroad for their children. However, like the US students, Canadians tend to be held back from full immersion in non-English-speaking institutions because of the students' weak foreign-language skills. The opportunity for a bilingual French–English public-school education has certainly increased the percentage of linguistically mobile students in Canada beyond the US numbers but not to the same extent as in Europe. The variety of experiences made available to Canadian students through field schools and island programs is an enormous strength that opens up areas unattainable by direct exchange.

Credit-transfer mechanisms

> After returning ... I found that I had to start from the very begin-
> ning again in regards to matching credits to the courses I took at
> Keele.
>
> Canadian exchange student at
Keele University, 1995/96

> There was so much uncertainty with regards to transfer credits being
> given for a senior level course. It was very frustrating. Financially, I
> cannot afford to be paying out money for courses for which I will
> not receive senior credit.
>
> A non-Canadian visiting
Université Laval, 1996/97

The evaluation of overseas experiences and credit transfer is a thorny issue. The number of students across Canada who attend excellent academic institutions abroad with contractual partnerships with their home institution only to return and have their adviser deny transfer of some of their credits is shocking. Whole institutions or individual departments with long experience in international education tend to adopt the fundamental principle that students should not be disadvantaged by joining a university-approved study-abroad program. The acceptance of this principle compels more flexible and generous treatment when Canadians return from their exchange.

In Quebec, for example, international experiences for under-graduate students are seen as a way to provide students with a cultural experience, educational in the broadest sense. The Conference of Rectors and Principals of Quebec Universities (CREPUQ, Conférence des recteurs et principaux des universités du Québec) has an agreement system in which more than 250 universities worldwide can send students on a reciprocal basis and all credits are recognized at the home institution. It is assumed that if the institution is good enough to be a recognized partner it must be trusted to deliver satisfactory courses. There is only limited concern with the course being identical to something offered in Quebec; in fact, taking advantage of the differences in offerings is encouraged.

In the open approach of CREPUQ, students accept responsibility for their course choices and the coverage of prerequisite materials. This is most desirable, as it greatly diminishes the barriers to an overseas experience. However, in many institutions, faculty are not prepared to grant students such autonomy, and for them some new tools are needed. The European Credit Transfer System (ECTS), the international course-equivalency guide, is an approach with many advantages. Articulation across Canada and then to the ECTS would be an excellent start in streamlining credit transfer. Of course, for widespread acceptance of a standardized articulation process, the governing bodies of our institutions must have a systematic way to evaluate partners; accordingly, any articulation must involve local faculty on a discipline-by-discipline basis.

137

A portfolio approach to mobility offerings

International experiences for students can range from short-term academic tourism to a full year of interacting in another language, culture, and academic and work environment. Students, too, range from those who are sheltered and fearful to the courageous and curious, but all should be more international by the completion of their postsecondary experience. In a country where the majority of students attend university while living at home, we need to acknowledge that signing on for a full year in an unknown environment may represent a significant hurdle. A portfolio approach, with various types of mobility offerings at each institution, is needed to meet the requirements of various student groups. The more intrepid students will always come forward, even without help from the university, but we need to reach those larger numbers of students who require some extra encouragement.

To build trust and support for these types of programs, faculty, too, must gain experience with sending their students abroad. Departmental leadership is essential, but faculty buy-in comes with a series of positive experiences. For example, although a full year abroad provides a more intensive experience, faculty who are new to the exchange process may be more comfortable having students spend only one term abroad, because it poses less risk of undermining the integrity of the degree. As well, for some professional programs, students may jeopardize their ability to meet licencing requirements if they spend too much time away. As a result, international program planning should include increased liaison with appropriate licencing bodies. Canadian faculty should not assume that an overseas experience will prohibit a student's meeting licencing obligations in Canada. Academic program leaders in Canada have often successfully advocated the merits of such experiences with a professional organization, with the result that the organization relaxes requirements for students with parallel (not identical) international experiences.

However, internationalization is a gradual process. We are not responsible for completing the process in our students, merely for taking them as far as they can go. By developing profiles of the groups of students on one's campus who share values and attributes, one can tailor initiatives to specific populations of students and can set goals that are appropriate to their needs.

An example of an international program targeting a particular student group is an undergraduate program with a student population dominated by the sons and daughters of new immigrants from Hong Kong. For these Asian parents, an open exchange program without supervision was out of the question. In response, a tailored 5-week island summer program in Europe was developed (Tretheway 1992). The director hosted an information session for parents and stressed that Canadian faculty would teach and live on site with the students. Under these conditions, many students were then permitted to travel and gain some direct experience with Western European culture and traditions. Some used it as a stepping stone to a full-term exchange program later in their degree:

> My parents would not allow me to even apply for an exchange program, even though I would only be gone for one term, and I had already spent 2 years at UBC [University of British Columbia], away from them. They only said yes to summer school after they met the professors and knew we would be taken care of. Even though I was 21, they would never have let me travel on my own!
>
> P.W., a Chinese–Canadian student at the University of British Columbia, summer program, 1992

Students want more opportunities to go abroad, better information about the opportunities, more assurance that their academic work will be recognized for transfer credit, and some hope of financial assistance for overseas study. Virtually all students report that their international experience, regardless of duration, was a highlight of their time at university:

> Most of the people I spoke to before I went on exchange would say that their year abroad was the best experience of their life. I used to think that they were "keeners," the sort of people who say that every year. The thing is, I find myself saying the exact same thing; giving the same sort of answers that I usually reserve for my grandma just to make her happy — only I'm genuine.
>
> Canadian exchange student at the University of Nottingham, 1994/95

Those who stay home

Internationalizing our students is an incremental process and, as such, is linked to activities beyond exchanges and travel. The introduction of programs, international courses, and increased foreign-language study can contribute to internationalization, but experience shows that these have often occurred without significant disruption of the culture and practice of the institution. The way in which transnational student gatherings are encouraged and attended; the access to foreign books, case studies, and computer networks; the availability of foreign-language word-processing opportunities; and the manner in which visiting staff and students are assisted are all extracurricular ways of highlighting internationalization and should be included in planning and targeting the deployment of resources. Changes to the curriculum to make the acquisition of cross-cultural skills and cultural awareness explicit and desirable for all students require an additional fundamental change.

139

Educating the whole student

Professional programs at universities and colleges tend to look at program-wide issues in evaluating and developing their offerings. In schools like pharmacy, dentistry, management, and engineering, competencies beyond the main academic content, such as public speaking or medical history, are embedded either as special courses or as an integral part of the overall curriculum. International opportunities for students in these disciplines are easier to stimulate because of the already established commitment to "professional readiness" and some overarching sense of a complete education that goes beyond a mere collection of courses. In less career-focused programs, the education of the student beyond a list of course requirements is less often discussed, much less funded. In response to a question about the lack of science students on educational exchanges, a science dean replied that "labs are almost the same everywhere in the world so there is not much advantage for science students going abroad." Nonacademic goals are insignificant in this kind of thinking, and yet I am sure that the mission statement of his faculty, like those of other large and small institutions, expresses commitment to developing graduates prepared to function as leaders in the society of the future. Certainly, the Canadian future requires international, intercultural, and multicultural skills. And why should science students be denied the advantages and opportunities offered to others in the institution? But in the more general programs in science or the humanities, who takes the responsibility to make sure that this happens?

Many dedicated faculty have become involved in developing international work and study experiences for Canadian students, but many are also becoming frustrated at the lack of recognition for their contributions. This is especially true at the large research-based institutions, where the research mission remains paramount. Most explicit reward structures support research excellence, and the implicit system identifies the strong researchers as being more valuable than the great teachers or service providers. Even when these skills coexist in talented faculty members, it is research capability that is the most lauded. There is very little time for developing suprapro- grammatic or broader based educational experience, especially at the undergraduate level. The pleas for shifts in the reward system have been made for years, but the results are modest. More incentives need to be developed for faculty to support internationalization initiatives for students but also to increase the faculty members' own international skill set.

Work abroad

In addition to study experiences abroad, Canadian students are seeking work experiences as a part of their education. Cooperative education was established in Canada more than 40 years ago as a way for students to gain practical experience and understand the application of the knowledge they were acquiring in classrooms. It is estimated that more than 30 000 students from Ontario alone participate annually in these programs, but only a small percentage of these students leave Canada for their experience (Zarek 1999). There are some notable exceptions, and increasingly the attempt is made to find overseas placements so that cooperative education can help address the need to prepare graduates to work in a more global business environment. However, finding and supervising suitable employers is an expensive proposition, especially when targeting parts of the world less accustomed to interns and cooperative-education students. Demand for places usually exceeds the number of those available, and virtually all cooperative-education offices across Canada report higher numbers of applicants than they can place.

Our most successful programs should be a template for new initiatives. Capilano College in British Columbia continues to be recognized for excellence in its Asia Pacific Management Co-operative Program, as it stills seems innovative 12 years after accepting its first 30 students. Experienced postbaccalaureates receive a year of intensive language, culture, and business training, before finding a year-long placement in Asia. The majority of graduates find permanent employment that builds on their international experience, and a recent report indicates that the economic impact of graduates on two-way trade and investment between Canada and Asia over 10 years is in the hundreds of millions of dollars. Dr Scott McLeod, the director of the program, stated that the ratio of return on investment in this program to the Canadian economy is more than 200 to 1 (McLeod 1997).

Many MBA and bachelor of business programs have made international work projects or internships available, but very few make them a requirement. In Toronto, York University's International MBA includes language and culture training and requires an international internship in the country of specialization. In the early 1990s, the University of Victoria began to offer a BComm with a specialization in international business. In less than 2 years, it developed placements in Asia for all of its students — an astonishing feat. There are established and successful consortia like the Co-op Japan Program for engineering and science students. It was founded by the universities of Victoria, Waterloo, and Sherbrooke and now has 17 participating members and excellent experience in developing orientation, language training, and overseas support programs for their placements in Japan. Hundreds of Canadian students have benefited and returned with a specialized skill set to offer the Canadian economy.

The desire for international experience continues to grow, but students are limited by language capabilities and the high costs of finding and supervising such experiences:

> Reflecting on my year abroad I must admit that it was a year of extremes. Some aspects of life in Hong Kong far exceeded my expectations while in other areas I remained frustrated until the day I left … . Many students found internships in their area of career interest. My internship changed my life.
>
> Canadian exchange student at the
> University of Hong Kong, 1993/94

Before the emergence of exchange and cooperative-education programs at our universities and colleges, students themselves organized opportunities to get international experience through organizations such as the Association for International Exchanges of Students in Economics and Commerce (AIESEC) and the World University Service of Canada (WUSC). First established in Europe in 1948, AIESEC has 50 000 members in 87 countries. From a high of 237 students in 1986, the total number of students placed in Canada has dwindled to 74 in 1998. AIESEC can only offer positions overseas on a reciprocal basis: the total number of placements offered to incoming international students is equal to the total number of positions offered to Canadian students overseas. The Canadian executive reports increasing difficulty in locating Canadian businesses willing to employ foreign students for the summer. Perhaps the numbers of cooperative-education programs linked to Canadian universities and colleges has increased to the point that firms traditionally supplying placements simply do not have additional room for foreign students. In any case, now that Canadian students have choices offered by their own institution and often for credit, AIESEC has become a less prominent player in finding international work placements for Canadians.

The volunteer agencies are another source of international experience for Canadian students. WUSC has also been active for five decades in sponsoring international students at Canadian universities and colleges, and, like Canadian Crossroads International and Canadian University Service Overseas, WUSC provides many opportunities for young Canadians to gain international experience. Unlike AIESEC, which places students in the private sector, WUSC's network of individuals and postsecondary institutions focuses on development-related projects and training organizations in less affluent parts of the world.

Government-sponsored internships

New federal initiatives providing internships for underemployed graduates are to be applauded. They are now in their second year of operation. Sponsoring agencies, such as the Canadian International Development Agency, seek out placements with salaries and preparation funding for new graduates. Although a full evaluation of the experience is not yet complete, certainly a significant number of young Canadians have received international exposure, as well as some opportunity to gain experience in their field. With further evaluation of the sponsoring organizations and intern experience, it may be possible to determine which kinds of placements will make the greatest contribution to the Canadian economy in future.

International student recruitment — a strategic assessment

Over the years, international students have attended Canadian universities in slowly increasing numbers, despite ad hoc recruitment efforts and meagre expenditures. There is some irony in the fact that in the early 1990s, when many institutions became more aware of the value of the foreign student as a force for a more internationalized education for Canadian students, the overall number of foreign students entering our universities for full-time studies declined. Concurrently, both provincial and federal governments began to see incoming foreign students and their differential fees as a way to enhance the resources available for postsecondary education without further depleting government coffers.

The Canadian postsecondary-education sector is confident that Canada has much to offer the international community of students, but we now find ourselves in a highly competitive environment, one in which education is dealt with as a commodity. In many academic circles, with the shift to an environment in which financial potential is so prominently featured, there is a great deal of discomfort. A highly subsidized education and a sincere attempt to provide equality of access have been hallmarks of the Canadian postsecondary-education system. The majority of institutions have enjoyed strong enrollments from high-quality candidates, and demand has generally exceeded supply. Efforts have always been made to secure top candidates from everywhere in the world for particular institutions through scholarships, recruitment visits, and the like, but, on the whole, students have made their choices without heavy marketing campaigns, glossy brochures, or slick education fairs.

To some extent, the enriching effects of having international students on campus were taken for granted by Canadian institutions. Long before governments showed direct interest and "globalization" became a catchphrase, those committed to the goals of internationalization provided support and encouraged interaction between incoming foreign students and the local student population. Although these interactions were often confined to the social realm, they unquestionably contributed to a more sophisticated worldview in those Canadians who came to know the foreign students.

The francophone universities in Quebec have not suffered the same decline in enrollment as the rest of Canada. The majority of incoming students are from francophone countries, so Quebec may not be subject to the same competitive pressure. Special tuition arrangements between Quebec and the Government of France eliminate price differences, and the province has been generous in its support of foreign students, especially those from Africa, who make up almost 40% of the total francophone foreign-student population.

The recruitment challenge

As latecomers to active recruitment, Canadians have an opportunity to gain from the experiences of their competitors. Worldwide, the economic incentive has become primary, whereas academic and cultural

144

rationales remain at the institutional level only (de Wit and Knight 1997). Even without a revenue incentive, we are now forced to compete for students from other nations and cultures because others are actively recruiting and redirecting potential students away from Canada. The obvious contribution that overseas tuition revenue can make to the system — as is evident even in publicly funded systems like those of Australia and the United Kingdom — has changed funding expectations at the federal level and has the potential to alter those of provincial ministries as well. Increased tuition fees for overseas students in at least some jurisdictions now seem inevitable. That this should be cause for concern may be difficult for those outside Canada to comprehend; having access to education (and health care) without regard to one's income is a key component of the sense of "Canadianness" and the value system the Canadians themselves use to delineate their culture from that of their very large neighbour, the United States.

The approach in Quebec is distinctly different from that in the anglophone universities in the rest of Canada. Although de Wit and Knight (1997) reported that cultural and academic rationales were predominantly found at the institutional level outside Quebec, cultural and political values seem to motivate the Quebec government in its approach to international students. Indeed, because the government retains any differential tuition charges from international students, the incentive to recruit more students is much more embedded in a long-term strategy of good reputation.

The competitors

Because the highest profile education providers in the United States have been private institutions, overseas students have been part of their student bodies for decades. The best known places, like Stanford or any of the Ivy League schools, continue to select on merit and ability to pay (although some scholarships are offered) and have not compromised academic standards in the process. However, the Canadian education community is well aware of some smaller and less prestigious institutions that may have adopted less stringent admission criteria in exchange for much-needed tuition revenue from foreign students. An *Open Doors* press release, dated January 1998, stated that international students bring more than 7 billion United States dollars into the US economy on a yearly basis (IIE 1998).

Economic difficulties in the United Kingdom shifted the emphasis in international postsecondary education from aid to trade almost 20 years ago. Organizations like the British Council have successfully presented education in the United Kingdom in a coordinated, cohesive manner and systematically made it a billion-dollar industry for the United Kingdom.

A decade ago, Australia followed the British model, taking a countrywide approach to the systematic recruitment of full fee-paying international students. It chose to use the education system to help integrate the Australian economy with those of the Asia–Pacific region (Back et al. 1997). The government provided additional funding for a comprehensive internationalization plan for its own nationals that included curriculum-development initiatives, mobility programs for the Australian student population, and the research and mobility needs of scholars. Financial incentives encouraged universities to adopt internationalization goals, and government influence smoothed any immigration "red tape."

Some local stakeholders

On Canadian campuses, there is still debate about the desirability of actively recruiting more foreign students, setting high fees, and investing in programs and systems to ease foreign students' entry. International-education professionals, faculty members, credential evaluators, and the general public have somewhat different perspectives, but each must be understood if we are to develop strategies to move forward.

Among the general public, there is the perception that our universities are working at capacity; therefore, international students are seen as taking the place of some deserving Canadians in a taxpayer-supported institution. The real benefits of international classmates for Canadian students are still not widely understood, and so Canadians do not necessarily welcome their increased presence. Visitors to campuses in the larger centres of the country commonly mistake the multicultural reality of Canada for evidence that the university is already full of students on visas.

International-program professionals tend to see the positive social, cultural, and educational contribution that a diverse group of international students can make to a campus, and these professionals generally support the choice to open our campuses to more international participants. When international-service organizations first emerged on our campuses, the professionals in these organizations worked closely with church and other service organizations, and very limited budgets, to provide reception and ongoing support for students sponsored by the various aid organizations. The international-service organizations are needs responsive, not for profit, and service oriented. The recent focus on the revenue potential of international students raises anxiety in these organizations about issues of elitism, sufficient support, and appropriate placement that may emerge as the numbers of international students increase.

Faculty throughout the country are always interested in attracting the best scholars to their programs, regardless of their nationality. Many have been leaders in internationalization efforts to date and have enthusiastically endorsed the option of having more international students on our campuses. But many are uncomfortable with setting high tuition fees, selling education like a commodity, and basing admission to the university on the student's ability to pay. Also, concern is expressed about the decrease in the quality of education in the classroom when there are too many students with linguistic difficulties. This is compounded in those universities with very high populations of landed immigrants with weak English-language skills, such as the University of Toronto and the University of British Columbia (UBC). There is also the concern that if institutions rely too much on foreign tuition revenue, they may be tempted to compromise entry standards to meet budgetary requirements.

Admissions officers are asked to screen students based on a set of criteria imposed by the academic governing body. In the past, in anglophone universities, screening for English-language ability has been common, and, in many institutions, the brilliant student with weak language skills was not even considered. The unscrupulous behaviours of some applicants, coupled with the high demand for places in many Canadian institutions, has forced many admissions officers into the difficult role of gatekeeper. Somehow, they must achieve a balance between enforcing standards and projecting a welcoming and encouraging attitude to applicants of many cultural backgrounds.

In Quebec, a French-language competency test is generally not a condition of admission. The attitude is that students know that they are studying in French and will be expected to perform well enough in that language or risk failing their courses. If they have an admissible grade-point average, they are granted entry. It should be noted that francophone institutions have a variety of support courses in the French language, both in summer and year round, so students can

concurrently work on their language proficiency and discipline studies. This approach is common in European schools. Although this is
not the place for an extensive discussion of the merits of having students pass a language-proficiency test as a criterion of admission,
anecdotal evidence from Quebec suggests that leaving the responsibility for language development up to the student has been a successful strategy. Language is not a barrier; effort is rewarded; dropout
and failure rates are minimal; and the numbers of international students continue to grow.

147

Resource allocation

A decision to join the Canada-wide initiatives to bring more international students to campuses should be made with a good understanding of the implications for the services currently in place.
Without a careful audit, to merely add to what is currently in place
would be unwise. The current staff of admissions, awards, student
reception, and counseling can be used to meet the anticipated needs
of incoming students. They can also inform the strategic planning
process by defining the current barriers in an institution and identifying issues specific to a particular ethnic group or geographic region.
Commitment must come from top administrators and often the
board of governors, and they must develop policies on tuition fees,
the number of foreign students, admission standards (such as language
skills), and the ways these are related to the Canadian applicants.

In Australia, the national government set regulations to allow
international students no more than 25% of spaces on any campus,
and the institutions then worked on plans appropriate to their circumstances (Goldring 1984). Because of the division of legislative
powers in Canada, we cannot borrow directly from this experience,
but governmental dialogue still needs to occur. Alberta, British
Columbia, and New Brunswick have provincially funded organizations dedicated to international education, and recently Prince
Edward Island embarked on some joint institution–government marketing initiatives in Asia. In British Columbia, UBC negotiated with
the provincial ministry for a 15% increase in total enrollment of full
fee-paying international students. As previous full-time enrollment
calculations included all students, establishing additional full-time
enrollment as a separate quota not only provides new revenue but
also frees up spaces for Canadians in the funded student allotment
previously occupied by visa students.

If an institution wishes to increase its international enrollment,
then new funds must be dedicated to this undertaking. A financial

plan that includes enrollment projections, promotional materials, recruitment travel expenditures, and new service costs can clearly demonstrate the potential long-run benefits of opening the institutions to greater numbers of foreign students. Some proportion of foreign-student tuition revenue should be dedicated to the provision of scholarships to attract outstanding applicants and support able students who would otherwise be unable to attend the institution.

An increase in the number of international students requires additional investment in services. Students who have been actively recruited and are paying high fees have expectations of good support services (Patterson 1996). By providing reception, orientation, counseling, and ongoing support to international students, one can diminish the difficulties in adjusting to what is for many of them a very different educational system. This investment is needed not only to improve the students' chances of academic success but also to reduce strain on all university services, including those in the classroom. International-student support units in Canada are accustomed to "doing more with less," so staff fears of exorbitant demands on campus should be central in planning the necessary services.

Some system of revenue sharing to allow faculties and departments to gain some financial benefit from having additional international students would be essential. Students from diverse educational traditions have diverse expectations of the workload, deadlines, class participation, and student–faculty relations and create an additional burden on the faculty (Vertesi 1992). Further, a lack of common cultural experience limits the examples and metaphors instructors can use to enliven the material they teach. Successful internationalization of the classroom depends on a positive response from faculty, who must believe that the benefits outweigh the costs. Idealistic arguments alone are simply not strong enough to induce what is sometimes significant change in both pedagogic style and workload in the professorate.

Establishing recruitment targets

Student recruitment should not be an ad hoc process but should match institutional strengths and attributes to the applicant's requirements. All Canadian institutions offer credible educational experiences. Relative to the rest of the world, Canada is a land of beautiful natural settings and is safe, clean, and tolerant of diversity. These strengths can be promoted by all institutions and should form the basis of the general marketing of a Canadian education to foreign students. Beyond these, each institution needs to understand its unique qualities and recognize the wide variety of students seeking an educational experience abroad in an English- or French-speaking environment. What seems a drawback to one student segment may be an attraction for others.

149

For example, some Asian students look for cities with significant Asian populations, like Vancouver or Toronto, where they can be close to relatives or easily find familiar food or surroundings. Others arrive at the University of Toronto or UBC and are very disappointed that they are not surrounded by Caucasians only. Intrepid foreign students may be much more satisfied in less racially diverse communities. No matter how "natural" some connections seem to be, there are some general guidelines to include in planning for targets. Students are more likely to come to Canada when they

- ✦ Know Canada through immigration patterns, large alumni populations, or world institutions or events, such as the North American Free Trade Agreement, the Olympics, music, and movies;

- ✦ Have established travel links to Canada, such as nonstop flights, or flights that do not require transit through the United States;

- ✦ Are part of a growing middle and upper-middle class, who can afford a postsecondary education abroad;

- ✦ Have Canadian embassy or CEC support for international-education initiatives; and

- ✦ Can easily obtain exit visas and take currency out of their home country.

A recently published study (Lawrence 1997) on how students from 10 Asian countries made their selections to study abroad reveals in all cases that the first criterion was the country. This emphasizes the need to promote Canada as a desirable destination for foreign students in general, before marketing efforts focus on individual institutions. Students who have chosen North America indicate that the reputation of the institution and the specific program influenced their choice, whereas students going to Australia and the United Kingdom stated that they were looking for a broadening experience. Much more research on student decision-making is needed to make a wise use of the resources in attracting students to Canada.

150

Box 2
Recruiting foreign students: questions from universities

Canada, like many other countries, is engaged in recruiting foreign students. It does this through its network of Canadian Education Centres (CECs). Although the idea of enlisting more foreign students enjoys broad support from Canadian universities, our way of going about it often raises questions. Why is it, for example, that the CECs, which are often housed in Canadian embassies, should have to charge universities a membership fee, when our embassy cultural programs used to distribute information free to the universities? Isn't there a risk that CEC activities, such as education fairs, are simply duplicating the efforts of provincial agencies or other university groups and organizations? Are the CECs to some extent competing with our own universities when the CECs set up shop in countries where these universities have been active for some time? How can we measure the extent to which this network is really helping to enrol more foreign students in Canadian universities, given it is impossible to determine what influenced the students' decisions? In short, if the costs to the universities are so high and the results are so difficult to assess, we may question whether the efforts of the CECs are really good for the universities and whether it might not be better for the universities, and for Canada, to take a different approach.

Eliminating barriers

When the Department of Foreign Affairs and International Trade (DFAIT) embraced international-student recruitment, it brought much needed attention to the immigration issues facing recruiters and international students. More active consultative committees are bringing government and university officials together to try to streamline the prompt handling of visa requests. Obviously, the establishment of the CECs is meant to alleviate pressure on the embassy staff, and in some locations these are very effective partnerships. However, some of the procedures that interfere with the timely issuance of student visas have little to do with the CEC.

The processing procedures for health certificates, visa changes and renewals, and foreign-student work opportunities and the requirement that foreign students have all funds available for the complete degree program need to be reevaluated. Ridiculous regulations, such as that the visa application provide all information about future place of residence, should be adjusted to reflect the reality of the university setting, where even places in residence may not be assigned until only a few days before term.

Admissions procedures

Professionals in international admissions have made enormous progress in cataloguing and assessing educational structures and institutions worldwide, so fundamental credential evaluation should be much less of an issue. The future of international admissions includes more on-line registration with faster approvals and turn-around times, although the current systems will be maintained for those students without access to technology. Once again, detailed investigation of the applicant's home-country conditions should help to identify those procedures that require tailoring, if recruitment is to be successful. For universities in Canada without a semester system, the September starting date may limit successful recruitment from areas of the world where the yearly timetable differs from Canada's, such as in the southern hemisphere. The University of Calgary recently opted to allow foreign students to begin their studies in January or April because a high incidence of unexpected delays in visa processing was holding students back an entire year.

Language training and bridging programs

Language evaluation remains troublesome. Against the explicit advice of the Educational Testing Service, which developed the official Test of English as a Foreign Language (TOEFL) (ETS 1994–95), scores on TOEFL (or some other test of English) have been used extensively as a screening device at Canadian universities. Although admission procedures require transcripts and other documentation, the language-proficiency scores are frequently used as the first hurdle before further evaluation of a file is carried out. Study after study has shown that TOEFL is not a successful predictor of academic success (Hughey and Hinson 1993), but admissions criteria in many institutions have not changed. There are still stories of faculties raising the TOEFL requirement even higher, after receiving students with good TOEFL scores (550–600) who nevertheless could not communicate orally. In many institutions, it is not widely understood that the most commonly used English-proficiency examinations measure only passive proficiency and neglect the more active skills of speaking and listening, which are also essential to student success.

There are two approaches to take when confronting a student with a language deficiency. The first, to block their admission, is becoming less frequent. The other, to evaluate on academic merit beyond language skills and provide or suggest remediation, is an essential part of any successful recruitment of international learners to our campuses. Increasingly, schemes are being developed involving "conditional admission," together with bridging or transition programs in English language (for example, at the universities of Carleton, Alberta, York, and Western Ontario, to name a few). Several universities offer credit for language-development courses for non-native speakers (for example, at the universities of Carleton, Saskatchewan, and Québec à Montréal) and allow students to begin their academic program while continuing to up-grade their English or French.

The Europeans have been much more flexible about language requirements for their highly mobile students (Teichler 1996b). In many institutions the student may take courses in their native language even when it is not the language of their host country. Sometimes classes are taught in the host language, but students can elect to be evaluated in their mother tongue. In Canada, the University of Ottawa has provided bilingual courses and evaluation in both of Canada's official languages. In any case, universities that have not already done so should establish clear policies and entry tracks for their increasing nonnative-speaking international (and domestic English-as-a-second-language) populations.

Linked to (but not the same as) language preparation are programs that stress the performance expectations and culture of Canadian universities. Sometimes offered as part of an extended orientation, these programs should cover learning and instructional styles, faculty–student relations (for example, Canadian faculty members expect to be questioned), workload, level of self-discipline, student responsibilities, commonly used terminology, assignment-deadline expectations, group-work responsibilities, mid-term- and final-examination formats and deportment, and introduction to Canadian culture, history, social structure, and politics. Whether given for a fee (like UBC's University Readiness Program), for credit (for example, the Capilano College Study Skills course), or as part of the entry program for international students, these programs reduce the incidence of misunderstanding between faculty and foreign students and lead to more successful integration and student success.

Positive implications of internationalization for all students

Having more international students on campus has practical implications for what we teach and how we teach it, even in the short run. However, instructors in Canadian universities are not being asked to change their teaching style only to cater to foreigners — national background is the most obvious dimension of learning differences in any group of Canadian students as well.

Pedagogical dimension

Across Canada, many institutions are increasing the number of non-Canadians in their classes; yet, generally, classes are still taught in traditional Anglo-American lecture-and-discussion format. Perhaps the pressure of teaching to rows of individuals unresponsive to old jokes, silent during class discussions, and bewildered by group projects will be enough to motivate faculty to consider new approaches. Students raised in North America enjoy being taught with humour, expressing their own ideas, and seeing their professor as a guide and facilitator (Flowerdew and Miller 1995). Behaviours appropriate to this model may be highly offensive to students from other cultures. Canada has very little tradition of instructional training for faculty in universities and colleges, but without question, success in a multicultural classroom depends on some adjustment in the teaching styles otherwise successful in Canadian culture.

153

Professors need to develop new pedagogical techniques to encourage the participation of students from cultures where asking for help is unacceptable. Students from cultures where they are rewarded for regurgitating facts cannot instantly become critical thinkers, nor can those from a tradition of students' remaining silent in the classroom suddenly "role play" or speak up in class discussions. They must be nurtured to display more interactive behaviours, especially as it is through their increased participation that their Canadian classmates will benefit from internationalization:

> When I was first in Canada and a professor talked to me in class, I was so embarrassed. Now I am back here in Japan — our professors say that we noisy students are suffering from the UBC effect!
>
> Japanese exchange student in the Ritsumeikan–UBC
> Academic Exchange Program, 1996/97

We need to shift our focus to the development of the best pedagogical techniques to fit the audience or, better still, to provide alternative approaches to the same material, allowing the student to choose. Of course, many excellent teachers across the country do this already, but it must happen more systematically. Innovations and adjustments in instruction initiated because the student body is more diverse can also benefit the other students, as they, too, may find in this innovation a delivery suited to their learning style. Many of the changes are small, a matter of nuance, but they are cumulative and can have a very positive affect on learning outcomes for students, regardless of background.

Instilling an international perspective throughout the curriculum

More attention must be brought to the issue of instilling cross-cultural perspectives in all the material that we teach. The international students in the class should therefore be regarded as a resource in that they compel the professor to provide multiple reference points for viewing the subject matter under review. Obvious examples of this can be found in lectures and discussions of international case studies or literary pieces, but professors will also have less obvious opportunities. Should foresters, for example, always learn good forestry practice relative to Canadian environmental conditions or should they be exposed to some comparative forestry techniques as part their core requirements? This small change in one course might signal that everything else that is being taught is local and pertinent in some geographies only and that graduates will have much to learn when going to new environments.

The international students in all courses are an untapped force for internationalization. One of the most trivial techniques for increasing their potential impact is to make the professor and tutorial leaders aware of who they are in their classes. By calling on these students, the faculty member brings new information to the class and signals to other class members the value of these different perspectives. Given the multicultural nature of Canadian society, many Canadian students can contribute in this way as well. Certainly, in many classes, the topics may not be suitable for this technique. Nevertheless, some variation of it can be developed for every type of teaching format, if the faculty member is motivated:

> I couldn't believe it. There we were in a strategic management class, doing a case on the EU [European Union]. The prof knew I had been in Belgium but never even let me speak during the discussion. I knew more than he did. Maybe that's why he didn't ask.
>
> Exchange student from
> Louvain-La-Neuve, 1993/94

Faculty should also call on Canadian students who have had a university-sponsored international experience, whenever possible. They have an enhanced impact because they are likely to return to more senior classes, which are usually smaller and more conducive to discussion, and to be familiar with a participatory classroom culture (in fact, some schools use frequent class participation as a selection criterion). They feel an intense desire to share what they learn, and they choose to comment on issues salient to their home culture — in this case, Canada.

To further the benefits to the Canadian students who do not study or work abroad, it is best to increase the impact that a highly diverse student population may have. A direct effect can be produced in the formal-education setting of the classroom, but the effect can be greatly enhanced by increasing the opportunities for social inter-action between the Canadian and the non-Canadian students. It is a mistake to assume there will be widespread spontaneous socializing between Canadians and foreign students. Here, too, some incentives are needed to encourage Canadians to get over their shyness. Some examples of the means to accomplish this are the following:

+ Student-society or senatorial positions representing foreign-student needs and responsible for activities that bring students together;

+ Requirements for "buddy" or other international volunteer activity from Canadians as a condition of acceptance to over-seas exchange or cooperative-education programs; and

+ A recognition system for Canadians serving as buddies, such as a social event hosted by the president or dean.

Conclusion

International students, whether they come for a term or a complete degree, require similar services but should be seen as different planks in the university's internationalization platform. Exchanges provide opportunities for study in institutions and in parts of the world to which Canadian students might not otherwise have access. High fees, stringent language entry requirements, or political regulation can be overcome through institutional partnerships. For example, instead of the 13 260 GBP a year tuition fee at the London Business School, exchange students from McGill University pay only their home rate to their university before studying at the London Business School (in 1999, 0.612 pounds sterling [GBP] = 1 United States dollar [USD]). Students on exchange are permitted to go to Italy, Mexico, or many other places, bypassing the usual language testing. It is their respon-sibility to comprehend enough to successfully complete their term.

Exchanges can be a source of foreign students who would not otherwise come to Canada. German students do not pay tuition in their system and have a countrywide international-mobility financial-support system. Most are simply not motivated to pay high tuition fees overseas while degrees at home are subsidized, and yet, they are excellent additions to the Canadian classroom when on exchange programs. Strategic partnerships can add ethnic balance to the international student group and raise the profile of Canada as a destination for other foreign students.

The past decade has seen a profound increase in international activities for students. Where universities have been slow, students themselves have organized programs, such as study tours to China and Latin America, internships, and group projects overseas. Individuals seek out organizations that send them abroad to work so that they will gain the experience they need for their future; the proportion of students doing so is still small, however. There have always been intrepid individuals on campus who need little encouragement to seek out new experiences and expand their horizons. However, most young Canadians are not so bold. A March 1998 survey of undergraduates in a large business faculty in which educational exchanges had been operating successfully for more than 10 years found that 75% of students thought that study-abroad programs were "a desirable part of an undergraduate program" but that fewer than 33% had any intention of applying to these programs (Stanbury 1998). The mere opportunity is obviously not enough. We must convince the other 67% that they, too, must develop international skills, and we must offer more ways for them to acquire these skills.

Returning students are an extremely potent force for the internationalization of campuses. Having spent time in another culture, they recognize differences that are salient to the education of other Canadian students who chose not to travel yet still need to increase their intercultural knowledge. What is required is an approach institutionally coordinated both within and between levels to increase the impact on our programs. Only in those institutions that invest in social as well as academic activities that bring domestic and foreign students together over and over and provide a forum where their students can speak out about their international experiences will the presence of foreign students have any effect on the majority of Canadian students who never go abroad.

Support from the federal and provincial governments is essential to increasing the external profile of Canadian education, but we also need a concerted public-relations effort to remind Canadians of how we benefit from having international students on our campuses. Just as our university decision-makers need more information from national sources on emerging international-recruitment opportunities, the government also needs more dialogue with the education providers so that our rhetoric does not outstrip what we can be reasonably offer. At the macrolevel, we must take the following measures:

- ✦ Develop a coordinated plan to raise Canada's profile as a destination for international students;

- ✦ Establish measurable targets for numbers of incoming foreign students;

- ✦ Improve our investment decisions by assessing the impact of various marketing initiatives, such as fairs, written materials, and web links;

- ✦ Coordinate our coverage of major educational events to share costs across various players;

- ✦ Assist in the development of further international work opportunities for Canadians overseas and for foreigners in Canada;

- ✦ Solidify mechanisms for communication between practitioners and legislators to address regulative barriers to entry of full-time and exchange students;

- ✦ Enforce national standards for ethical practice and for provision of foreign-student services; and

- ✦ Develop a national–international credit-transfer scheme to decrease the administrative burden of exchange programs and to secure transfer credit for Canadians.

But in the end, no matter what the DFAIT initiatives are, no matter how competently the CECs promote Canada, and no matter how well organized provincial jurisdictions become, our success will depend on the actual experiences of the students on the campuses.

At present, the Canadian dollar allows us to offer real price incentives for international students to choose Canada. This is a tolerable short-run strategy because it creates an incentive for students to "experiment with our brand," rather than choosing something more familiar, like the United Kingdom or United States. But in the long run, surely we do not want to base our international reputation on being the lowest priced provider of a university education. To really increase the quality of what we have to offer international students implies a level of intercultural sophistication and generosity that will take training, resource reallocation, and commitment from everyone on campus from food-service providers, to professors, to information clerks, to senior administrators, to housing staff, to student organizers. Word-of-mouth reputation is an enormous motivator in international students' choice of a country for their education (Lawrence 1997). The most potent marketing tools we have are satisfied alumni.

Universities and colleges where administration and faculty understand the true significance of internationalization are the ones that actively invite students from other cultures and treat diversity in their classrooms with respect. They ensure that revenues are reinvested in the further development of programs and services. And they build reward systems that encourage faculty to include intercultural perspectives in their teaching. Anyone can write internationalization into their mission statement and sign a few agreements. But the leading institutions in this field manage to actually change the habits of faculty beyond the superficial, train their staff to be generous toward diversity in their student body, and convince their students of the importance of intercultural skills in their careers and personal growth.

158

Chapter 7

New Forms of International Cooperation

Fernand Caron and Jacques Tousignant

This chapter deals with the international relations of Canadian universities and, more precisely, the probable evolution of these relations over the coming years. We shall support our analysis by looking at a number of models of international relations currently in use among universities: some, because they are new and deserve to be examined to see whether they hold promise for the future; others, because, although they may be conventional, the universities still regard them as important. This chapter then attempts to identify those of the various kinds of cooperation that are most likely to shape the future of our universities and to guide the manner in which they go about their fundamental mission of education, research, and service.

Other chapters in this book point to the particular routes that international cooperation is likely to take in the near future: the offer of study-abroad programs (Chapters 5 and 6), distance education

---

NB: At the outset, we would like to say how useful we found the documentation that the Association of Universities and Colleges of Canada kindly made available to us from its files. It provided an essential complement to the information we had already.

(Chapters 6 and 8), and the use of new technologies (Chapter 8). Here, we consider the likely evolution of international university cooperation as a whole.

Some current and new characteristics of international cooperation in use by Canadian universities

International university activities are typified, as we see it, by three factors: a wide variety of activities, more institutionalized cooperation, and more structured activities in international research and development.

A wide variety of international activities

University people are themselves the first to admit surprise at the way new initiatives keep cropping up in international cooperation. The area of student mobility, in particular, displays a wide variety of models that institutions are constantly adapting, depending on the discipline, the level of study, the importance the institution attaches to international ties, and whether the projects are entirely self-financing. Take, for example, the various formulas that have been conceived in many universities for making MBA courses and undergraduate management-science studies more international.

This great diversity can be explained by the fact that in Canada there are no broad public cooperation programs, such as we find in universities in the European Union, that might serve as a channel for an important part of international cooperation. It also likely reflects a continued lack of the institutional planning needed to develop international relations and financial support for them in many universities. In fact, members of the university community have often been obliged to act without any clear institutional support, and they are accustomed to working with anyone they think appropriate, in the way they think best, and in the places that most closely suit their interests. The absence of any major public programs, as well as the continued failure of institutions themselves to take responsibility, implies as well that the financial support provided for international relations is often modest. This makes it difficult to develop large-scale projects and tends to promote the proliferation of small-scale initiatives.

The lack of major public programs has had its beneficial effects, however. For one thing, it has long obliged the more dedicated internationalists to draw on their imagination and seek out all kinds of formulas for getting their projects under way — hence, the astonishingly broad range of activities and the great freedom with which projects can be adapted to particular circumstances. This creativity and this diversity are important to preserve while we strive to promote broader and more generous public programs.

More institutionalized international cooperation

When it comes to international relations, a growing number of Canadian universities are no longer content to leave this strictly to the individual initiatives of professors, students, or administrators. Some institutions are actively promoting and supporting international relations — they plan and set their priorities depending on the discipline, the region, and the kinds of partners desired. Instead of leaving each sector of international activity to evolve on its own, they establish links among them to reap greater returns. For example, in many places, it is no longer regarded as sufficient merely to expand the number of international agreements, take in a growing number of foreign students, or provide for more individual study opportunities abroad for our own students. The intent now is to ensure that all of these factors are mutually reinforcing and are henceforth used in support of clearly defined institutional objectives, which are essentially to broaden the international scope of research and to transform university communities into real centres of international culture and education for the benefit of all and not just for the benefit of restricted groups. Not all universities have yet reached this point, but it is a trend that can be observed in more than one institution.

More structured activities in international research and education

University research has long been broadly international. It is now becoming more so, given the breadth of the issues it is being called on to address and the need to develop multidisciplinary approaches for which the required experts and technologies may be scattered all over the world. What is new is that universities are seeking more than ever to make sure that this increasingly international research will contribute explicitly to producing young researchers who are at ease with international life in all its dimensions.

162

In the context of a movement now well under way, universities are also devoting more of their energies to designing and offering their students new areas of training with a distinctly international profile. These programs are no longer aimed only at postgraduate students, but at the broad undergraduate body as well. The greatest changes to date have probably been in the realm of the administrative sciences, but, little by little, engineering, education, health sciences, and indeed all the other disciplines are becoming involved, because to varying degrees all professions and, in the end, all jobs have an international component. It is more important than ever, therefore, for all students to be able to work in an interdependent and global setting in their own chosen disciplines. Offering an education with an international flavour is becoming an integral part of university training and a determinant of its quality. As in business and government, so in the university it is now recognized that this is a key dimension of the mission of the university itself. No longer can this dimension of education be looked on as a mere frill to be indulged in only if one has the time and the means to do so.

The internationalization of universities, as this movement is now coming to be called, is gradually embracing all universities. It is the organized, formal, institutional development of the international dimension in all its forms and its integration into all spheres of university life, with active participation from both the administration and the professors, as well as other groups within university communities. To give an idea of the scope of this phenomenon, in the academic year 1994/95 alone — the year of the last Association of Universities and Colleges of Canada (AUCC) report (AUCC 1995c) — more than 15 of the 89 universities in Canada adopted formal internationalization policies, in addition to those that already had such policies. What must that number be in 1999?

This formal commitment from a growing number of universities to the process of integral and integrated internationalization helps to explain many of the changes that have taken place or are now under way in the international relations of Canadian universities. We are witnessing a proliferation of international networks of all kinds, and more and more universities are adopting criteria to guide their choice of projects for scientific collaboration and development assistance. They will continue their efforts to expand the mobility of their students and will ensure that foreign students and teachers join our university communities in ever greater numbers to help build up their international character.

New partners, new partnerships

New partner countries and new issues

The recent changes brought about by the generalized globalization of trade, the major political events that have occurred in recent years, and decisions made by governments at both the federal and the provincial levels have meant new challenges for Canadian universities, as well as some unique opportunities.

163

Thus, we find that countries or regions that were not formerly considered prime partners for Canada and its universities have suddenly taken on greater or renewed importance. This is true of several countries in central Europe, African countries (such as Rwanda), Chile, Haiti, Mexico, Asian countries like Viet Nam, and others. And this list is sure to grow and to change in the coming years.

At the same time, new areas of activity have been added to the traditional ones. Cooperation activities in agriculture, education, health, forestry, and hydrology are still very important, but they have been joined by more recent activities concerned with the environment, community development, and the advancement of women. In recent years, there have also been growing demands for massive university intervention in the areas of democratic development, governance, human-rights training, civil law and justice, dispute resolution, and training for the public service. A whole new chapter is opening for international university cooperation.

The future of bilateral and multilateral agreements

Universities have always employed a large dose of pragmatism in selecting their international partners. Thus, we now find a great variety in terms of both partners and forms of association, in addition to the conventional bilateral agreements with which universities have been fully familiar and that still have their place. Most of these arrangements are entered into freely, whereas others reflect the specific requirements of subsidized programs, such as federal initiatives relating to student mobility in the member countries of the North American Free Trade Agreement (NAFTA) and in those of the European Union (under which there must be at least two participating universities from each country). As well, partnerships may last for the duration of a project (from 2 to 5 years) or they may be established to pursue objectives over an indefinite number of years. Finally, these agreements may be formally established, or — and this is becoming more frequent — they may simply be based on the good faith of the partners. More than ever, we find all these models coexisting. And the universities, bolstered by their experience in this area, are swift to choose the formulas that best suit each of their projects.

A well-known model is the bilateral agreement between two universities, one in Canada and the other abroad. It has variants whereby the two signatories may be joined by a limited number of other partners on both sides. The basic formula has stood the test of time and gives every indication that it will continue to be a popular option. Then again, there are multilateral agreements with strictly limited, permanent numbers of participants. Examples of such agreements abound, and university professors and administrators can nearly all point to agreements of one or the other sort in which their own university is a partner. By way of example, we have the China programs of the University of British Columbia (UBC) and UBC's 20-year agreement with the Japanese University of Ritsumeikan; the Bali Sustainable Development Project of the University of Waterloo, with two Indonesian universities; and many others.

These agreements usually arise from, and are promoted by, the leadership of a few professors or administrators. For the most part, they involve multiple facets and produce significant results with minimum administrative costs. Because participants can come to know each other very well over time and develop professional friendships, business can be dealt with briskly and in full confidence, and subprojects spring up frequently: joint research, meetings of professors and researchers, student exchanges, and even teacher exchanges, with the result that they learn each other's languages, influence the choice of subject matter for reports and theses, etc. This is an excellent type of agreement that should be encouraged, together with the other already existing models for cooperation.

University groupings created through international projects

University groupings created through international projects — which come to be known as networks once they have acquired a certain stability — can arise from either the initiative of their partners or the requirements of certain public cooperation programs. Universities have learned to value the special benefits of this form of collaboration and seek to promote more such arrangements. With several universities involved, it is possible to take on larger and more complex projects and take advantage of complementarities. It is also easier in this way to ensure the continuation of certain projects over the medium and longer terms (such as by setting up a new department or launching a new program of studies), and it tends to enhance the project's credibility with funding agencies.

One of the most interesting of the spontaneous groupings of this kind is undoubtedly the Canadian Higher Education Group (CHEG), which brings together five Ontario universities and a private company to undertake certain international projects. The Commonwealth Universities Study Abroad Consortium, with 9 Canadian universities and 35 foreign institutions, is another example of this type of spontaneous association, as is the Inter-American Organization for Higher Education (IOHE), a vast grouping of more than 350 institutions of higher learning from throughout the western hemisphere.

Also, a number of more or less temporary and informal groupings have resulted from university participation in international public programs. Such partnerships, which were at first regarded as a constraint — especially by francophone universities that often found themselves dealing with anglophone partners — now seem to be increasingly popular among the universities, and to such a degree that the number of partners involved in any one project often exceeds the strict requirements of the program. The Canadian Program for North American Mobility requires at least six institutions of higher education (two in each partner country) to form a consortium to collaborate on a given project; this number is often exceeded in practice.

As well, the Canada–European Union Cooperation Program extends formal invitations to the members of consortia formed under the program to take on other institutions as associate members, and indeed this frequently happens: in some projects we find up to four, and in one case seven, Canadian universities associated. The program for University Partnerships in Cooperation and Development of the Canadian International Development Agency (CIDA) also involves setting up major networks of institutions, often in several countries. Thus, for example, we have the Groupe interuniversitaire de Montréal (inter-university group of Montréal), comprising research professors from four Montréal-area universities, under the leadership of the Institut national de la recherche scientifique (national institute for scientific research), a member of the Université du Québec system, also within the CIDA framework, working on urban development in Central America and the Caribbean with such partners as the Latin American Faculty of Social Sciences and several universities in the region. By the end of this 10-year program of intensive collaboration, one will see profound changes in all its partners. In addition to such associations, a great many international networks, either recently created or more long standing, are devoted to research, such as the Coastal Resources Research Network, which embraces researchers in 90 countries.

Growing diversity of partners: university–business partnerships

The partners have become much more diverse, as have the purposes underlying these groupings. This is a development that we may regard as irreversible. Universities are now more likely than in the past to work not only with other universities but also with community colleges and the CEGEPs (collèges d'enseignement général et professionnel [colleges for general and professional education]) of Quebec; governments and ministries, both Canadian and foreign; public and private agencies, such as the United Nations Educational, Scientific and Cultural Organization, the World Bank, and the Inter-American Development Bank; nongovernmental organizations (NGOs), etc.; and private businesses. The nature of the project determines which partners the universities seek out.

Cooperation projects frequently involve a number of aspects, including human-resource development. Consequently, among the partners on any project, it is now common to find private companies working side by side with universities and colleges. Two examples illustrate this trend. The Ryerson Training Program is a consortium of Canadian universities, colleges, and private companies working in Brazil to reduce pollution and manage industrial waste. The partners divide responsibilities among themselves for the project's several interrelated aspects: human-resource training, sale of equipment and technical services to Brazilian companies, and even joint research between Canadian and Brazilian universities. We may also point to the McGill University project in China, in which the university works with the Royal Bank of Canada, the Great West Life company, and the Chinese partners to train managers for the banking and insurance industry and thereby develop the Chinese financial-services sector. There are many other such partnerships.

Cooperative arrangements between universities and businesses are becoming more frequent, and this trend is very likely to continue. The motivations behind such agreements are many: for example, it is becoming a common practice for universities to ask companies to accept student trainees, here or abroad (in administrative sciences and engineering, for example), or one partner (either a company or a university) may approach the other to provide the expertise to solve a specific problem or take over a particular aspect of a project, depending on the respective strengths of the partners.

The nature of the relationship between the private company and the university, along with the models they use, will change according to the purpose at hand. But not all models are equally useful. Each of the partners must be fully aware of their own interests and those of the other party, and they must work together to assess the possibility of properly serving those interests. The university, for example, will need to determine whether it is expected to provide research or teaching and to ensure that in either case it will retain control over its own specific fields of activity. Creating a consortium such as CHEG would seem to be a particularly interesting approach in this respect. The five member universities and private company take part in their joint projects as equal but distinct partners; in fact, the role of each partner and in particular the activities to be performed by the company were the subject of a general agreement negotiated in detail and at great length between the partners, although they can adjust it to suit the nature of the projects. At the other end of the scale, there is the private company that is imposed on a university or that exerts its project-management authority over the university in cooperation programs carried out nearly entirely with university or college resources. The three CIDA programs for institutional strengthening in the Maghreb — Pricat in Tunisia, Pricam in Morocco, and Prical in Algeria — are examples of this. Applying models of this kind can easily result in disputes because the company can all too readily intrude into the specific fields of activity of the university.

167

Box 1
Canadian Higher Education Group

Membership

+ Carleton University, McMaster University, University of Guelph, University of Waterloo, University of Western Ontario, and the Hickling Corporation

Nature of the program

+ Resources pooled to undertake specific, large-scale international development projects — five universities and a private company

+ Expected output — greater international visibility, more expertise in international management and in approaching certain clients and major donors

+ Unincorporated partnership of equals — projects selected by the group, as partner or as contractor in each project, with all partners involved in the Management Committee

+ Internal rules established jointly, in advance — annual contribution to development fund ($5 000), cost recovery, fees prorated for work performed, profits shared equally among the six partners

Contact information

+ E-mail: hickling@hickling.ca

+ Internet: www.cheg.edu

New government initiatives

Over the last few years, Canadian and foreign governments have been increasingly active in establishing the basis for agreements related to higher education and research, which normally constitute a specific aspect of accords that are above all commercially oriented. These arrangements are entered into with more or less conviction, depending on the case, and without any major financial commitment. However, the result has been to provide higher education with a number of programs for fostering exchanges. Obvious examples are to be found in the programs for student mobility created within the framework of NAFTA: those with the European Union; the France–Quebec agreements intended explicitly to intensify economic and cultural relations between the two societies; and the Ontario program for cooperation with four European regions (Baden–Würtemberg, Rhône–Alps, Catalonia, and Lombardy). All of these have the effect, directly or indirectly, of bringing a greater element of student mobility into higher education systems.

This new-found interest of Canadian and provincial governments in the international contributions of universities is a step forward. Governments have their own political and economic objectives; it is up to the universities to seize these new opportunities and, as in other circumstances, to act as responsible partners. This means, first of all, insisting on respect for constitutional jurisdictions and, second, recognizing each partner's specific capacity to participate in the design and management of programs.

A broader role for higher education associations

Another novelty, at the provincial and national levels, is the university association designed to represent universities in dealing with national associations in other countries and to foster more intensive cooperation in research and university training. These initiatives are resulting in solid international links and a broader awareness, extending beyond national frontiers.

Thus, the AUCC has become the recognized representative of Canadian universities among Mexican national organizations such as the National Association of Universities and Institutions of Higher Education and the National Council of Science and Technology and among Chilean organizations such as the National Commission for Scientific and Technological Research. In Quebec, the Conference of Rectors and Principals of Quebec Universities (CREPUQ, Conférence des recteurs et principaux des universités du Québec) negotiates agreements for student exchange programs between Quebec universities and universities and technical institutes in France, other countries of Europe, and the United States. In 1996, CREPUQ also negotiated with the French Conférence des présidents d'université (conference of university presidents) and Conférence des directeurs d'écoles et de formations d'ingénieurs (conference of directors of engineering schools and institutes) a France–Quebec framework agreement on the recognition of degrees and the validation of studies, as well as a framework convention on thesis coadvisers from both French and Quebec institutions. IOHE provides a fine example of a large international university association. Its activities are winning increasing respect, both domestically and abroad.

Precedent-setting trends in study programs

Fortunately, many institutions are devoting increased attention to the international dimensions of their study programs. Greater stress is now placed on building an international component into postgraduate programs (internationalization of the MBA program, for example), and international elements are incorporated more systematically into programs at the undergraduate level as well. Universities are modifying their syllabi, adding courses, creating new concentrations, and even developing new programs (as with the three new bachelor's-degree programs in international studies now offered at the University of Toronto). Opportunities are proliferating for foreign-study semesters and work–study abroad at the undergraduate level. Such activities are in fact mandatory in certain programs, and they can be used to earn academic credits.

Today, the professors and administrators responsible for managing such programs must deal with a whole set of international cooperation agreements relating to student mobility, study periods abroad, selection and integration of foreign students, and host arrangements for guest professors, researchers, postdoctoral students, etc.

Two initiatives for double accreditation

Two initiatives deserve particular attention because they represent the first efforts in an area that is bound to become the subject of many agreements: training in two systems, leading to double accreditation (two degrees).

What is involved here is the integration of complete study programs offered by institutions in different countries into a single curriculum or even a single program. These can be undergraduate or postgraduate programs. Students registering for them are offered the chance to benefit from an education with the stamp of the two original programs. Over the course of their studies they undergo a good deal of immersion in the society and culture of the partner country. Canadian universities are only beginning to experiment in this direction. European universities are ahead of our own in this respect, thanks to the experience that their faculties have accumulated through ERASMUS (European Community Action Scheme for the Mobility of University Students), now called SOCRATES. This program amends and enriches programs of study to allow for this type of initiative.

In Quebec, as well as in the rest of Canada, several projects of this kind are under consideration. But it seems that only one is currently active, the International Double Accreditation Program in Automated Production Engineering (Programme de formation internationale bidiplômante en génie de la production automatisée). This has been offered jointly since 1994 by the École de technologie

---

Box 2
International Double Accreditation Program in Automated Production Engineering

Membership

+ École de technologie supérieure (ETS, school of advanced technology), Université du Québec à Montréal, and Fondation EPF (École d'ingéneiurs [school of engineers]), Sceaux, France

Nature of the program

+ Single integrated academic track, with a Quebec and a French program

+ Two engineering diplomas in automated production, recognized in France and in Canada, with the right to practice professionally in North America and Europe

+ Studies and work terms in industry, alternating annually for 4 years between ETS and Fondation EPF, with a preliminary year in France for the French students

+ Students selected by jury, after admission to ETS or Fondation EPF, according to the admission standards of each establishment

+ Instruction divided into basic courses (11%), basic sciences (11%), mathematics (9%), specialty courses (28%), international culture (6%), four industrial work periods (35%), and foreign-language studies

Contact information

+ E-mail: ltremblay@etsmtl.ca

+ Internet: www.etsmtl.ca/progetud/7285.htm

supérieure (school of advanced technology) of the Université du Québec à Montréal (UQAM) and the Fondation EPF (École d'Ingénieurs [school of engineers]) in Sceaux, France. Under this program, French and Quebec students constitute each graduate class. Instruction and work assignments in industry alternate between the two countries, for 5 years in the case of French students and for 4 years for Quebeckers. This ensures prolonged immersion in two professional and social cultures. The result is both an enriching living experience and a broad educational experience. Students earn double accreditation and two degrees from the two institutions, which grants the right to practice in North America and the European Union.

171

Another innovation of a similar kind is a codirected doctoral program in Quebec, which has been in place since 1996 and has already attracted a number of Quebec students. Under an agreement between France's Conférence des présidents d'université (conference of university presidents) and Conférence des directeurs d'écoles et de formations d'ingénieurs (conference of directors of engineering schools and associations) and Quebec's CREPUQ, a doctoral student now has the opportunity to pursue his or her studies simultaneously in France and in Quebec under the joint direction of two thesis advisers, earn two degrees, and receive training in both countries.

"Sandwich" doctorates

The "sandwich" doctorate is not new, but it is growing in popularity and certainly deserves support. At this time, it is of increasing interest to developing countries seeking doctoral training for their young professionals; it is also attracting a still-limited number of our own students. In this type of doctoral program, a student acquires a portion of his or her training in a top-ranked foreign university, in both industrialized and developing countries. The formula is relatively flexible and contains the following elements: university enrollment and thesis defence in the home country and a period of time in a foreign country to carry out a portion of the related academic and research work. This formula offers several advantages: a strong professional grounding in the home country; an education that is enriched through immersion in a foreign setting, which is of particular interest to universities in developing countries; an expanded number of foreign students in the advanced study programs of the host institutions; and reduced international costs for each study project, allowing funding agencies (in Canada and in the developing countries) to finance more students.

Offering educational services abroad: a route worth exploring

Exporting courses and programs is another idea that is not new but that has gained in intensity and taken on new forms. The administrative sciences, in particular, but also education, health sciences, and engineering, are in great demand in foreign countries.

Regular programs

There have been a number of experiments in which an institution in Canada accepts responsibility for offering one of its programs abroad until the foreign institution is in a position to shoulder the burden itself. This is how Saint Mary's University, responding to an invitation from the Gambian government, recently began to offer a bachelor of arts program in a country that still does not have a university.

Universities will also continue to be invited by developing countries to conduct programs of study leading to master's degrees, postgraduate diplomas, and undergraduate degrees for classes of students brought together specifically for this purpose (over a period of 3–5 years). These programs are offered mainly in the areas of education and health sciences but also in engineering: for example, the Université du Québec à Trois-Rivières (UQTR) offers a master's-degree program in educational administration in Africa, and the University of Manitoba offers a program leading to a certificate in nursing sciences in China.

In another fairly new practice, foreign countries request specific programs to be given that are not intended to be incorporated into their own higher education system but are expected to retain their "originality" and are desired precisely for their specific nature. This is the case with several MBA programs. An example is the one offered by UQAM. The Dominican Republic has expressed great satisfaction with it. This program is given locally in Spanish to Dominican managers and has the added advantage of providing the Dominican managers with insights into the North American economy. Morocco has asked to have this program to counteract the influence of France's approach to management. This program is of particular interest to small and medium-sized enterprises. In fact, even a prestigious university like Paris–Dauphine has decided to add this Quebec MBA to its already diversified programing, as the Quebec program can be expected to enrich the range of management styles offered to French students, particularly working managers seeking additional training and skills upgrading.

Special programs abroad: an inevitable development?

The intensive training sessions offered by several universities abroad remain a sector of dynamic activity and one that is bound to become more interesting from more than one point of view. Yet, the universities are facing competition. It is up to them to make the best use of their teaching resources and institutional guarantees.

173

Universities are increasingly seeking to enhance the institutional fallout from these activities, which can all too often remain marginal from the point of view of other university interests. They are, for example, inviting their regular students to take part in these sessions as instructors, tutors, monitors, etc., either abroad or at home. One illustration of this comes from the Richard Ivy School of Business at the University of Western Ontario, which offers intensive introductory courses abroad, dealing with the key concepts and practices of the market economy. Every summer some 45 students from its MBA program are given the chance to spend several weeks teaching abroad, mainly in Eastern Europe.

Then there is the phenomenon of "exporting within the country," that is, offering in Canada intensive sessions designed specifically for foreign officials and managers. These sessions are of particular interest to business people from Japan and China (UBC and Saint Mary's University), Central Europe (York University), Africa (École des hautes études commerciales in Quebec), and other countries. Other groups, especially in the areas of education and health, are eager to take these intensive training courses. This is a useful formula and one that can provide significant benefits for the host institution.

What interest do the universities have in these growing activities to provide instruction abroad? For one thing, this is one of the rare cases in which the universities can generally reap a financial benefit, particularly when they are dealing with large companies, which is, in fact, the primary reason for offering these programs abroad. But what of the potential impact of this foreign teaching activity on the internationalization of training in the home institution? If there are too many of these initiatives, they may distract faculty from their primary task at home and create human-resource management problems at a time when such resources are shrinking. Yet, we must give due weight to the fact that faculty can develop international skills and experience in this way, to the greater benefit of their students in Canada. Moreover, it has been found that more and more master's-degree and doctoral students are engaged in these projects. And over the medium term, as Canadian universities become better known, they can attract greater numbers of foreign students. We should therefore foster this international activity with a clear vision, measuring in each case the benefits of the project in terms of the primary mission of the institution and remembering that the host country must be able to integrate this "foreign" training into its own culture.

Toward international institutions for teaching and research

It is encouraging to finally see international institutions for university training and research pooling their resources. In addition to international networks devoted exclusively to university research — which are growing in number and increasingly active — several more or less formally constituted "transnational" institutions are now also devoted to education. In francophone academia, a large network for higher education has already demonstrated its worth, the Association des universités partiellement ou entièrement de langue française–Université des réseaux d'expression française (association of partially or entirely French-language universities–university of francophone networks). In the same vein, we can mention the project now under consideration for the University of the Arctic, involving Canada, Finland, Norway, the Russian Federation, Sweden, and the United States. The objective would be to create a geographically dispersed institution devoted to defending and promoting the environmental, cultural, and economic integrity of the Arctic regions and bringing together faculty and students from each of these countries. We can also add the College of the Americas, an initiative of the IOHE, which is promoting the establishment of training and research systems among universities throughout the western hemisphere (the Americas). In this initiative, faculty provide instruction to students at different levels of university studies, as well as to teachers, researchers, and managers.

Using the Internet and other communication and instruction media to promote international cooperation

The use of the Internet and other new information technologies in education is discussed in detail in Chapter 8, so we will touch here only briefly on the various media, old or new, now supplementing the classical face-to-face contact between teacher and student.

For several years now, some Canadian universities have been using various forms of distance teaching to respond to the specific needs of developing countries. A still widespread practice in Asia and in Africa, as well as in North and South America, is to send out paper documents to students by mail or other means so that they can work on them individually or in groups with the aid of tutors. Increasing use is made of cassettes and videotapes as well. Video conferencing is still beyond the reach of most developing regions because they lack the appropriate infrastructure and the costs are still too high; even in Canada, the use of video conferencing to provide training courses is limited, although the situation appears to be changing rapidly.

Recently, however, the Internet can fairly be said to be bringing about a profound transformation in the ways we exchange information and overcome the constraints of distance. International cooperation activities are directly involved here. Although the universities make little reference to the Internet when they describe their international projects in AUCC competitions, it is true that virtually the whole world is making wide use of it for e-mail, discussion groups, document transmission, Internet telephoning, etc.

A few examples will serve to illustrate the very promising outlook for electronic communications. A mathematics professor and researcher in mathematical didactics in Cali, Colombia, has seen his professional life literally transformed in the space of a few months, thanks to his access to the Internet. There are hundreds, even thousands of teachers and researchers like this mathematics professor in Cali. There are also several Canadian universities offering regular, intensive sessions in host countries with Canadian faculty, alternating these sessions with work periods during which students use the Internet to stay in regular contact with the Canadian faculty and access articles and documents they would never find at home. An example is UQTR, which offers its master's-degree program in pulp and paper sciences in Venezuela. Another example worth mentioning is the Global Young Entrepreneurs Network at York University, which essentially relies on electronic communication to train and develop young business leaders from around the world.

A particular method of exchange: student mobility and its arduous growth

We make specific reference to student mobility as a means of international training, not only because it is particularly effective, but also because we feel that it is currently receiving more attention than it deserves when measured against the challenge of providing an international education for all students within an institution.

Box 3
Global Young Entrepreneurs Network Program: a résumé

Membership

✦ Institute for Leadership Development, York University, and United Nations Trade Point Development Center

Nature of the program

✦ A group of young people (aged 20–30 years) are drawn from all continents, from business or from public or nongovernmental organizations

✦ Instruction is offered in management and international trade, understanding the economic and social aspects of globalization, leadership training for young executives

✦ Use is made of electronic communications (Internet) — transcontinental dissemination of courses, customized answers to questions and problems from young network members, direct communication between members and mentors, opportunity to set up subnetworks and to discover business and collaborative opportunities

✦ The Global Young Entrepreneurs Summit is hosted every 12–18 months, on one continent or another, aimed at promoting young entrepreneurship, management and leadership training, and the expansion of the electronic-access network for young entrepreneurs and managers around the world

Contact information

✦ E-mail: ild@yorku.ca

✦ Internet: www.yorku.ca/org/ild/index.html

Proliferating initiatives

Initiatives to ensure student mobility are proliferating under the joint pressure of the students themselves, education departments, and institutions: study tours ranging from a few weeks to a few months or a whole year (or even longer, in the case of joint study programs); working assignments in companies and in foreign organizations; student "trade missions"; etc. Here again, it seems to be students in the administrative sciences who are benefiting the most, thanks largely to the support of businesses, which put their international networks of affiliates and customers at the service of students.

Tours of study and work abroad are no longer limited to initiatives organized by individuals or small groups but are becoming increasingly institutionalized: these tours are now part of regular study programs and are becoming mandatory in some programs, or can at least be claimed for university credit. Increasingly, they are organized by the institutions themselves. Moreover, the fortunate beneficiaries of study and work terms abroad can share their experiences with their colleagues on their return. Several universities now view such activities as very important; they often constitute decisive experiences for the students; and they contribute strongly to an understanding of international situations, as well as to the acquisition of the skills needed in international dealings.

But this method should not be used to the exclusion of all others. The number of lucky beneficiaries of such mobility will always be too limited. The ability to pay for study abroad remains a major problem and has always limited its growth. As we shall see, even with the support of public programs, this problem has not been solved. Thus, we find institutions and students undertaking all sorts of initiatives to finance their overseas plans. For example, Dalhousie University decided to devote a significant part of its recent tuition increases to promoting student mobility, and Simon Fraser University set up a special fund to help bring foreign professors and students into its advanced studies programs, using the tuition fees paid by domestic students for their own studies abroad.

New public programs

Several public programs to support student mobility have appeared in recent years, sponsored both by the federal government and by various provincial governments. For example, the federal government sponsors the Canada–European Community cooperation program for higher education and training, with an annual budget of $1.3 million and 19 projects under way in 1998; the North American program for mobility in higher education, with an annual budget of $1.2 million and 30 projects under way in 1998; the CIDA University Partnerships in Cooperation and Development program, whose projects can include mobility for students; and several programs related to specific countries, such as Malaysia and Taiwan.

The provinces also offer programs to facilitate student mobility, through either administrative measures or provision of partial funding for the extra costs involved in mobility (generally, overseas travel and certain other costs). Thus, thanks to official framework agreements, students from Quebec and Ontario can spend up to 1 year of their undergraduate studies in foreign universities:

+ Students from Quebec, particulary, can pursue studies under the CREPUQ agreements between the universities of Quebec and more than 400 universities in some 16 countries, including 157 in France and 79 in the United States; the agreement with France on mutual recognition of diplomas and validation of studies; and the agreement on doctoral-thesis coadvisers with France; and

+ Students from Ontario can pursue studies in Germany and in the Rhône–Alps region under the framework of the Ontario Baden–Würtemberg Student Exchange Program, the Ontario Rhône–Alps Student Exchange Program, etc.

178

Foreign students: new expectations

Foreign students fall into two categories: those who register in Canada as regular students and those who come to take part in intensive sessions or to follow courses of study of a few weeks' or months' duration. In the former, the focus of attention has shifted from sheer numbers of students to the need to integrate them into the university community and the institution's scientific life. Their contribution is now clearly essential if our universities are to become the truly open and international institutions we hope to offer to our own students. Universities are also very happy to take these foreign students into their master's-degree and doctoral programs, which might otherwise be less stimulating or even threatened with closure.

Are there sound financial reasons for welcoming these students? On this point, there are divergent views. On one hand, the contribution that foreign students make to internationalizing Canadian education is widely recognized, and it is seen as having considerable value; on the other hand, taking in foreign students imposes direct and indirect costs on our institutions, and these are higher than generally imagined, especially if universities continue to act responsibly. The recruitment of foreign students is still regarded as something of a business, and agencies like the Asia–Pacific Foundation's network of Canadian Education Centres actively promote such recruitment. One thing is certain: foreign students have their place in every one of our institutions, and reasonable investments should be devoted to them.

The offer of intensive training sessions to foreigners on Canadian campuses is another kind of business several universities are engaged in. These courses include language training and a whole range of specific instruction in business, health, and other areas. They are frequently lucrative for the institutions involved. Moreover, some of the students attending them may be induced to come back later to enrol in regular programs. On the other hand, the impact of such sessions on the internationalization of campuses may be fairly limited, especially if insufficient attention is paid to involving regular

Canadian students in these activities (as some universities do) or not enough effort is made to promote real cultural interaction with the visitors. All too often, we find ourselves promoting our own culture enthusiastically, without really seeking to discover the cultures of our visitors.

Some observations on mobility

The number of students who can benefit from mobility is fairly small, especially at the undergraduate level, and is likely to remain so. Across Canada, the proportion of these undergraduate students is probably no greater than 2%, although the participation rate is significantly higher in some programs (in administrative sciences, particularly).

It is worth recalling that mobility is only a means and that the end is still to offer all students an education that provides them with a sound international understanding and, in a certain number of cases and to varying degrees, equips them with international skills. It is therefore important to use all available means, including building an international dimension into study programs themselves, encouraging the students to learn foreign languages, and taking systematic advantage of the presence of the professors in the institution with extensive international experience, guest professors, and the like, and the contributions of foreign students.

The current public and semipublic programs for student mobility are certainly useful. They are part of the solution. However, they offer fewer financial incentives than programs in place in Europe. The Canadian programs (including those in Quebec) are designed as if the majority of students and their families had the financial capacity to sustain the extra costs involved in studying abroad. This is an illusion. A recent survey conducted in Quebec confirmed what we know to be the case in Europe and may readily suppose to hold for Canada as well, that the additional costs of studying abroad represent a major stumbling block to students in search of mobility. And now that provincial governments are less preoccupied with keeping tuition fees at socially acceptable levels, there is even more risk that mobility will become the privilege of a fortunate minority, as to some extent it already has.

We are facing a double task in terms of student mobility. First, we need to ensure that mobility is accessible to the greatest possible number of students; mobility is expensive, but the benefits for those who experience it and even for their institutions are ample reward for the investments made. Second, we need to find ways to ensure that some of the benefits of mobility — which will always accrue primarily to individuals and limited groups — can be expanded to the student body and to the institution as a whole.

180 Conclusion: directions for the coming years

Over the next few years, the following elements should form the basis for the internationalization of our universities: new partnerships between universities, of course, but also between universities and colleges, businesses, and NGOs; new international associations embracing higher education institutions; new study programs with a more international perspective; greater support for student mobility; a greater understanding in governments of the international component of the university mission; and more integration of international aspects into the planning and development of universities in Canada.

In addition, we draw particular attention to three further recommendations for future action: keeping institutional priorities flexible, placing greater stress on foreign-language learning, and using universities to promote diversity and imagination.

Keeping institutional priorities flexible

Does becoming more international mean that universities must constantly enter into new agreements of all kinds? Is it proper for them to accept all the invitations they may receive to join new networks or team up with new partners? There is a clear risk of diluting their focus and efforts, and some international commitments can certainly distract professors and administrators from their basic duty of serving the students on their home campuses. In every institution where this has not been done already, the promotion of international cooperation needs to be integrated into an overall plan, along with the other dimensions of internationalization and, indeed, the pursuit of the institution's fundamental mission. It is now more important than ever that each institution — including each unit, department, and research centre — determine its international priorities and adopt criteria to guide the selection of their target countries and regions, their preferred areas of activity, the complementarities they hope to achieve, etc.

Placing greater stress on foreign-language learning

Although international agreements are multiplying and mobility is growing in Canadian universities, the same progress has not been made in foreign-language learning; nor are any spectacular moves apparent in this direction. In fact, a survey conducted in 1996 by the AUCC and the Canadian Bureau for International Education revealed that learning foreign languages is ranked ninth among the priorities of Canadian educational institutions and governments and seventh in the private sector (AUCC 1996a), even when all kinds of measures are in place to promote education with an international dimension. This is surely an astounding finding and one we should be examining very closely.

We are still far from adopting the attitude of Europeans, who for the last 10 years have invested millions of dollars through the Program to Promote the Teaching and Learning of Community Languages for students and instructors in higher education (involving 13 languages!). This is part of a move to increase student mobility and build the new Europe. Europeans consider foreign languages among the most important necessary conditions for discovering and understanding foreign cultures. People in Europe are convinced that mastering a foreign language will give them a greater ability to penetrate and experience another cultural system — with everything that each culture conveys to foreigners in terms of new values, different sensibilities, and particular ways of organizing society — and that it helps them to place their own cultural system in its relative context. If we confine ourselves to our mother tongue, we run a great risk of never escaping our own cultural setting, no matter how many trips and study tours we may undertake.

Many francophone students go to France, but they also go to Latin America, the United Kingdom, and the United States and to English-speaking Canadian universities. As soon as they leave Quebec, they are forced to use another language. Anglophone students are probably more prone to continue using their mother tongue, even when they go abroad for some time to a non-English-speaking country, as they can count on English having the status of the current international language, however rudimentary and limited in nuance that English may be in many places.

This lack of interest in foreign languages is a source of real concern, if what we are seeking is a true recognition of the value of other cultures and if we hope that international exchanges will promote mutual respect and enrichment. This lack of interest is especially surprising to find in the setting of a university, an institution supposedly devoted not only to professional training but also to solid-ifying students' own cultural base and understanding and promot-ing the cultural heritage of diverse peoples and humanity as a whole.

Using universities to promote cultural diversity and imagination

182 Given the expansion of international relations and contacts of all sorts, does it not seem inevitable that the institutions participating in this process of internationalization are undermining cultural her-itages? For the moment, this risk does not appear to be very great, because of the extreme caution universities exercise in their approach to pooling their activities. But even if they adopted a bolder approach, this fear would be unjustified, because in the first place the pooling arrangements are clearly defined and their objectives are freely adopted by all the partners involved; in the second place, the part-ners continue to show complete mutual respect, without allowing either to become dominant. It is true that neither individuals nor institutions can escape totally unscathed from true intercultural encounters; it is also true that they will emerge from them enriched and, paradoxically, more sure of themselves.

The introduction of public programs in support of international activities, along with the regulations accompanying them, will inevitably imply a certain risk, as well as a tendency to try to cen-tralize and standardize everything, as if whatever is big and unidi-rectional must necessarily be more efficient. Do we really want to force the universities to do everything in the same way? The "old international hands" are well aware that there are many paths to effective international cooperation and that it always requires imag-ination and flexibility.

Bolstered by their experience, our universities will continue to engage in partnerships of all kinds, here and abroad, constantly renewing their approach to their basic mission of education and research and preparing their students for a professional life with a large international component.

Chapter 8

The Impact of Information Technology on National and Transnational Education

Jon Baggaley

With the emergence of each major communication technology, Canada has played a prominent role in its development. The nation's geographical vastness has caused it to attach particular importance to the educational development of its communities, and, unlike other countries of a comparable size, Canada has been blessed with the funds to explore the uses of information technology for this purpose. In the late 1990s, however, Canada's advantages are no longer as distinctive in this respect as they once were. Educational organizations in the developing world are rapidly becoming as well endowed with technology as Canada and are looking with cautious optimism on the educational opportunities of the Internet and multimedia. They are also looking to Canadians to share the benefits of their experience to help them to harness the new media effectively. This chapter will consider the ways Canada can work profitably with international partners to realize educational technology's potential. It will examine the problems of maintaining the techniques and skills demanded by the educational media and the disappointments with which the history of educational technology is littered. It is hoped that by the time the chapter is read, the Internet and other computer-based multimedia will not have gone the way of the dodo as so many other educational technologies have done — wasted through unimaginative use and squandered through mismanagement.

184 Teaching the global village

One of Canada's first advantages in the modern age of information technology was its good fortune to have as favourite sons two of the most notable communications theorists of this century: Harold Innis and Marshall McLuhan. Both thinkers drew attention to, inter alia, the global importance of media in communications. From the 1920s to the 1950s, Innis placed an interesting emphasis on the powers of transportation media to unite and transform culture (Innis 1950), and, in the 1960s, McLuhan led the world to think about the impact of the print and electronic media as no other contemporary thinker had done previously (McLuhan 1962, 1964; McLuhan et al. 1967). He suggested that the media would put an effective girdle around the globe, transforming it into a "global village," and he identified the contribution of the media themselves to the messages they convey. In fact, Innis had been even more specific on this question than McLuhan, in stressing that the impact of a technology arises from the techniques associated with it. Both of these influential Canadians made it self-evidently clear that media techniques would, if misused, fail as often as they succeed in delivering their intended messages.

If there is one type of technologist who should be particularly aware of the possibility of messages being misunderstood, it is the one who applies media in education. To the detriment of many educational technologists, however, they have failed to take the teachings of McLuhan and Innis to heart, blinkered as they tend to be by the exciting, even if unproven, possibilities of each new medium. They may actually have been encouraged in this optimistic attitude by McLuhan's prophesy of the global village. However, as any other son of a small-town Alberta community, McLuhan surely must have realized that this village would not be all harmony and caring; indeed, the global community soon discovered that the culture created by the broadcast media was as much one of warfare and pain as of enlightenment.

Thirty years later, despite McLuhan's prediction, the media have proven no more successful in creating a dominant educational perspective for the globe than they have been in creating any other form of universal enlightenment. But in the 1990s, this may be changing. A new medium has emerged with such cost-effectiveness and universality that it promises a greater level of international understanding than any previous medium. The Internet has taken over from television as the most powerful information technology.

One of McLuhan's observations about television indirectly explains the Internet's current potential. McLuhan observed that television was, at that time, the one medium powerful enough to carry all the others. Broadcast television, McLuhan pointed out, is capable of carrying all types of aural and visual information. It conveys sound, colour, light, shade, movement, the human voice, and the images of all other media. When McLuhan noted this, no other medium could claim the same ability. In the mid-1990s, however, the Internet began to assert itself as a new medium capable of carrying all the others, television included. In the next 10 years, television and the Internet will doubtless merge into one, and the hybrid will be a new supermedium for the next generation. The debates about its appropriate use, however, will be the same as those that people have waged regarding the use of any communication medium for centuries.

Before television was the printing press, a source of controversial material from its inception. Before that, the "word" was carried by traveling actors and minstrels, whose messages were considered every bit as pernicious as any TV program or pop song today. In the 1890s, cigarette-card collecting was held to be a similar danger to society, filling the minds of its male youth with no good thoughts for hours on end. Interest in every medium and pastime yet invented — snooker, pool, television, video games, and now the Internet — has been regarded as a sign of a misspent youth at one time or another. Yet, no medium is better or worse than the content it conveys and the uses to which it is put. To those who happily watched TV wrestling or sorted cigarette cards with their fathers on a weekend afternoon, the gratifications yielded by these media were unbeatable.

In the 1970s, the "uses and gratifications" of media became a major criterion in the scholarly assessment of their social value (Blumler and Katz 1974). At the same time, in the educational corner of media communications, evidence was amassed about the subtle impact of various media production techniques. Canada took an international lead in the design of effective techniques and processes for television's use, not merely at the broadcast level, but also in the service of Canada's many isolated communities. Canadian film and video specialists took their cameras to record material in remote communities across the country, north and south, for use in educational and social programs. Two of the most influential of these early programs were the "Challenge for Change" program, created by the National Film Board of Canada, and the "Fogo Process" of Memorial University in Newfoundland (Gwyn 1972). The techniques they developed generated a new international awareness of the potential of media in community development. Canada's example in this respect has since been followed on every continent and has demonstrated that the techniques of the traveling player–educator are as effective in the late 20th century as they were in medieval days and as powerful when assisted by a video camera as when accompanied by a strummed lute.

Numerous pioneering Canadian technologies have assisted in this process. In the 1980s and 1990s, for example, the Teledon and Alex systems both promised to bring useful audiovisual information, on demand, into homes and workplaces across the land. Unfortunately, each of these systems failed in the marketplace for want of adequate updated content. Other Canadian innovations, including some of the early pay-TV enterprises of the 1980s, failed because they were either too expensive or too esoteric, or not esoteric enough. In short, Canada has had no shortage of innovative flair in the media and communications field and plenty of disappointments, and it has demonstrated a distinctive theoretical and practical expertise in the use of every information technology yet devised.

The collective wisdom about the reasons for Canada's adventurous spirit in the communications industry points to the following factors:

+ The nation's vast political landmass, second largest in the world;

+ The absolute need to surmount the communications and cultural problems that the vast landmass has created; and

+ The pioneering flair that brought many nations together as Canadians.

The unusual range of the nation's educational-media experience, from urban to rural, has taught that effective education is as much a matter of communication process as of product, which is an understanding more commonly found in nations that cannot afford teaching tools as expensive as television or the computer but have become ingenious in using far simpler devices. In more affluent nations, teachers are apt to move on from one promising medium to the next, after their first failures to use it properly, a tendency that leads them to overlook the possible reasons for

+ Their own failure to adopt the appropriate applications;

+ Their own failure to create adequate resources to supply the medium with effective content; and

+ Their own failure to account for the classroom processes needed to enable students to efficiently interpret this content.

For example, at a recent media conference (held, incidentally, on the Internet), some Americans and Canadians decided that educational television is a medium *manqué* and that the tool of choice is now the Internet (World Bank 1996). But if educators have failed to make efficient use of the rich television medium over the years, can they have any greater hopes of harnessing the Internet? If they heed the lessons of their previous successes and failures, they may succeed, however, as even a cynic would have to admit that the Internet has some new advantages.

The Internet as a supermedium

The Internet is the first medium to allow unimpeded, interactive access to information from anywhere in the world that has a supply of electricity. A computer with Internet software can be run from the cigarette-lighter socket of a jeep in the fields of Africa as easily as on the streets of New York (Baggaley 1997). It can communicate by increasingly inexpensive satellite means from either of these locales to the other. The Internet can bring live music and comment from the radio stations of the world to one's desktop; with a little extra effort, it can carry the images of television and can be carried on it. It allows the world's students and teachers to share information previously inaccessible to them; and distance-education programs and institutions are developing around this concept on every continent. On this basis, the "developed" and "developing" worlds are drawing nearer to one another with remarkable speed, and Canadian scholars who take sabbatical leave in parts of the developing world are shocked to find that the facilities there are often superior to those of their own universities back home. This lament is heard increasingly as Canada's educational institutions continue to suffer through their 1990s' era of relative economic hardship. They hope to emerge from

188

this low point with new structures and priorities in place and new methods to attract a wider student revenue base.

For this purpose, Canadian educational institutions are extolling, almost in unison, the benefits of online and distance-based course delivery and the Internet's unique ability to carry it. However, even the largest of universities do not possess the ability to implement an online strategy overnight. The pedagogical approaches of traditional institutions do not readily lend themselves to media delivery, and the institutions themselves often lack a cohesive view of the steps they need to take in developing or converting their courses for this purpose. For example, one Canadian university recently stated that it needed to increase student numbers to augment revenues and fulfill its obligation to offer degree certifications to students in remote parts of the province. To achieve this, faculty members throughout the university recognized the importance of developing distance-education courses for delivery by television and the Internet. A need for university cuts, however, led simultaneously to the closure or restructuring of programs throughout the university, including the one department with the human resources needed to create the required mass of distance-based course materials. The lack of shared institutional perspective among the university's administration and faculty led to the abandonment of its distance-education plan, although it was identical to schemes bringing new revenues into universities and colleges across the continent.

If the educational institutions succeed in creating a technological infrastructure for their course delivery, they still face the hurdle of generating a continuous supply of effective teaching materials. The current demise of educational television as a popular institutional medium is largely due to the unforeseen complexity of its production process and the inordinate amounts of time and resources needed to produce an adequate supply of programing. The challenge of placing educational programs on the Internet will be no less taxing. A teacher who has been accustomed to entering a classroom and lecturing extempore can be shocked to find that delivery at a distance requires all course materials to be prepared in advance, not just the classroom handouts, but also a text containing the spoken words and illustrations, for each lecture. If the only adequate medium for teaching a particular topic is television, the teacher may also be challenged to produce a fully featured videotape for every class; and even with the assistance of an expert institutional media service, producing this can tax the time and patience of the greatest media enthusiast.

In addition, the materials have to be kept up to date, and copyright clearance needs to be secured for the use of every passage, picture, or diagram created by other authors. At present, copyright clearance of course materials for electronic delivery is by no means automatic (see the next section), and teachers may be unable to use many of their favourite slides and quotations when they move their materials online. In general, effective distance education involves far more work for the teachers than might be expected. Even institutions with a specific distance-education mandate are feeling the pressures that online delivery creates. For example, a 1998 survey at Florida Gulf Coast University revealed that a majority of faculty are distinctly opposed to its use in their teaching. "The problem," the faculty members said, "is that teaching via the Internet — using e-mail, chat rooms and other electronic means — is a demanding proposition for professors ... because of the large majority of student–teacher contacts" (McKinnon 1998, p. F1). Indeed, the addition of technological bases for teaching seems to have given rise to an assumption that teachers can now return to the time-honoured one-on-one model. However, to the teachers of Florida State and elsewhere, this is clearly no less time consuming and unrealistic via distance media than via conventional means.

Ironically, teachers who have not experienced the logistic burden that educational automation involves are apt to voice the opposite fear, that information technologies will make them redundant. Robertson stated that by 2000, students would be learning with the help of "virtual communities," smart agents, and mentor networks and that without schools to staff, teachers would no longer be necessary (Robertson 1998). The vocal opposition that this prospect is likely to generate will be sufficient to sink many distance-education efforts, whatever the merits of the opposing arguments.

It is to be hoped that moderation will prevail and that solid evaluation studies will lead to a sensible harnessing of the new media. By 2000, Internet technology will be capable of providing untold new advantages: transmitting, for example, a high-quality, live audiovisual image of the teachers themselves, thereby allowing them to combine personal and impersonal forms of distance-based teaching as appropriate. At this point, the wheel of invention will have come full circle, and if we are not careful, the new media will be used as unimaginatively as educational television was used in the 1970s. The 1990s' conception of the Internet will be discarded, as was an earlier conception of television, as being too full of poor programing and advertising to be educationally respectable. Last-ditch attempts will be made to share Internet programing among higher education institutions, but this move will be resisted as faculty members point out that other institutions' materials are inappropriate for their students. The main users of the Internet for information delivery will be the corporate sector, which will continue to develop extremely efficient training materials distributed via CD-ROM and other multimedia delivered on the Internet and the World Wide Web.

It is in the commercial sector where the Internet's most prized ability will be maximized: its ability to enable all sides of a communication link to interact. The lack of effective interactivity was television's major limitation. Phone-in programs and talk-shows were the best it could achieve by way of audience participation, however much its producers and presenters longed for it. The Internet, however, will make each medium it carries fully interactive. Managers on the road and in the air will videoconference with hundreds of staff members at their desks; families and friends will unite around the world for fireside chats on each others' television sets; and teachers will begin to use educational technologies in a new way, not as a means to produce old-style productions, but as a forum for interactive communication. If the function of media is seen as being to generate communication processes, rather than products, the Internet may become a completely cost-effective, interactive medium, capable of linking teachers and students as effectively at a distance as in the classroom. Otherwise, the old mistakes will be repeated, and the virtues of the Internet will be forgotten in the excitement of a new wave of information media. If the history of educational technology holds true, the Internet will be far from the supermedium it promises to be.

The international move to distance education

However, Canada can play a major role in anticipating the pitfalls of media-based education and helping to optimize its international benefits. Canadians can advise on the use of new media, such as the Internet, just as they did previously in identifying techniques for the use of video and film in remote communities of Newfoundland, Saskatchewan, and the Canadian north. Knight (1995) indicated that Canadian universities are increasingly aware of, and interested in, opportunities for international collaboration, and they rate international development projects highly (fifth out of 18) among their priorities for international collaboration. As other nations establish the technological infrastructures for development projects, Canada can help to make them work and, in the process, learn about the innovative educational applications of low-technology media developed by less affluent nations before acquiring the means for high-technology education. In educational collaborations involving the Internet — which all nations are discovering more or less simultaneously — the gap between "developed" and "developing" will speedily close, and the international benefits will be reciprocal.

Of particular value in this respect is the fact that Canada is home to world-leading institutions that have delivered their courses by communications technologies since the early 1970s. Quebec's Télé-Université and the Athabasca University of Alberta are small organizations by comparison with the "mega" distance-education universities of other countries (Daniel 1997), but they have been in operation for longer than most of their larger cousins and are no less adept at survival. They can each give ample advice on how they designed and sustain their infrastructures for producing high-quality teaching materials, and they can also apply their experience of bringing effective media education to remote and underprivileged communities as they show newer institutions how to avoid the cardinal sin of educational technology: its tendency to polarize society into "haves" and "have-nots." This particular danger of technology-based education is well recognized by educators at distance-education institutions, especially those with an open-learning mandate.

Box 1
Athabasca University

Canada's oldest distance-education university — Athabasca University in Alberta — has followed the model of the "virtual university," operating without the bricks and mortar of traditional campus-based universities since its inception in 1970. It is also an open university, committed to providing lifelong learning through open access to high-quality university-level programs, regardless of the barriers of time, space, educational experience, and, to a great degree, level of income. From the outset, Athabasca University has taught 100% of its courses by broadcast and other media, including print, telephone, radio, television, and teleconferencing. Its student enrollment is drawn from all parts of the world and usually numbers in the range of 11 000-14 000. During the 1980s, computer-based materials were added to its suite of delivery media, and in the mid-1990s, it began adapting and producing course materials for distribution over the World Wide Web and on CD-ROM. In 1999, Athabasca University has more than 350 undergraduate and graduate courses on its books. By 2000, it hopes to be in a position to present the courses in its disciplines via traditional educational media or the Internet, or both, depending on the advantages of each. New course-development and course-sharing agreements — notably, those with the Télé-Université in Quebec — are broadening both institutions' international clientele and generally strengthening Canada's own role in the global distance-education field.

This is because, with the widespread use of computer-based media, distance education and open learning are coming into conflict. To be totally true to both concepts, an open university has to maintain the best distance-education approaches possible for the students with access to a state-of-the-art Internet-capable computer as well as students who can afford no computer at all. The earlier media of television, radio, telephone, and postal service were by and large accessible to all Canadians, and a distance-education university could safely expect its students to attend its courses via these media without undue hardship. The Internet, however, requires students with access to a well-stocked computer, a condition that a truly open university cannot in all conscience dictate. For this reason, every course that is either developed, converted, or revised for online Internet delivery must also be prepared for delivery at a comparable high level of quality on the more accessible, traditional media. As the design and attributes of all media are different, parallel sets of materials have to be developed for each course, and the logistics of maintaining this vast collection presents no small challenge.

It is of course tempting for those teachers convinced of the benefits of online education to concentrate on developing courseware for this student majority to the exclusion of the dwindling lower tech minority. The reverse temptation can also occur. A teacher whose discipline has been well served by more traditional media can disregard new opportunities to embrace new, potentially more powerful media. If their media selections are justified by ongoing evaluation studies, each of these attitudes may prove to be correct. However, no distance educator can afford to overlook the fact that the proportion of distance-education students with access to a computer is typically far higher (three times so in the case of Athabasca University students) than that in the student population at large. Either the students in distance-education institutions are being drawn predominantly from computer-owning sectors of society or they are being subtly encouraged to purchase computers after enrolling in their courses, and neither of these possibilities is compatible with the goals of open learning.

There is a current unfortunate trend in the philosophy of open learning to think of it as only an ideal, a goal for distance educators to aspire to. Regardless of whether this mind-set is justified, it appears that the growing use of computer-based media such as the Internet is already polarizing society into those who can and those who cannot afford distance education. To reconcile the increasing reliance on high technologies with the requirements of the open-learning mandate, distance educators are placing an increasing emphasis on community-outreach services and parallel uses of computer-based and traditional methods. For this reason, the Indira Ghandi National Open University in Delhi and the Bangladesh Open University in Dhaka are placing a high priority on the use of older technologies (radio and video, for example) in rural outreach. Canada can use its process-based traditions for media education to assist such efforts while encouraging the evolution of the new multimedia as effective transnational tools, capable of continually adjusting their educational messages to the students' varying needs.

For instance, the International Development Research Centre (IDRC), based in Ottawa, is responsible for a major drive to establish communications infrastructures and practices throughout the world. Its Pan-Asia Networking Program provides a model for similar initiatives in Africa and Latin America. Through its Acacia Program, IDRC is training African technologists and educators to use their new networks to alleviate environmental and community-development problems and create electronic networks to share their experiences. IDRC, together with other international agencies, also hosts Bellanet, a secretariat dedicated to coordinating development strategies among information technology specialists. Another Ottawa-based agency,

---

Box 2
Commonwealth of Learning

Founded in 1987, the Commonwealth of Learning (COL) was the first intergovernmental organization with the mandate to encourage development of distance education and the sharing of open-learning–distance-education materials, expertise, technologies, and other resources for students throughout the Commonwealth and other countries. Its 54 member countries are from all continents and oceanic regions, North and South. More than 40 of these countries are active users of COL resources, which address all the needs of the education, information, and training sector, not exclusively those of higher education. COL's main activities are directed to the following objectives:

+ To promote the use of communication and information technologies for distance learning;

+ To facilitate access to affordable, high-quality learning materials and resources in support of formal and informal education;

+ To provide access to training in the adoption and use of distance-learning technologies and techniques; and

+ To provide information and advice about distance-learning systems, programs, and technologies to practitioners and developers.

COL's current initiatives include the integration of a series of national learning grids in Australia, Canada, India, South Africa, and the United Kingdom, with particular emphasis on school education.

Global Access Television (WETV), is the coordinating centre for a major initiative in the satellite delivery of television for international development. With affiliates in 30 countries, the WETV consortium provides clear evidence that television has not yielded to the Internet as the medium of choice in all parts of the world.

At St Francis Xavier University in Antigonish, Nova Scotia, the Coady International Institute continues to spread the international benefits of its 40-year experience with participatory (people-based) development techniques. Simultaneously, the Vancouver-based Commonwealth of Learning (COL), one of the largest distance-education secretariats in the world, is providing information technology services to the peoples of the Commonwealth, a notional one-third of humanity. Since 1997 the distance-education needs of the global francophone community have also been catered to by the Université virtuelle francophone, an intergovernmental agency based in Canada.

Other forms of collaboration in distance education involving Canada and international partners include initiatives to develop the following:

✦ An infrastructure for the implementation of educational technologies, involving Canada's Open Learning Agency and the Telesecundaria in Mexico;

Box 3
Université virtuelle francophone

The Université virtuelle francophone (UVF, virtual francophone university) is based in Montréal and represents 320 universities and governmental bodies in 52 nations (African, European, and Arab countries and those in the Indian Ocean region). The organization has the following objectives:

✦ To unite international francophone expertise in distance education;

✦ To build partnerships of excellence between North and South; and

✦ To increase the dissemination of knowledge throughout all regions of the world.

UVF's activities are based on a competitive model that aims to stimulate the best of distance-education methodologies and encourage their constant improvement. In developing its collaborative training activities, the organization's initiatives seek to make balanced use of the new technologies to ensure cost-effectiveness, pedagogical development, and the adoption of a participatory process that is satisfactorily respectful of diverse identities and cultures. UVF's emphasis is on establishing multilateral research and teaching teams to reinforce links between research, training, and community service. The organization is also stressing the need to define international equivalence for educational programs and courses and to promote opportunities for students to "cograduate" from more than one international institution.

+ A joint curriculum for technology-based learning, involving the University of British Columbia and the Monterrey Institute of Technology in Mexico;

+ A distance-education training program, involving Laurentian University and the South-West Institute of Technology in China; and

+ Provision of accountancy courses by Athabasca University for students of the Tokyo Accounting Center seeking North American accreditation (Baggaley et al. 1998).

The list of Canadian information technology initiatives goes on, many of them drawing support from the extensive aid resource provided by the Canadian International Development Agency. This extraordinary proliferation of Canadian support for information technology projects suggests that knowledge and the sharing of knowledge are becoming effectively border free. However, one must remain cautious about the long-term international prospects for these multimedia initiatives. Despite their vast potential, the development of a totally international, "virtual" educational system is likely to face at least as much opposition at the international level as at the local one. The more the "have" nations offer their distance-education resources for others' use, the more the recipients are apt to fear an imperialist motive. The emergence of national distance-education institutions, formed specifically to resist external influences in their area, is already occurring, and a recent international forum held in Japan concluded that the most practical approach to forming international educational networks may indeed be to "think global, but act local" (Latchem 1998).

Following a review of current moves to form global, virtual universities, Cunningham et al. (1997, p. 180) concluded that "despite the activity in this area already, there is no guarantee that totally off-campus delivery will succeed," and they went on to remark that

> Questions of accreditation, articulation, language, accessibility, ownership, intellectual property, and copyright would have to be dealt with … . Economic and teaching/learning models would have to be developed, implemented and supported — and then these would need to prove to be efficient, effective and sustainable. Reliable and robust communication and technology infrastructures would need to be established. The requirements and expectations of a target student cohort would need to be identified and then fulfilled.
>
> Cunningham et al. 1997 (pp. 189–190)

Intellectual property and copyright issues have been hotly debated in academia since the time when early use was made of educational film and television in the 1960s, and these issues remain moot today. The development of distance-education courses raises particularly awkward questions about the rights of those who design and teach them. It is well established in the majority of Canadian universities that faculty members are the rightful owners of their academic materials, discoveries, and innovations, even in the face of institutional pressures to the contrary. Thus, the teacher can expect to be the first beneficiary of any form of commercialization arising from his or her work. However, distance-education institutions are in a better position than traditional ones to make the case for their entitlement to benefit financially from their employees' academic output. This is because a distance-education institution is essentially two types of organization in one. It is a teaching institution, but it is also a commercial publishing house. In producing and distributing course materials for the use of its students and in being drawn into agreements to share these materials internationally, the institution, as well as its academic authors, can expect to benefit from the revenues that accrue. So the development of distance-education courses is creating scope for a head-on conflict between university and college managements, on the one hand, and their teaching staffs, on the other, and for pressures to redefine the roles of the institution and its faculty in the distance-education process. Property rights agreements differ widely between institutions, and standardized versions of them in the international context may prove difficult to attain and impossible to monitor. The recent strike at York University, one of the longest in Canadian history, points to the strife that may lie ahead as institutions grapple with these issues.

The proliferation of the new multimedia technologies further complicates intellectual property and copyright issues, as ownership and usage of electronic course elements are even more difficult to define than those of print materials. Moreover, conventional publishing houses, which have their own plans to diversify in the educational market and their own commercial interests to protect, have begun to see distance-education institutions as their competitors and are increasingly reluctant to grant them access to the multimedia materials that distance-education teachers need for their courses.

Although information technology promises much, it will certainly deliver less if such problems are not resolved.

Bringing media to the people

Perhaps we have been dazzled by technology and have come to expect too much from it. Perhaps McLuhan unwittingly misled us when he suggested that the media are *extensions of people*; without people to use them well, that is, as *extensions of the media*, the machines are useless. In seeking to package our educational wares for the widest possible audience via bigger and broader media, such as television, we may have lost sight of the extent to which all learners are different and relish the ability to question and deny the ideas they are taught. For years, television producers have believed that the remote, impersonal nature of television could be overcome with the winsome use of this medium. Yet, the only provable failure of educational television, in its pre-Internet form, has been its inability to provide effective two-way interaction and continually adjust its content to the students' needs. Educational technologies can bring teaching and learning to a diaspora of students unable to access them otherwise, but the manner in which they have been used has fostered a one-way notion of teaching, rather than the ideal dialogue. It is therefore fortunate that the media as a whole are now converging and may emerge from their 20th-century chrysalis as a fully interactive supermedium for the years ahead.

But the new technologies will still need to be demystified for the benefit of those who wish to use them. The Canadian tradition of taking media, such as film and video, to the people has served this purpose well. It has exploited the major advantage of these media — their ability to make the images of the world more accessible — within a community-outreach framework that compensates for the technologies' lack of interactivity. In parts of the world that have not had access to high-technology infrastructures, simple media and ingenious techniques for their educational use are commonplace, and the traveling player–educator tradition has not died in these countries. So Canada and the developing world share a natural affinity for the process use of media in teaching, and both have a good opportunity to work together in developing the new multimedia. Neither has the economic resources to overcome the logistical problems that have obstructed the optimal use of earlier technologies, and each has something to offer the other in partnership.

Developing nations can take advantage of Canada's experience in planning and designing efficient technological infrastructures for distance education and producing and delivering high-quality educational courseware. Meanwhile, Canada can learn from the insights

197

198

its international partners developed before they had access to cost-effective educational technologies. Agencies such as COL and IDRC may be the first to identify the strategic alliances needed to shape the new technologies' effective global use, as they have a special knowledge of complementary national strengths and the development priorities simultaneously shared by diverse nations. Funding agencies are already welcoming the economic advantages of the Internet because as much as project partners may enjoy traveling to one another's country, they are forced to admit that much collaboration across the miles could be served by e-mail, file-transfer methods, and desktop conferencing.

Canadian universities still firmly believe that the most important justification for international cooperation is the opportunity for students to gain enrichment through travel (Knight 1995). But the universities can rest assured that communication technologies will not eradicate the need for international exchanges. These are needed in each discipline to provide training in the use of the new technologies and approaches; indeed, the major benefit of the communications technologies is their ability to help sustain projects in the long term. Canada will continue to share in the benefits of international exchanges, as it has throughout its history, and to apply its national expertise in areas such as instructional design, formative evaluation, and action research to help overcome the one-way modes of presentation all too commonly generated by current technologies.

Canada's expertise in the social uses of the media might not have been developed in the first place without the transfer of ideas from another nation. Significantly, this nation was the only one with an even larger political landmass — the former Soviet Union. Canada's "Challenge for Change" and "Fogo Process" projects were deeply influenced by, and built on, pioneering uses of media developed by young filmmakers such as Vertov and Medvedkin during the Russian Revolution. Indeed, in considering the educational-media practices of the last 40 years, one finds that Vertov initiated all those we have since identified as best practices, and none of the worst (James 1996a, b). His work provides a useful checklist of the instructional design, formative evaluation, and action-research principles to emulate in our attempts to bring the Internet, along with the next supermedium after that, to an international audience.

Opportunities for research and interchange, as well as for course provision, will be stimulated in this transnational melting pot. To permit the efficient transfer of learning and accreditation across borders, new subdisciplines, such as "prior learning assessment," are emerging, and numerous private distance-education organizations are challenging the perception that the accredited university is the sole credible knowledge source. As the immediate needs of the developing world are for assistance in areas not emphasized in the traditional curriculum (for example, environmental studies, health education, and social marketing), conventional university expertise is no longer seen as being as relevant to transnational education as when education was geared to local interests. Carefully applied, the new media can be the basis for a world in which all types of educational experience are conveyed between nations, regardless of international boundaries, and can bring about the "death of distance."

Conclusions

New media, particularly the Internet, have the appropriate attributes to overcome the shortcomings of previous communications technologies. The Internet is a two-way, immediate, multimedia medium and has the capacity for communication on one-on-one, one-to-many, and many-to-many bases, regardless of distance. As long as we recognize the need to demystify the new media, maintain high-quality materials for them, and assist students in interpreting the diverse values they reflect, such technologies can truly bring about the death of distance in our educational efforts. They can also have profound effects on our educational planning, enabling us to scan the entire globe for partners with needs and priorities identical to our own. With luck, the focus of our attention will shift away from the differences that separate us regionally and toward the similarities that unite us internationally. Unless this shift is resisted, provincial and even national control over education and culture will become less relevant and increasingly unenforceable.

The breakdown of the old lines of demarcation may well cause bewilderment among educators. However, the new clusterings around special interests, problems, and needs for mutual support will be reassuring — even virtual support is more comforting than no support at all. Ultimately, the notion that Canada or any nation might have a distinctive role to play in the process of globalized education might become entirely obsolete. Canada may share with other nations new educational roles in diverse international communities. Or again, owing to Canada's unusual diversity, it may play a unique role in teaching the world how to use the communications media for tackling social ills.

Chapter 9

Issues and Trends in Internationalization: A Comparative Perspective

Jane Knight

Introduction

Purpose

The previous chapters in this book addressed the changes, challenges, and activities of international cooperation during the past four decades in Canada. The first objective of this chapter is to build on this analysis and identify current trends related to Canadian universities' international work. The second objective is to place the international dimension of Canada's higher education sector in a context that includes other countries and regions of the world. These two aspects are discussed simultaneously throughout. The third objective is to stimulate reflection on several major questions and challenges facing the higher education sector regarding the international aspects of teaching, research, training, and service.

These three objectives are rather ambitious, and it is therefore prudent to identify the scope of the chapter. First, the emphasis is clearly on Canada. Reference to other countries and regions is primarily oriented to Australia, New Zealand, Southeast Asia, the United

202

States, and Western Europe. This chapter is based on information and insights obtained from recent comparative studies completed as part of the Programme on Institutional Management in Higher Education (IMHE) of the Organisation for Economic Co-operation and Development (OECD) project on internationalization (de Wit 1995; Knight and de Wit 1997) and various seminars and workshops. The purpose of the comparative analysis is to learn more about trends and challenges facing internationalization in Canada by highlighting and understanding the situation in other countries. More attention has been given to a qualitative than a quantitative approach in discussing the trends and issues.

The issues and trends identified in this chapter are primarily at the macrolevel, that is, at the system or sector level. There is no intention to minimize the importance of issues facing individual institutions at the operational level. It has also not been possible to discuss all the key issues specific to individual disciplines, stakeholder groups, or special-purpose institutes. Although these issues are of no less importance to the discussion, the focus of this chapter is on issues at the macrolevel, as they are more likely to be relevant to the Canadian higher education sector as a whole.

Assumptions

Being clear about the assumptions underlying the discussion in this chapter is important. As the previous chapters have demonstrated, there has been an interesting evolution in the nature and purpose of the international dimension and work of Canadian universities. The meaning, rationale, strategies, and outcomes of international work have changed and matured over the past several decades. Because this chapter is looking at current issues and trends and future challenges, it is necessary to articulate the fundamental understandings assumed in this discussion.

The major assumption relates to the definition of *internationalization*, as this concept means different things to different people, institutions, and countries. (In fact, one of the issues discussed below is the interpretation and use of the term *internationalization*.) The concept of the internationalization of higher education can be described and used in a variety of ways. First of all, it can be applied at the national, regional, provincial, or institutional level. It can also be described in terms of policy or program considerations. For the purposes of this chapter, the concept of internationalization is oriented to the institutional level. This is consistent with the organizing framework of the book. *Internationalization* is defined at the institutional level as "the process of integrating an international and intercultural dimension into the teaching, research and service functions of the university or institution of higher education" (Knight 1994, p. 3). There are several key concepts included in this definition, which merit further elaboration.

The first is that internationalization is a process, a cycle of planned and spontaneous initiatives at both the program and policy levels. A process approach responds to the evolving needs, resources, and priorities of the institution. Fundamental to the process approach is that both organizational structures and systems of the institution, as well as academic activities, are involved. This differs from other approaches, which place more emphasis on internationalization of specific activities or outcomes (Arum and Van de Water 1992). It is important to note that a process approach should be based on explicit goals for internationalization and their relationship to outcomes.

Another important element in this definition is the notion of integration. Integration ensures that the international dimension is central to the mission of the university and can be sustainably integrated into the policies, practices, and systems of the institution. Careful attention is also given to including both the international and intercultural dimensions. This rests on the belief that the diversity of cultures inherent to a country, especially Canada, is as important as the diversity and similarities between nations. Internationalization of higher education is not limited to a geographical interpretation of the concept. Finally, it is acknowledged that internationalization is part of the university's efforts to fulfill its primary functions, namely, the teaching and learning process, research and scholarly activities, and service to society.

Macrolevel issues and trends

Meaning and use of the term *internationalization*

In the previous section, diversity in the meaning and application of the concept of internationalization of higher education was noted. This illustrates the richness and complexity of the concept, but it can lead to confusion about how to use the term, as well as to dilution of the importance attached to it by governments, institutions, and nongovernmental organizations (NGOs). *Internationalization* emerged in common usage in higher education during the mid-1980s. As often happens, the term has been borrowed or adapted from other sectors. *Internationalization* and *globalization* are now part of everyday language, whether one is talking about the environment, trade, communication, or even fashion. Even though *internationalization* and *globalization* are often used interchangeably, it is necessary to distinguish the meaning of these terms in discussions of the higher education sector.

There have been many terms used over the years to describe the international dimension of education. These terms reflect the priorities and perspectives of that particular time in history and, of course, the orientation of the user. Some of the related terms often used as synonyms include *international academic relations* and *cooperation*, *international education*, *multicultural education*, and *globalization of education*. There is a tendency today to use *internationalization* in a retroactive way and have it apply to concepts and activities popular in the 1960s and 1970s. This approach is neither useful nor wise. Recognizing the development of the vocabulary of the international dimension of higher education is important. By doing so, we respect the evolution of these terms and the differences in their meaning and use. Furthermore, we acknowledge the emergence of the concept of internationalization and how it is interpreted and used in the study and practice of higher education today.

Although it is not the purpose of this chapter to study in detail the differences and similarities between these terms, it is important to explore further the relationship between globalization and internationalization. One can describe globalization in a number of ways. The description that is most relevant and appropriate to the discussion of the international dimension of the higher education sector is as follows:

> Globalization is the flow of technology, economy, knowledge, people, values, ideas ... across borders. Globalization affects each country in a different way due to a nation's individual history, traditions, culture and priorities. Internationalization of higher education is one of the ways a country responds to the impact of globalization yet, at the same time respects the individuality of the nation.
>
> Knight (1997, p. 6)

Thus, internationalization and globalization are seen as different but linked concepts. One can think of globalization as the catalyst, but of internationalization as the response, albeit a proactive response. The key element in the term *internationalization* is the notion of the relationship between or among nations and cultural identities, thereby implying that nation-state and culture are preserved. A country's unique history, indigenous culture or cultures, resources, and priorities shape its response to, and relationships with, other countries. Thus, national identity and culture are key to internationalization. The homogenization of culture is often cited as a critical concern or effect of globalization; internationalization, by respecting and helping to preserve nation-states, is therefore seen as a very different concept.

It would be remiss to leave the discussion of the relationship between globalization and internationalization without introducing the concept of civilization. A controversial hypothesis (Huntington 1996) suggests that peoples and countries with similar cultures are coming together and that this is emerging as the predominant force in international relations, not the globalization of the economy. Furthermore, devotion to one's own cultural identity is gaining increasing importance, which counters the argument that culture is being homogenized because of the impact of globalization. A key premise of the hypothesis is that groups of countries with similar cultures, classified as civilizations, will have strong alliances and a metaimpact on the world stage. This leads to an exploration of the relationship between diverse cultures–civilizations, as opposed to that between nations. Internationalization, which is often seen to be based on the concept of people–culture and state at the national level, is therefore being challenged or at least interpreted in a rather interesting and different way. How multicultural countries, such as Canada, fit into this hypothesis warrants further exploration.

Rationales

Why a country or a higher education institution believes internationalization is fundamental determines the nature and extent of its support and action in favour of internationalization. Although this is rather self-evident, the importance of having an explicit statement of the rationale for internationalization and a set of clear objectives cannot be overstated. The rationales for internationalizing higher education in general and institutions in particular are many and diverse. Rationales are changing and closely linked to each other; they can be complementary or contradictory, especially as they can differ according to the interests of diverse stakeholder groups. Furthermore, rationales can differ between and within countries. An examination of the motivation for internationalizing the higher education sector is a fascinating and complex task, but for brevity's sake the rationales for internationalization can be categorized into four groups: political, economic, academic, and social–cultural (Knight and de Wit 1995).

The political rationale is often considered more important at the national than at the institutional level. This is because international education has historically been seen as a tool for foreign policy, especially with respect to national security and peace among nations. Although this is still a consideration today, it does not have the importance it once had. At one time, bilateral cultural, scientific, and educational exchanges were seen as ways to keep communication and diplomatic relations active. However, in Australia, New Zealand, North America, and the United Kingdom, and to some extent in the four Asian economic "tigers," there is a growing trend to see education as an export product, rather than as a cultural agreement. With the massification of higher education increasing at an exponential rate, large and small countries are showing a strong interest in making the export of educational products and services and the import of foreign students a major part of their foreign policy. In fact, we can see major shifts in foreign policies, from seeing education as primarily a development assistance activity or cultural program to seeing it as an export commodity. This shift to a market orientation introduces the economic rationale for the internationalization of higher education.

The economic rationale has increasing importance and relevance in Canada and in other developed countries around the world. As a result of the globalization of the economy, a growing interdependence among nations, and the information revolution, countries are focusing on their economic, scientific, and technological competitiveness. An effective way to improve and maintain a competitive edge is to develop a highly skilled and knowledgeable work force and to invest in applied research. Both strategies involve the higher education sector. Thus, at the national level, there is a closer and closer link between internationalization of the higher education sector and the economic and technological development of the country. At the institutional level, the economic rationale is receiving more emphasis as universities are pressured to diversify their funding sources and decrease their dependence on government support. It is still unclear whether exporting educational products and services to international markets is indeed directly enhancing the international dimension of teaching, research, and service. This question is discussed several times in this chapter, as it is fundamental to what we mean by the internationalization of higher education and why we think it is important.

The academic rationale is directly linked to enhancing the teaching and learning process and achieving excellence in research and scholarly activities. The results of the 1994 Association of Universities and Colleges of Canada (AUCC) survey (Knight 1995, p. 4) indicated that the number-one reason for internationalizing higher education is "to prepare students and scholars who are internationally knowledgeable and interculturally competent." The second most important reason is "to address through scholarship, the increasingly interdependent nature of the work (environmentally, culturally, economically, socially)." Clearly, the academic motivation for internationalization was uppermost in the minds of university presidents at that time. Given the policy and economic changes in the past 3 years, it is interesting to ponder what the results of a survey would reveal in the next decade.

The social–cultural rationale for internationalization is changing in light of the potential impact of globalization. As discussed above, higher education has traditionally been a part of cultural agreements and exchanges. Today's globalized economy and globalized information and communication system suggest another aspect of the social–cultural rationale. In many non-English-speaking countries, such as Indonesia and Sweden, the preservation and promotion of national culture and language constitute a strong motivation for internationalizing higher education. Countries consider internationalization a way to respect cultural diversity and counterbalance the perceived homogenizing effect of globalization. The acknowledgment of cultural and ethnic diversity within and between countries is considered a key aspect of, and a strong rationale for, the internationalization of a nation's educational system. In Canada, respect for our multicultural diversity has not been seen as an important rationale for internationalization, as is evident from the 1994 AUCC survey (Knight 1995). However, it is acknowledged that the importance of learning about other cultures stems from an appreciation and knowledge of one's own culture.

As a rationale for internationalization, the preservation and promotion of national identity and cultural values is a sensitive issue. Although some countries see internationalization (as opposed to globalization) as a way to preserve culture, other countries see it as a way to promote their cultural values abroad. Canada falls into this latter category. Since 1996 the promotion of Canadian values and culture abroad has been the "third pillar" of our foreign policy (CIDA 1995), and the role of exporting educational products and services has been clearly defined. The juxtaposition of preservation and promotion of cultural identities and values is an issue taken up elsewhere in this chapter.

Related to the social–cultural rationale is the need to improve intercultural understanding and communication. Tied to this is the overall development of the individual as a local, national, and international citizen. Citizenship involves more than being a productive member of the wealth-generating sector, which the economic rationale clearly emphasizes.

In summary, it is important to repeat that these four types of rationales are not entirely distinct or exclusive. An individual's, an institution's, or a country's motivation is a complex and multileveled set of reasons evolving over time and in response to changing needs and priorities. It would be an oversimplification and probably unfair to try to label different countries according to their rationales for internationalization. What is more important and interesting is to note the changes in the rationales in different countries. The motivation driving the internationalization movement is discussed in the following sections.

National-level coordination, planning, and policy

In Canada, we are fortunate that many diverse groups, organizations, departments, and networks in the education, government, and private sectors have focused on the importance of internationalization. However, a shared commitment to internationalization does not necessarily mean a shared vision, rationale, or set of priorities, let alone a coordinated planning and policy framework. In fact, it must be asked whether the increased level of interest and attention at the national level has unintentionally led to a fragmented and perhaps less effective use of the efforts and resources directed to the internationalization of higher education in Canada.

Three recent reports (DFAIT 1994; Knight 1996; Tillman 1997) have identified the need to improve communication and coordination among key national players with vested interests in the internationalization of higher education in Canada. In addition to the coordination issue, several other national trends and issues identified in these reports are discussed in this section. A policy paper (DFAIT 1994), "The International Dimension of Higher Education in Canada: Collaborative Policy Framework," noted that, overall, a major weakness in efforts to bring about internationalization stems principally from a lack of coordination among governments, institutions, and organizations. The more specific areas of weakness mentioned include the following:

+ Poor integration, coordination, and coherence in government policies and programs, both among federal bodies and between federal and provincial governments, and no sense of urgency to act on this;

+ No investment in international activity and no coherent strategy for building on existing strengths and achievements; and

+ Ad hoc treatment of networking and partnerships.

Other issues identified include low enrollments in foreign-language classes, low levels of Canadian student and faculty mobility, diminished funding for higher education, no integrated marketing strategy for educational products and services, and limited appreciation of the influence of cultural factors on teaching, learning, and research.

A national survey (Knight 1996) conducted by the Canadian Bureau for International Education (CBIE), AUCC, and the Association of Canadian Community Colleges (ACCC) — major stakeholder groups in the government, education, and private sectors — identified a number of pressing internationalization issues. One of the few points on which all three sectors agreed was that there is a need for "more cooperation, new types of partnerships and better coordination among and within the sectors" (Knight 1996, p. v). In addition to calling for more coordination, they identified specific instances in which cooperation is needed. These include

+ A more systematic approach to the marketing and exporting of educational products and services;

+ Improved cooperation between the private and education sectors in arranging work placements, internships, and scholarships for study abroad;

+ Strategic partnerships between universities–colleges and the private sector for joint research projects; and

+ Stronger cooperation among federal government departments to resolve the issues related to foreign-student fees and visas.

Implicit in the call for cooperation is a need to recognize the differences and similarities among the sectors' interests. The purpose may be explicit — to enhance and sustain the internationalization of the higher education system in Canada — but the answer to the question "In whose interests?" may not be as clear.

Other issues identified in the stakeholder survey include

+ The need to achieve international standards in education;

Box 1
International cooperation and internationalization at AUCC: some key dates

The Association of Universities and Colleges of Canada (AUCC) is recognized as the focal point in Canada for promoting and exploring the implications of international relations among universities. It is interesting to note how AUCC has gradually taken on a management role — one that has not been without its controversies — and how issues relating to internationalization have been addressed in AUCC's biennial conferences. From these viewpoints, AUCC can be seen as a good mirror of Canadian universities' interests and concerns.

Some key dates in AUCC's history are the following:

1911   AUCC is founded.

1968   AUCC scholarship office takes over management of the Commonwealth Scholarship and Fellowship Plan and begins, for the first time, to administer international scholarships.

1978   The International Development Secretariat is created in AUCC, pursuant to an agreement between the Canadian International Development Agency (CIDA), the International Development Research Centre, and AUCC. The universities are asked to identify a person in their establishment to be responsible for international development. This gives rise to a network of international liaison officers.

1983   The International Development Secretariat publishes its *Directory of Canadian University Resources for International Development*, the first in a series of AUCC publications dealing with the international development activities of Canadian universities and their institutional links to partners in the South.

1985   Two databases are created: International Development Projects of Canadian Universities, based on information compiled from the publication mentioned above, and International Exchange Agreements of Canadian Universities. These tools contain information on projects and agreements dating back to the 1970s and are regularly updated.

1987   The International Development Secretariat and the section responsible for academic relations with industrialized countries merge under one administrative unit.

1988   The Canada–China University Linkage program is created, financed by CIDA. This is the first institutional program administered by AUCC; other programs focus on scholarships and grants for students and professors.
        The theme of the biennial conference is the Expanding Role of Universities in International Cooperation.

1990   The theme of the biennial conference is University Partnerships in a Changing World.

1992   The theme of the biennial conference is Seeking Innovation: Conference on International Cooperation among Universities.

1994   AUCC and the universities play a central role in creating the University Partnerships in Cooperation and Development program, financed by CIDA's Canadian Partnership Branch. AUCC is assigned the management of one of the program's two aspects.
        The theme of the biennial conference is From Competition to Cooperation: The Evolving International Strategy of Universities.

1995	AUCC formulates a declaration on internationalization and Canadian universities. It testifies to the changes already helping to internationalize universities and proposes a framework for further pursuing this process. AUCC publishes Jane Knight's *Internationalization at Canadian Universities: The Changing Landscape*, the first in a series of studies dealing with various aspects of the internationalization process in Canadian universities.
1996	The Scotiabank–AUCC Awards for Excellence in Internationalization is created to recognize university achievements in internationalization and publicize their initiatives throughout the university community. The theme of the biennial conference is Internationalization: Moving from Rhetoric to Reality.
1998	The AUCC Board of Directors approves an initiative with international financial institutions (IFIs) within the International and Canadian Programs branch. This initiative is aimed at positioning Canadian universities and AUCC to win IFI contracts. The theme of the biennial conference is Internationalization: Building on Our Experience.

✦ The impact of free trade on the globalization of the professions;

✦ The identification of competencies needed in new graduates working in a local and global environment;

✦ Fees, visas, and marketing for international students;

✦ Mixed messages on the importance of foreign-language teaching;

✦ Study abroad and work placements for Canadian students;

✦ The need for curricular reform to internationalize teaching and learning;

✦ Marketing and export of educational products and services;

✦ Needs and vested interests in research; and

✦ The impact of new information and communication technologies.

This represents an overview of the key and emerging issues identified by the stakeholders' groups in the education, government, and private sectors. Clearly, there is divergence among the sectors on the nature of the challenges and solutions to these issues. But it is important to recognize that there is agreement on the principal issues and, more importantly, on the need to improve collaboration and cooperation.

Following these two reports ACCC, AUCC, and CBIE undertook another joint project that resulted in a paper, "Internationalization of Advanced Learning: Toward a Planning Framework" (Tillman 1997). This paper moves the call for improved coordination forward by proposing a planning framework. The framework is action oriented and practical. It attempts to translate advocacy into action. It identifies the issue, describes the nature of the issue and the challenges related to it, details the desired outcome, allocates the primary responsibilities, and lists the important players. The major players and partners are federal government departments and the national NGOs with vested interests in the international dimension of higher education in Canada. It also refers to provincial governments and individual educational institutions.

The framework identifies three fundamental points and a number of specific challenges. The points are

+ Improving communication, coherence, and collaboration within and among key players;

+ Articulating a clear, global vision of international education as a public policy; and

+ Securing adequate funding (especially for support services).

The specific challenges cited in the paper are wide ranging and in most cases duplicate and reinforce the issues identified in the two previous reports. However, the strength of the planning framework is that it identifies explicit action and desired outcomes.

The challenges include conducting research and gathering data on student and faculty mobility, overseas alumni, and the economic impact of international education; enhancing the Canadian Education Centres (CECs) network; streamlining immigration and admission procedures for international students; increasing market intelligence for export of education products and services; improving quality assurance and assessment measures; improving recognition of credits; promoting greater private-sector involvement; and developing administrative flexibility.

It is evident that internationalization of higher education is "coming of age" or at least "coming on stage" at the national level. The call for public policy, greater coherence among key players, and adequate funding is stronger than ever and is being translated, albeit cautiously, into a more coordinated approach to defining the issues and to taking action. Canada appears in a rather unique situation when our national policies are compared with those of other countries around the world. Education is a provincial responsibility, so national-level policy on the international dimension of higher education is not articulated by a federal ministry responsible for education, as in other countries. However, this does not diminish the need for public-policy statements on this issue in Canada and information on other countries' approaches to internationalization.

The movement in Europe to develop a more articulate and comprehensive national policy on the international dimension of higher education is very interesting. It is recognized that in Europe the most influential and important actor in international education has been the European Commission. Institutional strategies have been initiated mainly as a result of support provided by the European Commission and, in a more limited way, by national governments (de Wit and Callan 1995). The European Commission programs, such as the European Community Action Scheme for the Mobility of University Students (ERASMUS), TEMPUS, and SOCRATES, have helped institutions to increase the mobility of students, faculty, researchers, and administrators, mainly in Europe but more recently from Europe to Asia, Latin America, and North America. Many would argue that the orientation of the European Commission programs has been more to Europeanize than internationalize education, but that is not the topic to be explored here. In any event, the European Commission has had a profound influence and a strong catalytic effect on the international dimension of higher education in Europe.

In 1996, for the first time, European universities and other institutions of higher education were asked by the European Commission to develop their own international policies and to demonstrate how European Commission-funded projects fit into institutional-level policy and planning (Kalvemark and van der Wende 1997). Clearly, this is a very different approach from that in Canada, where since the early 1990s most universities and colleges have had the international dimension articulated in institutional mission statements and there has been significant work done on the development of international policies and institution-wide strategies. However, the influence of the Canadian International Development Agency (CIDA) and the International Development Research Centre (IDRC) should not be ignored, as Canadian universities were required to demonstrate how CIDA- and IDRC-funded projects would fit into the overall international work and policies of the universities.

The 1996 initiative of the European Commission resulted in the Academic Cooperation Association (ACA) study, "National Policies for the Internationalization of Higher Education in Europe" (Kalvemark

214

and van der Wende 1997). The study found that in many countries national policies for internationalization of higher education do exist, but they are not always part of the wider higher education policy. This is a fascinating situation and may be more like the one that Canada is in. For instance, Austria has a variety of agreements, memoranda of understanding, and treaties to promote internationalization of research and higher education on a bilateral basis. New legislation in 1993 and 1997 on the structure and curriculum of universities in Austria has resulted in individual institutions' having more autonomy, which is expected to facilitate internationalization. Except for specific pieces of legislation, Austria is best described as not having a national policy on internationalization of higher education (Leidenfrost et al. 1997).

In contrast, Germany does have explicit national- and state-level policies on international and European cooperation that highlight the importance of student and staff exchanges (Kehm and Last 1997). Since 1974 Sweden has been the leader in acknowledging and clearly articulating the importance of internationalization in national education policies and budget bills. For example, the 1995 budget bill passed by the Swedish parliament was particularly interesting with regard to balancing cooperation with European and other international interests and commitments, as is evident from the following statement from the bill:

> Cooperation in Europe must not be developed at the cost of other forms of international commitment and cooperation education has a great responsibility with regard to the broadening of knowledge and understanding of societies and cultures in other regions. This is particularly true with respect to developing countries, where more than 80 percent of the world population is to be found. Universities and colleges must actively promote knowledge about the developing countries. They must also forcefully combat every form of xenophobia and racism.
>
> Quoted in Kalvemark (1997, p 177)

Consortia and partnerships

The proliferation of consortia and networks dedicated to international cooperation and work is one of the more striking trends. What is so interesting about these consortia is the diversity of their sizes, types, and rationales. Once again, competitiveness and, to some extent, the globalization of the market can be identified as key factors in the growth in these networks.

During the last decade, when "partnership" was the trademark of international development, there arose the need to establish consortia to bid on, and implement, major projects. Canadian universities have developed consortia among themselves, colleges and technical institutes, private-sector companies and industry, government agencies, and NGOs. The large scale and complexity of many development projects or contracts have dictated that partners with different niches of expertise collaborate to obtain and complete a major project. The universities in the United States were probably the pioneers in setting up these kinds of consortia, but now Australia, Canada, and Europe are fully engaged in this process. The success of these consortia is uneven. Partners experience a learning curve, as the collaboration and cooperation needed to bid on projects has not always been as strong during the implementation phase. In this era of larger and more multisector interdisciplinary projects, both the need for consortia and their numbers will most likely continue to grow.

International development work is not the only reason to establish these consortia. Since the Department of Foreign Affairs and International Trade (DFAIT) began to identify educational products and services as important trade commodities increased attention has been focused on the commercial activities of both public and private education providers. Manufacturing and service companies want to explore partnerships with public and private education providers to deliver the education and training needed to win international contracts.

Even in the area of international-student recruitment, in which competition among higher education institutions is increasing, the development of consortia is under way. Canadian institutions are just beginning to realize that the major source of competition is from other countries and not from other institutions within Canadian borders. Recruitment consortia are extremely well developed in Australia, the United Kingdom, and the United States, and now Canada is following their lead. The networks are of different kinds and sizes. For instance, there are large fee-based networks, such as the CEC network or smaller local and regional groups of high schools, colleges, and universities cooperating to attract students to a specific city or province.

Bilateral cooperation agreements with universities in other countries have been a part of international cooperation for several decades. More recently, we are seeing the development of international or global consortia of universities. One example is Universitas 21, which is a formal network of about 25 comprehensive universities from around the world. Regional networks, especially in the Asia–Pacific region, are also increasing. The Capital Cities Network is an example of a European regional network. The aims of these kinds of consortia are usually well articulated and include objectives such as international benchmarks, joint research and scholarly activities, increased numbers of mobility programs for students and faculty, collaborative bids on large-scale development projects, and development of web-based courses and curriculum materials. Consortia and networks are seen as different from membership-based organizations. However, it should be noted that the number of international and regional organizations oriented to higher education and, in many cases, specifically international education is also mushrooming.

In Canada, it is too early to have solid information on the benefits, impacts, sustainability, and implications of these newly formed national, regional, and international networks. However, it is not too early to make a plea for some kind of monitoring and analysis of the lessons learned from these new consortia and partnerships.

Quality assessment and assurance of the international dimension

There are two important aspects of the discussion of quality and internationalization. The first relates to how the international dimension contributes to the improved quality of higher education. The second is how one assesses and enhances or maintains the quality of internationalization initiatives. The purpose of this section is to discuss concerns and issues related to both these aspects, but more importantly to the second.

Any discussion of quality is always challenging and, at times, contentious, as quality depends on the "eye of the beholder," or the stakeholder. Measuring, or even defining, the concept of the quality of education, let alone the effect on it of the international dimension of higher education, is challenging. That said, it is still important to try to address some of the issues related to quality and internationalization.

The question of whether internationalization is an end in itself or a means to an end, with the end being the improvement of the quality of education, is often the subject of vigorous debate. An assumption implicit in this debate is that enhancing the international dimension of teaching, research, and service adds value to the quality of our higher education, given that we are living in a more globalized environment in which understanding and knowledge of the impact of globalization is critical. However, this is predicated on the rationale and goals of internationalization — a recurring theme in this chapter, which especially relates to the balance of academic and economic motives.

A full discussion of if and how the quality of higher education is improved or lowered by the international dimension is beyond the scope of this chapter. However, a short discussion of two examples of the concerns illustrates the complexity of the debate.

In many countries, especially some of the Asia–Pacific countries, internationalization is seen as almost synonymous with westernization (Knight and de Wit 1997). Based on that perspective, internationalization therefore contributes to the homogenization of world culture. This leads to a legitimate concern that Western concepts are replacing indigenous knowledge and belief systems. This question is closely linked to the issue of standards and standardization. The relevance of this concern to Canada rests on the nature of our cooperation with international partners, especially as the orientation of our foreign policy emphasizes the promotion of Canadian cultural values and the export of educational products and services.

Second, those who believe that economics is driving the current interest in internationalization propose that the quality of education may be in jeopardy. This relates especially to the issue of international students. Concern has been expressed (ACA 1997) that in some countries the desire to recruit more international students to a university or college lowers the entrance requirements and the prerequisite level of English. This casts aspersions on the quality of the students and the institutions' entrance standards, which in turn affects their retention rate, the level and quality of the teaching and learning process, and the curriculum. It should be noted that this concern is not limited to English-speaking countries but is also found in many non-English-speaking countries, where there is a growing interest in offering courses in English in an attempt to capture a "market share" of international students. Some countries in Europe and Southeast Asia would fall into this category.

These two examples illustrate the concerns raised about the contribution that internationalization makes to the quality of higher education in general. Identifying them as concerns is more appropriate than calling them trends; however, attention needs to be given to these concerns before they become critical issues and trends.

Another aspect of the quality issue is the assessment and enhancement of internationalization activities. In Canada, little discussion appears to take place, even less action, on the question of assessing and assuring the quality of internationalization strategies. Canada stands out as one of the few Western countries not formally addressing the quality issue. In Australia, Europe, New Zealand, and the United Kingdom, there are considerable debate and action on assessing, monitoring, and improving the quality of internationalization. The reasons for this interest range from accountability purposes, to benchmarking and competitiveness, to a desire to improve and expand the international dimension (Wodehouse 1996).

It is interesting to analyze the different approaches and instruments used to address the issue of quality assessment and enhancement. In continental European countries, it is usually an institution's decision whether to engage in a review of the international dimension and which approach or instrument to use. No organizations require it, but national agencies are making it an issue and developing the resources to help institutions undertake self-assessments of the international dimension. For instance, the Netherlands Universities Foundation for International Cooperation in Higher Education developed a set of guidelines, "Quality in Internationalization: Guidelines for the Assessment of the Quality of Internationalization in Higher Professional Education" (NUFFIC 1995). It is an assessment tool that institutions use to rate themselves on a five-point scale regarding various academic-program and organizational aspects. It is more qualitative then quantitative and is basically a guide to help institutions identify areas in which they need improvement. The strength of this tool is its comprehensiveness, the fact that it does not limit itself to just one or two major areas of internationalization, such as exchange programs or the curriculum. The Finnish Centre for International Mobility has also developed a self-assessment checklist, which institutions are using to evaluate and improve their international work (Snellman 1995).

Since 1996, the IMHE of the OECD, in collaboration with ACA, has had a special project on quality assessment and assurance of internationalization (IMHE 1997). It emerged out of a project on internationalization strategies, in which the issue of quality was identified as very important. An approach called the Internationalization Quality Review Process (IQRP) was developed and has been piloted it in eight countries, including Australia, Kenya, Malaysia, Mexico, Western and Eastern European countries, and the United States, but not in Canada (Knight and de Wit 1999). Basically it is a process to enable individual academic institutions to assess and enhance the quality of their internationalization efforts according to their own stated aims and objectives. The process includes procedures, guidelines, and tools to be adapted and used in both a self-assessment exercise and an external peer review. The emphasis is on the analysis of the strengths and weaknesses of the institution's international dimension and on identifying steps to take to improve it. IQRP covers a very broad range of areas, from governance and organizational systems, to academic programs, to research and scholarly collaboration, to students, to staff, to external relations and services. It does not take a checklist approach, as institutions undertake the evaluation according to their stated aims and objectives for internationalization. Although data gathering is an important step, the focus is on analysis, not on description of activities or quantitative measures.

The short-term goal of the IMHE–OECD project is to develop an instrument for quality review of internationalization efforts for institutional use. The long-term objective is to ensure that the international dimension is included in all quality audits, whether they are evaluating specific subjects or disciplines, the teaching and learning process, or institutional management systems and practices. This is consistent with the philosophy advocating the integration of the international dimension into the core functions of the university, not marginalizing it in a group of special activities.

Australia is an interesting case from the point of view of quality assessment and assurance. For various reasons, its quality audit systems are directly linked to government support and funding. Accountability and merit are key factors. Australia is putting new systems and procedures in place at the institutional level. Senior management positions, such as deputy vice chancellor for quality, are not uncommon. Because international-student recruitment, offshore programs, customized training, and research contracts are major revenue sources for institutions, interest has also been increasing in quality review and enhancement of international activities. At the institutional level, there has been some interesting work done to develop and combine a number of quality-assessment tools for international activities. Performance indicators with benchmarks are being developed. In other instances, international offices have worked toward ISO 9000 accreditation, the IQRP model is being used and adapted, and certification for offshore programs is being obtained. The diversity of these approaches and instruments illustrates the importance Australia attaches to the quality of internationalization and the work it is doing to develop the right approaches.

The quality of educational programs offered offshore, either through distance education, twinning programs, or satellite campuses, is also seen as important. The New Zealand Qualifications Authority has developed a certification process and system for all public and private education providers offering education programs offshore. Hong Kong has recently developed legislation requiring all foreign distance-education providers to be registered. These two examples illustrate that both providers and recipients of offshore or distance education are taking steps to monitor the quality of education. The Global Alliance for Transnational Education (Wodehouse 1997) is developing a certification program for transnational education, which is further evidence of the concern for quality assessment.

To date, quality assessment and enhancement have not been key issues in Canada, but as internationalization comes of age it will be critically important for Canada to address questions of accountability, merit, and improvement.

Sustainability and funding

In Canada, without question, the last decade has seen an increased interest in, and commitment to, the international dimension of higher education. The AUCC survey (Knight 1995) of university presidents clearly indicated that they are paying greater attention to internationalization. This is evident from the fact that by 1994 more than 80% of university mission statements referred to the international dimension. But is this rhetoric or reality? Is there any concrete evidence of this increased interest or is it primarily a moral commitment?

Box 2
Internationalization and quality standards

The issue of quality control of international activities is problematic. Why evaluate international activities at all? For what purpose and for what audience? Quality control of academic programs is a provincial responsibility. It is generally recognized that the objectivity of a peer-review process ensures high standards in a field of expertise. This same process generally works well for international research but is less applicable, however, to nonacademic activities. How then should the matter of quality control be handled for the less academic aspects of international activities? How can a quality-assessment strategy take account of the impact of international work on, for example, students? Because a successful international-education experience achieves both an academic and a nonacademic result, is a new mechanism needed to assess the academic results of formal courses and the new forms of socialization that are shaping students on and off the campus? To assess the quality of internationalization requires a clear understanding of what internationalization means, with agreement on all facets of the concept. Clearly, the debate is complex. The variations from discipline to discipline and the tendency of international activities to be more geared to praxis than to academic considerations goes some way to explaining why the issue of quality standards and control of internationalization remains largely in limbo.

One indicator of commitment is whether funding and resource allocation for international activities have increased or decreased. It is difficult to get an accurate picture of the financial investments made by the institutions themselves in internationalization activities. However, emerging economic trends suggest that funding increases when a financial return on the investment is possible. For instance, it is interesting to ask whether more funding is available to market and recruit international students or contract education offshore than to revise the curriculum or establish student- or staff-mobility programs. A review of job postings for international work in the universities is likely to show that more international-student-recruitment positions are being created than positions for managers of study–work-abroad centres. One can cite no hard data on this, but it appears to be an emerging trend.

Another trend related to the funding and feasibility of internationalization activities is the recognition of the need to diversify sources of funding. Universities and colleges acknowledge that they have to depend less on government funding sources and are now seeking private-sector support, funding from foundations, and entrepreneurial income-generating activities. At the national and provincial levels, funding for international scholarships and research grants for Canadian students and researchers is decreasing. Since the early 1990s the level of funding for university partnership programs from CIDA has also been decreasing. The recent creation and funding of the new national program on international internships for young Canadians needs to be applauded; yet, it must be recognized that this program has as much or more to do with youth unemployment as with the internationalization of higher education. Nevertheless, the opportunity for young Canadians to become more knowledgeable and skilled in working in international and intercultural settings is extremely beneficial.

DFAIT's new emphasis on the export of educational products and services means that international-education activities are now being seen as a source of income, and institutions are more inclined to invest in those international activities when they anticipate a clear return on their investment. The income is often seen as a replacement for the loss of other government funding. The question of whether income generation from international activities is used for general education purposes or is directed to supporting and sustaining various internationalization priorities and activities needs closer examination.

222

A related issue, which also merits further analysis, is whether income-generation activities in international markets — for example, foreign consulting contracts, selling education products and courseware, franchising courses for delivery by foreign institutions — are in fact internationalization activities that directly contribute to the international dimension of a university's major functions. This is a controversial issue and gets us back to the question of what the major rationales and priorities are for international education and work in the university.

A number of factors affect the long-term feasibility of the academic aspects of internationalization. Funding is just one. The expertise and support of faculty are others. The engine of internationalization at the institutional level is clearly the faculty and staff. Opportunities for professional development and for recognition and reward for international work are two areas in need of attention if internationalization is to be sustainable at the institutional level.

Another important consideration is the "institutionalization" of the international elements. In the first part of the chapter the process approach to internationalization was described. It focuses on both international activities (exchanges, curriculum, international students, development projects) and organizational factors (policies and systems) needed to integrate the international dimension into all aspects of the university. The process approach is fundamental to trying to institutionalize the international dimension into the priorities, planning, policies, and procedures for the higher education institution. The process, or integrative, approach is better understood and recognized in Canada than in many other countries of the world. This is partly because we take a comprehensive approach to internationalization and have recognized the importance of the dynamic relationship between curriculum, development projects, research, etc. In other words, the "whole is greater than the sum of the parts."

In Australia, greater emphasis has been placed on the recruitment of international students and twinning programs; only recently has it looked at the internationalization of domestic students by addressing the curriculum and trying to expand student-exchange programs, etc. (Back et al. 1996). In Europe, the European Commission programs, such as SOCRATES, ERASMUS, and COMETT, have fundamentally shaped the internationalization activities of many universities and other tertiary institutions (de Wit and Callan 1995). The European Commission programs have been successful in creating institutional partnerships and exchange programs. In the evaluation of many European Commission programs, this issue, plus that of the sustainability of these initiatives, is being carefully analyzed. Can individual institutions continue these new programs without the support of the European Commission?

In Canada, we have not had these kinds of national or provincial programs to support our internationalization work, and much of the responsibility has remained with the individual institution. Not having such external support may have hindered the extent of our internationalization efforts, but in the end it may have helped the individual institutions to be more independent and entrepreneurial in finding ways to support this dimension of activities. The major risk is that institutions may place more emphasis on the economic and commercial aspects of international work, rather than the internationalization of the academic experience for Canadian students. An appropriate balance is needed.

In Australia, it is a completely different story. A significant reduction has occurred in national funding, and the institutions have had to proactively diversify the sources of their funding. Since the advent of full cost recovery on international student fees and a systematic marketing effort "the single most important and the single largest revenue stream is international students" (ACA 1997, p. 49).

Impact of trade agreements and the labour market

Reference should be made to the growing influence of trade agreements and the labour market on the internationalization of higher education. With a more globalized economy we are seeing an internationalization of trades and professions. The creation of regional trading blocks, such as those of the European Union, the North American Free Trade Agreement (NAFTA), and Asia–Pacific Economic Cooperation (APEC), is resulting in a greater flow of products and services across borders. This involves a significant increase in the mobility of workers and the need for international standards and accreditation programs. This, in turn can have a major impact on the education and training offered by higher education institutions, both at home and offshore. Greater attention needs to be given to developing international accreditation systems for professions and trades that currently have only national-level accreditation.

Another important factor related to the labour market is the identification of competencies essential to functioning in a more international work environment. The research, to date, in Canada and in other countries has been sporadic, but the topic is now gaining more attention (Stanley and Mason 1998; Wilson 1998). A study by the RAND Corporation, *Global Preparedness and Human Resources: College and Corporate Perspectives* (cited in ACA 1997), examined how US higher education is responding to the needs of multinational businesses. The study concluded that corporations with a need for entry-level candidates with cross-cultural competence frequently seek non-Americans to fill these positions. To counteract this practice and to help graduates gain the prerequisite knowledge and skills, US corporations are now working more closely with colleges and universities. Firms are providing funds for curriculum development, faculty-exchange programs, and students internships. To respond to industry's human-resource requirements and the need to be competitive in world markets, the US higher education system acknowledges that it needs to produce more internationally competent graduates and to cooperate with the private sector in doing so.

In Canada, a recent survey (Knight 1997) of the private, government, and education sectors indicated that more cooperation between the academic and private sectors is desirable. Although the sectors agreed on the need for closer collaboration, they did not agree on the nature of this cooperation. The education sector suggested there was a need for private-sector involvement in the following types of activities: research partnerships, scholarships for Canadian students, support for chairs in international studies, and work placements for international students studying in Canada. The private sector proposed different types of collaborative activities, such as financial and technical support on joint international projects and the promotion and export of Canadian education and training services abroad. The sectors agreed that cooperation is needed to provide internships and work placements abroad for Canadian students and identify competencies to enable new graduates to work in the globalized marketplace. This was thought to be a good starting point for closer collaboration.

In Australia, university cooperation with the private sector has taken a more entrepreneurial approach. Building on its success in recruiting international students, Australia has taken the lead in developing offshore campuses in cooperation with a private-sector company. American universities have made similar kinds of arrangements in several Asian countries.

International standards and standardization

Often cited as an extremely important reason to internationalize higher education is the desire to achieve international academic standards. What are these standards, who sets them, and who monitors them? These questions are still unanswered in Canada and in other countries around the world.

In the 1994 AUCC survey (Knight 1995), senior leaders of Canadian degree-granting institutions ranked "achieving international standards" as number 5 out of 10 in level of importance as a rationale for internationalization. In the 1997 survey (Knight 1997), key Canadian stakeholders (government, education, and private sector) gave a ranking of "high importance" to this same issue. The basic reason for the high ranking in the second survey was the need for Canada to be competitive in the export market for Canadian educational products and services.

A recent cross-country analysis of nine Asia–Pacific countries (Knight and de Wit 1997) revealed that the achievement of international academic standards was a primary motivating factor for investing in, and emphasizing, the internationalization of the education system. Meeting international standards was seen as a way to make their educational systems equal to those of others and make them credible for domestic and international students and scholars. However, they also indicated that international standards can be a double-edged issue. Strong concern was expressed about the uniformity and homogeneity that can result from an excessive emphasis on internationally recognized standards. Standardization was seen as a possible outcome of achieving international standards. There are many complex factors at play in the discussion of this issue. It is prudent to be aware of the expressed concern about a "cookie-cutter" approach to education while trying to achieve international standards of excellence in scholarship and research.

In the same study, Asian colleagues also referred to the potential for westernization and what some called the "McDonaldization" of their higher education sector. Often, they equated internationalization with westernization. National and indigenous cultures are perceived as being at risk and as being gradually eroded. Mixed emotions and some controversy about the long-term impacts and benefits of the increasing number of twinning programs, foreign satellite campuses, and distance-education programs were apparent. The dilemma of improving the standards of higher education while putting indigenous knowledge and belief systems at risk was clearly recognized. Is this an issue that affects Canada? As Canadian universities and colleges become more active in exporting education and setting up offshore programs, it is important for them to be aware of the issues of the westernization and homogenization of cultures. In fact, these are issues somewhat familiar to us from discussion of our relationship with the United States. In conclusion it is important to note that international standards need to be looked at, not only in terms of achieving excellence and competitiveness, but also in terms of preventing uniformity and standardization of the content and processes of education.

226

Brain drain and elitism

Two other issues that deserves mention are the phenomena of brain drain and elitism. These do not have the same importance attached to them as the previously discussed issues, but they are worthy of discussion because they are of importance to Canada and other countries.

The potential loss of national talent has long been an issue associated with the increased mobility of students and scholars, and it continues to be a relevant issue today for both developing and developed countries. For instance, in Canada, DFAIT has recognized the issue of brain drain, primarily in the direction of the United States, as a significant national problem requiring attention. Canada is producing top-level graduates in niche areas, such as biomedical and information technologies. However, we are unable to attract these graduates to Canadian companies or even to multinational ones located in Canada. The salary packages, as well as the opportunities for diversity of responsibilities and job promotion, are definitely more attractive in the United States, and thus we are suffering brain drain to the south. We are, at the same time, attracting qualified professionals and scholars from other countries, primarily those in the Asia–Pacific region, who are beginning to fill the gap left by the brain drain to the south. Brain drain is perhaps better described as the "itinerant intellect," as it is really about international mobility or flow of brain power; it is no longer a one-way drain.

Of course, this remains a matter of major concern for developing countries, which are sending their brightest talent and future leaders to foreign shores for further education and training. The prospect of continuing to work and live in a country where a student has spent a considerable amount of time in undergraduate or postgraduate education, or both, is attractive to many. Although the desire to remain in a country for work experience after graduation is often seen as understandable, a prolonged or permanent stay jeopardizes the sending country's plans for developing the human-resource base needed to modernize its systems and infrastructure.

Another issue related to mobility, and to some extent, to internationalization in general is elitism. Many people think that international-education opportunities are only available to students or scholars who either are the most talented and thus able to access international scholarships or have the resources to finance their own work–study or research programs abroad — two reasons why international education is perceived as the reserve of the elite. For the member countries of the European Union there are many successful academic-mobility programs that over the years have provided excellent opportunities for students, researchers, and academic administrators to study abroad. Accessibility is a key issue in these schemes, and extra effort is made to make these exchange programs available, on a competitive basis, to as many participants as possible. That said, it is still only possible to accommodate 5–10% of the student population. Therefore, once again, international academic exchange programs have been seen as elitist because they cater to a very small percentage of the academic community.

227

Canada has no large-scale, nationally funded exchange programs like those in Europe, nor does Canada have numerous scholarship schemes. Study-abroad and exchange programs are usually organized at the institutional level, and the financial responsibility rests with the student or the sending institution. Because of the small number of students who participate, it is again often referred to as elitist. Semester- or year-abroad programs are not as popular in Canada as in Europe, the United States, and now several Asian countries like Hong Kong and Singapore. Again, finances are seen to play a major role in determining who participates. Elitism, again, seems to be at play.

Therefore, as long as internationalization is thought of in terms of academic mobility, elitism will continue to be an issue because of the small number of students and scholars who can participate. Thus, it is appropriate to consider a more comprehensive approach to internationalization. The integration of an international or intercultural dimension into the curriculum would be a key strategy to reaching a greater percentage of students. Access to information through new electronic information and communication systems like the World Wide Web are now providing rich opportunities for students to learn about other cultures and countries and even to undertake joint projects with students in other countries. If one goal of internationalization is to help students develop knowledge and critical-thinking skills to understand their own and others' culture, history, politics, and economy, then we must be creative and find strategies to bring this dimension into the learning experiences and course work of all students. Internationalization should not be perceived as an elitist concept.

Societal trends

Other important macrolevel trends need to be noted, but perhaps not elaborated on. When discussing trends, it is sometimes difficult to distinguish between the larger societal trends that are affecting higher education in general and those trends and issues that are part of one aspect of higher education, in this case, the international dimension. For example, the movement toward a knowledge-based society and economy (Strong 1996) is one trend that has profound implications for the higher education sector and obviously relates directly to the international dimension.

The development of new information and communication technologies is another example. The opportunities to internationalize the teaching process and to engage in joint research through electronic collaboration with experts, colleagues, and fellow students in other countries add to the international dimension. The availability of international sources of information has exploded through access to worldwide databases, web sites, and library collections through the Internet. Delivery of courses via the Internet or through CD-ROMs is introducing new possibilities for interactive learning, the teaching and learning process, and the role of teachers. The "sage on the stage" is also becoming the "guide on the side."

Distance and time are no longer barriers, and therefore opportunities for offshore or international delivery and access are growing rapidly. The excitement of having new ways to internationalize the curriculum, the learning process, and scholarly activities is tangible. However, unbridled enthusiasm is as much of an issue as the sceptics' cynicism. Careful thought and attention need to be given to why, when, and how the new information and communication technologies enhance higher education and its international dimension. The key challenge is to determine how these emerging technologies can be used to enhance the learning process, extend its benefits, and bring international expertise together to focus on shared problems in new and creative ways.

Another trend is an increasing focus on regionalism, or the geographic grouping of neighbouring countries, as opposed to an area within a country. As seen earlier, new networks, associations, and mobility schemes are emerging at the regional level. The University Mobility in Asia and the Pacific (UMAP) program is a good example of this, the impacts of having closer regional links resulting from new regional trade agreements, such as NAFTA, APEC, and the European Union, have been noted especially in relation to the mobility of the workforce.

The role of the European Commission in promoting academic exchange programs within the European region is well known. An interesting new initiative from the European Commission involves mobility schemes between regions. The recent European Union–Association of Southeast Asian Nations program and European Union–Latin America program are examples of these schemes and help to focus in another way on the increasing importance of regionalization. Much of the discussion of regionalism has accepted the perspective of regionalization versus internationalization. The "versus" approach is not very productive or helpful in exploring this theme. The key issue requiring further analysis is how to achieve the most appropriate balance of interests at the national, regional, and international levels. When we juxtapose the need to recognize the interdependence of nations to solve some of the global challenges facing us with the need for technological and scientific competitiveness, the importance of finding the optimal balance between national, regional, and international interests comes into a clearer focus.

Microlevel issues and trends

This section focuses on a series of microlevel trends and issues. These relate to the strategies and activities that directly enhance the international dimension of the three primary university functions. Many of these trends and issues have been addressed in previous chapters dedicated to teaching, research, and outreach; therefore, the discussion in this section is brief but does make reference to the situation in other countries.

Academic mobility

The mobility of students and scholars is one of the best known and successful strategies for internationalization, both in Canada and in the rest of the world. The Colombo Plan systematically introduced the mobility of scholars to the Commonwealth countries. In fact, many Australian, Canadian, and United Kingdom universities view the Colombo Plan, along with other international scholarship schemes, as being fundamental to shaping their international cooperation.

Following on the heels of such scholarship programs were institutional-level linkages, with the support of national aid agencies such as CIDA. European countries and Canada also refer to the important role that bilateral cultural agreements play in the mobility of students, scholars, and professors.

Today, there are many different kinds of bilateral, regional, and international mobility programs. The best known ones are sponsored by the European Commission. These include the famous ERASMUS program for university student mobility, developed in 1987. The Program to Promote the Teaching and Learning of Community Languages, which focuses on languages exchanges, came into being in 1994, followed by LEONARDO, which is dedicated to vocational training. The European Union has created a new umbrella program, SOCRATES, to include some of the former programs. All of these programs have led to the perception among many in Europe that internationalization is equivalent to student mobility (de Wit and Callan 1995).

Two other regional mobility schemes are UMAP, which is dedicated to student exchanges within the Asia–Pacific region, and the North American Regional Mobility Program for student exchanges in North America. Another example is the Commonwealth University Student Activity Consortium, established in the early 1990s. These constitute only a selection, but they amply illustrate the interest in student mobility. However, it must also be remembered that on average only about 5–10% of students per institution have the opportunity to participate in an exchange program.

Although exchange programs are the most numerous and the most popular, other types of mobility schemes are available to students, faculty, and scholars. The Fulbright program is an example — one of the largest and best known scholarship programs that promotes the mobility of scholars. Canada's participation in the Fulbright program has been increasing since the early 1990s. In contrast, international scholarships and research grants for Canadians through the three Canadian granting councils have unfortunately been decreasing over the past several years. Semester- or year-abroad programs, which are very popular in the United States but not as numerous in Canada, are another aspect of mobility.

The number of international work placements or internships made as part of an academic program is growing. Germany and the Netherlands probably have the most developed systems to facilitate these experiences for students. In Canada, increasing interest is shown in providing for international internships as part of cooperative education programs and some postgraduate degrees. This type of academic-related work placement still has no national-level support; however, a recent initiative of Human Resources Development Canada provides international internships for young Canadian graduates. These internships are intended to provide work experiences for unemployed youth, especially in international development agencies and businesses. This program was developed in response to several factors. The high youth-unemployment rate is perhaps the most important factor, but the need to prepare young people to work and live in a more globalized, competitive, and interdependent world is another relevant reason for the emphasis on international work opportunities.

International students

The trends in the size and direction of the international-student flow is of great interest and significance at this time. Several factors are changing the dynamics of this flow. Mention has already been made in this chapter of the increasing competition among countries — especially Australia, Canada, the United Kingdom, and the United States — for international students, as well as to the national agencies and networks established to recruit more international students. Even the language of recruitment has changed significantly. Enrolling international students has a distinct commercial orientation. Discussions of strategies to "capture a market share" are more common than those on how to "increase the retention and academic success rate" of visa students.

From 1985 to 1992, Australia, New Zealand, the United Kingdom, and the United States established differential fee rates for international students. In Canada, it was not until 1996 that our foreign policy changed and increased attention and funding were allocated to recruiting international students and exporting Canadian educational products and services. This new emphasis has been a major factor in the current pressure to gain a market share of international students for Canada.

The massification of higher education, especially in the countries of the Asia–Pacific region, has played a significant role in the size and direction of the flow of international students. This is why countries such as Hong Kong, South Korea, Malaysia, Singapore, Taiwan, and Thailand have traditionally been the source of students; and, assuming that economic conditions remain positive, they will continue to send students. However, these countries also see the opportunity to take a market approach to the whole issue of international students and are beginning to promote themselves as a regional centres for international students from neighbouring countries such as China and Indochina. Factors such as smaller distances, less culture shock, and lower costs are given as reasons for neighbouring countries not to send their students out of the region.

The quest for international students by the "big four" (Australia, Canada, United Kingdom, United States) is now moving to Central and South America and the Middle East, where once again national higher education capacity is not large enough to enrol all qualified students, and a growing middle class can afford to send their children abroad for a foreign education. The Eastern European market is seen as a longer term investment.

The final point to be made in this section concerns a rather disturbing trend. The arguments for recruiting students are now becoming mainly economic. Recent research from national organizations in Canada on international students includes studies of economic impacts, export readiness of higher education institutions, Canada's competitiveness in the international student market, and the prospects for expediting visa and admission requirements. What is lacking are reports on how to monitor and increase the academic success rate and retention of these students and how to respond to their academic, linguistic, social, cultural, and financial needs. The important point here is that economic and academic motives for enrolling international students do not have to be mutually exclusive. What is critical is to achieve the appropriate balance between these two motives so that they reinforce each other.

International development cooperation

Participation in international development projects with the support of CIDA has been a key aspect and cornerstone of Canadian universities' international cooperation since the 1970s, and development education has been an important adjunct to the development work. As already discussed in previous chapters, the extent and nature of university international development cooperation are clearly changing and in some cases diminishing. CIDA has significantly reduced the number of university partnership projects, as a result of its budget restraints, and the number of bilateral projects involving universities is decreasing, as a result of the emphasis on working with the private sector. In short, international development work is not as strong an agent for internationalization as it once was. This is an unfortunate situation, as it involves a reduction in the number of opportunities afforded through international development projects for research, curriculum change, student participation, development education, and faculty development in Canadian institutions.

The same situation is found in the United States and to some extent in the United Kingdom. However, it appears that in the Nordic countries, development cooperation continues to have a strong role in the internationalization of the universities. Australia, Germany, and the Netherlands have also had a strong history of university involvement in international development work. These countries are experiencing a similar but less severe decline in university involvement than in Canada. It is interesting to note that at many international conferences and workshops on the international dimension of higher education, international development cooperation seems to have a very low profile; it is certainly less noticeable than other topics, such as international students, offshore and distance delivery, curriculum change, and academic mobility, for instance. Is this a reflection of the importance attached to international development work in the late 1990s and the direction for the next decade?

233

Foreign languages

In Canada, a substantial decline has occurred in the number of universities requiring a foreign language for graduation (Knight 1995), and generally students' interest in the study of a foreign language has decreased. In a few instances, new undergraduate and postgraduate programs in international business require students to gain a working knowledge of a foreign language as a prerequisite for working in international business. Appreciation of different cultural norms and values is part of this kind of language instruction as well.

Because of the exponential increase in the number of people speaking and learning English around the world and because English is the current working language of business, students in English-speaking countries do not realize the importance of learning other languages. In non-English-speaking countries, students are hungry to study English and, in some cases, other foreign languages as well. Foreign languages are seen as the passport to travel, study abroad, international work, and internship experiences, as well as to an international career. Therefore, we are seeing a growing number of students from Europe and several Asian countries who are fluent in English and often additional languages other than their mother tongue. Insight into different cultures and cross-cultural communication skills often characterize multilingual individuals, and these are important skills in today's world. In short, students who only speak English risk being perceived as parochial and finding themselves in a not necessarily advantageous position. A major challenge in Canada is to encourage universities and students to recognize the importance of learning about other cultures, including, but not exclusively, learning another language.

In non-English-speaking countries, such as the Netherlands and Thailand, more and more courses are taught in English. In some cases, this is done through a twinning relationship with a foreign university; in others, the university has its own qualified English-speaking teachers. Originally, the target students were domestic, and the motivation for teaching in English was to increase their students' future opportunities for study and work abroad. A secondary motive is now coming into play, which is to attract international students who want to study in English at their university, even though English is not its native language. Although these universities are interested in internationalizing their campuses, they are also strongly interested in generating income from foreign students.

There is a substantial amount of discussion about these programs, regarding their quality, whether they should be serving more domestic students, and how cost-effective they really are. This trend is not directly relevant to Canada. However, it is necessary to be aware of it because it illustrates how strong the competition is in the world today to attract international students.

Twinning programs and offshore campuses

The 1990s will be remembered as the decade of great interest in and speculation about twinning programs and offshore campuses. Australia and the United States are taking the lead in developing these kinds of educational arrangements. Canada's involvement has been limited, to date, but interest is growing.

Asian countries, especially, do not have enough capacity in their national education systems to provide higher education to their huge number of qualified students. These countries are implementing creative alternative measures to resolve this difficulty, and thus we see the growth in the number of twinning programs. A twinning program means that students complete the first half of their degree or diploma program in their own country, and then they usually travel to the domestic campus of the foreign partner for the second half. The degree or diploma is provided by the foreign institution. In Canada, no hard data are available on the number of universities involved in these types of activities or to what extent. A recent survey of the 38 universities in Australia (Back et al. 1996) showed that 27 of them were in twinning arrangements with more than 93 overseas institutions, involving 13 000 students. These programs were predominantly in Malaysia and Singapore, but arrangements like this were also active in China, Hong Kong, Indonesia, South Africa, Thailand, and Viet Nam.

Establishing offshore campuses is yet another trend in the international marketing of education. In selected Asian and Middle Eastern countries, private companies were found to be optimistic about the return on their investments in the education sector. As a result, new campuses are built with private money, and foreign universities, with the approval of the national governments, are establishing diploma and degree programs. In some cases, existing campuses are renovated, and public-sector funds are also invested. However, the key issue is that the foreign university is responsible for the development and delivery of the educational programs, and the degree designation is from the foreign university. Data from the same survey (Back et al. 1996) indicate that seven Australian universities have established offshore campuses in Fiji, Hong Kong, Japan, Kuwait, Malaysia, Singapore, and United Arab Emirates. To date, no Canadian universities have built or set up in any way campuses to offer a range of degree programs in foreign countries, although in several cases Canadian universities are delivering their degree programs, often MBA programs, in a foreign location.

What does the future hold for Canadian involvement in twinning programs or offshore campuses? Because of demographic trends the massification of higher education in Asia and South America will increase, and it is forecast that the number of students needing higher education opportunities will continue to increase until 2025. Therefore, if the supply of students is available, Canada's foreign policy continues to emphasize trade, and the higher education sector is forced to diversify funding sources, it is likely that Canadian universities will become more creative and entrepreneurial in their approach to the international market.

Reflections and questions

Reviewing the macro- and microlevel trends and issues discussed in this chapter makes one reflect on some overarching themes and challenges facing the internationalization of higher education. One of the most critical questions that continually surfaces relates to the rationale and goals of enhancing the international dimension. The academic and economic rationales clearly have more importance today

236

than in yesteryears, when the political and social–cultural rationales had more prominence. However, the increased emphasis on the economic rationale raises the question of what internationalization really means. Without offering any direct benefit to academic or scholarly activities is it really internationalization? Or is it an income-generation activity in an international marketplace that funds the work of the university but does not necessarily introduce any added value to the education of Canadian students or the research work of Canadian scholars? This question has no straightforward answer, as there are many stakeholders with diverse vested interests and motives. However, it is an important question to ask, if only to ensure that institutions, NGOs, and the government are clear and explicit about their rationales and goals for the internationalization of the higher education sector.

Probably the most pervasive and consequential trend discussed in this chapter is the growing interest in the market and commercial aspects of the international dimension. Canada seems to be following the lead of Australia and the United States in this respect. Technical and scientific competitiveness, the commodification of educational products and services for export, and shrinking government funds for higher education, along with the need to diversify funding sources, are just three of the factors responsible for the new emphasis on a market approach to international education.

IDP Education Australia (Back et al. 1997) has described the shift in emphasis of Australia's international dimension in higher education as a movement from aid, to trade, to internationalization in the last three decades. Like Canada, its universities' interest in international cooperation was rooted in the Colombo Plan and development work. In 1986, a national-policy change in Australia resulted in a shift to a trade emphasis. Since the mid-1990s there has been increased interest and investment in student exchanges, curriculum changes, and other activities to internationalize the educational experience of Australian students. However, from a Canadian perspective, one can say that Australia is still a leader in the export of education and that it is still extremely active in the trade phase. The Australians have been very open about how much they have learned from Canada's academic orientation in the internationalization of its higher education sector, and we have a lot to learn from the Australians in the area of offshore education.

The irony of these comments about the Canadian experience is that many Canadian educators would describe our shift in a different sequence, that is, from aid, to mutual benefit (which includes internationalization), to trade. Canada's increasing orientation to a trade and market approach, which started 10 years later than it did in Australia, is just beginning to have its full impact. It is perhaps more accurate, or maybe just more cautious and diplomatic, to describe Canada, at present, as attempting to find the optimal balance and link between the academic and economic aspects of international education.

If one had a time machine to allow us to fast forward to 2005 or 2010, what would we see as the impact of the "internationalization years" of the higher education sector? This may seem like an impractical exercise, but perhaps it is important in helping us reflect more on what we are doing and why we are doing it. The changes and benefits we would most like to see would include solutions to global issues, such as the environment, through cooperative international research and technology transfer; Canada's serving as a leader in the knowledge industry and information-service sectors; more knowledgeable young Canadians skilled to live, work, and contribute in local, national, and international environments; and greater access to higher education and lifelong-learning opportunities through electronic and other forms of international communication systems. These would be only a few observations from a Canadian perspective.

However, we may be unable or even unwilling to imagine other changes, such as the homogenization of national identities and indigenous cultures; unequal access to information sources and systems, contributing to a "knows" versus "know-nots" dichotomy; a new elite class or cadre of international business people and bureaucrats (Hersh 1997); the commodification of education in commercial products; and a new form of neocolonization through the sale of franchises for educational services. The larger question is what role is higher education playing, consciously or unconsciously, in the creation of a world culture or the enhancement of cultural pluralism.

Reality, of course, lies somewhere between these two extremes. The real purpose of trying to imagine the future is to ensure that we are taking a hard look at why we are internationalizing higher education today and the possible impacts at home and abroad. The increased interest and attention focused on internationalization are welcomed, but this should not come without serious consideration of the goals we are trying to achieve. Even though we have taken a process approach to internationalization, it is absolutely crucial that we never lose sight of the objectives we are trying to achieve in the short and long terms.

In conclusion, it is important to reiterate that many of the observations, comments, and insights in this chapter are based on
information, data, and learning from diverse reports, documents, and
conferences. Very little formal research has been done on most of
these topics. Therefore, it is important to close the chapter with a call
for research and analysis of the trends and critical issues in the international dimension of higher education. It is interesting to note that
Teichler (1996a), after reviewing the major issues of research on
higher education policy during the past four decades, predicted that
internationalization of higher education would be the theme of a new
focus of both higher education policy and research for the next
decade. In light of the evolution of the international work of universities in Canada over the last four decades, as presented in previous chapters, and the trends and issues highlighted in this chapter,
the research focus on the international dimension of higher education is needed and welcome.

Chapter 10

Conclusion

Jean-Pierre Lemasson and Sheryl Bond

Characteristics of the internationalization of Canadian universities

Throughout this book, we have stressed the idea that the internationalization of Canadian universities has been and continues to be a gradual process that over time and in unplanned and varied ways has come to affect all university activities. Starting with the commitment of a few individuals, it has gained increasing numbers of converts, who have worked to entrench and disseminate their objective while integrating their work fully into the basic missions of the university. Some periods were more productive than others, but each successive stage has led however haphazardly to a broader range of possibilities, worked toward an increasingly complex set of objectives, and led to the discovery of correspondingly complex means of implementing them. Today, a little more institutionalized and better integrated into teaching, research, and community service, internationalization is beginning to make its systemic mark on the objectives and strategies of every institution, even if resources are not always mobilized with the same determination. Although the age of the pioneers is well behind us, individual initiative remains crucial to maintaining the momentum, and, as in all university affairs, the commitment of the professors is a determining factor. From this viewpoint, any approach to global planning that fails to take account of the various levels of decision-making will be doomed. Internationalization can only be institutionalized through consensus, or it will remain a mere idea, albeit an idea pursued above all by those who want to push back geographic frontiers and share the knowledge and ideals that underlie the universalist's vision of the university.

Development assistance as the common source of the internationalization of Canadian universities

We can state with assurance that the processes of internationalization in the various Canadian universities have proceeded from a common historic root in the form of development assistance. The community-service mission, often undervalued in favour of teaching and research, was the first to be internationalized. Training human resources and strengthening university institutions in the Third World (as it was known after World War II) represented the very heart of early Canadian university initiatives. These initiatives did much to lay solid institutional underpinnings for internationalization by bringing foreign students to Canada in increasing numbers and engaging universities in the management of contracts awarded by the Canadian International Development Agency (CIDA). Little by little, nearly all university institutions became involved in development assistance and found themselves adopting a vision that became an essential feature of the Canadian higher education system. CIDA played a key role in bringing this about. Through progressive adjustments to its programs, it not only increased the number of university actors but also created conditions for an ever greater commitment from university management.

What was original about development assistance in Canadian universities was that early on they expanded their activities to include human-resource development and institutional strengthening for their counterparts in developing areas of the world. The result was a unique combination of knowledge and know-how that had no equivalent in other developed countries and was exemplary in terms of the variety of the recipient countries and contributing disciplines. In fact, Canadian universities came to constitute a unique pool of expertise for providing training in developing countries. Although as James Shute has rightly pointed out, this expertise has perhaps not been sufficiently recognized and documented, Canadian universities were the only ones to play such a central role in the development assistance strategy of any donor country until the early 1990s.

New forms of internationalization

Today, development assistance has lost much of its importance as the common point of reference once shared by nearly all universities in all provinces. Several factors have conspired to undermine this common institutional identity and orientation that, as we have seen, were particularly notable in academic sectors such as agriculture, health, and business management.

241

Since 1991/92 successive governments have pursued neoliberal policies. Official development assistance amounted to $3.18 billion in 1991/92, or 0.49% of gross national product (GNP). By 1998/99, the aid envelope had shrunk by 25.8% and represented only 0.27% of GNP. As a result, CIDA has lost a major portion of its budget, and its interests and activities are increasingly focused on the private sector. A significant constituency thinks it is better to use aid funds to promote the export of goods and services and create jobs in the private sector; not only have the resources allocated to universities been cut, but the universities themselves have also been expected to make a financial contribution as proof of their institutional commitment! All of this has occurred at a time when the universities have been suffering funding cuts, which in recent years have reduced their operating budgets by as much as 30% in some provinces. Development assistance has thus become a secondary concern, and its influence has waned to the point at which doubts are raised about its survival in certain universities.

At the same time and in a similar context of economic crisis, countries such as Australia and New Zealand have made it a central point of their international activity to recruit foreign students. With the creation of the Canadian Education Centres (CECs), Canada embarked on this path through the Department of Foreign Affairs and International Trade, and we can witness the importance that education marketing has assumed today (DFAIT 1998). Moreover, agencies devoted exclusively to recruiting foreign students have appeared at the provincial level (BCCIE 1997; EduQuébec 1998; Nova Scotia 1998; ACIE 1999), and a majority of universities are now actively engaged in recruitment through specialized mechanisms or units. We may wonder what such recruitment activities have to do with the internationalization of universities, apart from obvious financial considerations. Ten years ago, more foreign students were studying in

Canada than today. Yet, at that time, their presence within our institutions was not considered a dimension of internationalization as such. Only today, essentially after the fact, have we begun to appreciate the value of having foreign students in our midst, but in the days when they were more numerous and universities had no deficits, their presence was scarcely noticed. If we really believe that hosting foreign students is a key element in the internationalization of Canadian universities, we have yet to appreciate, or to take full advantage of, their potential contribution to academic and para-academic activities, as Catherine Vertesi suggests (Chapter 6).

Our students' mobility is considered another defining dimension of internationalization. Frequent mention has been made of European initiatives, such as the European Community Action Scheme for the Mobility of University Students. Originally intended to create a new and truly European generation, trilingual if possible, these initiatives have been taken as a model by governments in the North American Free Trade Agreement and have also made their mark on relations between Canada and the European Union. In practice, the modest level of resources invested to date at both provincial and federal levels raise questions about the real degree of government interest. Although much is made of the issue at the political level, it is clear that the impact of the debate on student mobility remains marginal in quantitative terms. Nevertheless, student mobility is without doubt now regarded as a major aspect of internationalization, both by universities and by policymakers, although admittedly the effort far outweighs the results.

Over the last 10 years, then, initiatives in the area of internationalization have become diversified, and new stakeholders have appeared both within the universities and beyond them. The development of internationalization among Canadian universities has become more complex; new institutional functions have been added; and whole new entities have been created, raising inevitable questions about internal coordination. With few exceptions, internationalization is generally not being implemented within an integrated framework. In fact, as a result of the involvement of Human Resources Development Canada in student-mobility programs and the creation of new bodies, the number of stakeholders has multiplied. In some cases, such as in that of recruitment, we can even say that the provincial initiatives are working to some extent in competition with the CECs. In short, from a common approach to internationalization, universities have now moved to a stage at which they are much less bound by a common model.

Major features of the internationalization of Canadian universities

It would of course be ideal if we could draw up a thoroughly objective balance sheet on the internationalization of Canadian universities, based on a few systematic indicators. As we have seen, however, the information available for assessing the situation is highly fragmented. Apart from data on foreign students, the only comprehensive statistics available are those on the number of agreements signed by Canadian universities with their counterparts abroad and on the number and value of development assistance contracts. The databases CUE (Canadian University International Exchange Agreement, on international exchanges by Canadian universities) and CUPID (Canadian University Projects in International Development) are managed by the Association of Universities and Colleges of Canada (AUCC) and are available at its web site (see Appendix 1). Apart from these admittedly useful data, we have no statistical tool to apply to what has become an infinitely more complex subject. Jane Knight's studies (Knight 1995, 1996) remain very valuable reference works, as attested to by several chapters in this book. Yet, focused on policy and institutional aspects as these works are, they do not allow us to fully understand the way internationalization actually works in practice. Knight makes this point herself, in the conclusion to her chapter. In fact, with the exception of the work of Yves Gingras, Benoît Godin, and Martine Foisy (Chapter 4), we lack the quantitative tools to grasp the systematic characteristics and specific features of Canadian universities. Under these conditions, we must rely primarily on qualitative analysis and incomplete lists and surveys, which can at best serve to highlight the most notable elements. In the future, given the challenges articulated below, we can only hope that additional research on this topic will be undertaken.

Without a dominant model for internationalization supported by significant government funding, universities have found themselves left on their own to meet the challenges of the internationalization of the universities, free to choose their own path and obliged to devise their own goals and strategies in light of their individual circumstances and their (generally limited and uncertain) financial means. Faced with relative indifference from governments as measured by funding levels, the universities have had full freedom to pursue the forms of internationalization that have seemed most appropriate with the modest means available. It is indeed a prime characteristic of universities in Canada today that they pursue objectives and practices in internationalization largely using their own funds or those that they themselves can raise for the purpose.

243

244

A second characteristic, related in part to the above, is the remarkable creativity and wealth of initiatives in internationalization to be found across Canada. We may say that not a single Canadian university has remained inactive in the process of internationalization. From modestly scaled regional institutions to the big urban universities, nearly all are building active and varied links with foreign partners. In the areas of teaching, research, and community service alike, an impressive number of projects and activities have been launched and are in full flight. Fernand Caron and Jacques Tousignant (Chapter 7) have given a clear demonstration of the profusion of new forms of internationalization, each more original than the last. Of course, without a tradition, such an approach can give rise to some of the best but also some of the poorest initiatives.

A third characteristic, again related to the preceding ones, is the importance that grass-roots groups have assumed as key players in opening Canadian universities to the world. In one respect, we can see here a continuation of the universities' pioneering approach to development cooperation. In the more recent context, we observe that internationalization begins with the university community and its efforts to find adequate local sources of funding for its projects on a case-by-case basis. It is most often the availability of local resources that can make or break the feasibility of such undertakings. Under these conditions, internationalization is seen as a lever to reinforce local knowledge and know-how and to meet the challenge of globalization, seen as both an opportunity and a threat. There are many ways of raising funds, and certainly a key dimension of success is persuading partners to contribute. In this regard, particular attention should be paid to the role of parents, the universities themselves, municipalities, and businesses, which are all regularly solicited for funds. Whether we are speaking of aid-type projects or business-development initiatives, it is difficult to imagine a successful undertaking without some form of local-community support.

A fourth characteristic relates to the great diversity of countries from which partners are being selected. From this perspective, we find that the internationalization of Canadian universities really means a globalization of their outreach. Whereas analysis of copublications offers clear evidence of the growing diversification of scientific collaboration, it also demonstrates the geographic breadth of this process by identifying the countries with which Canadian universities have signed collaboration agreements or where they have, on a more restricted basis, carried out development assistance projects. This breadth is hardly surprising when we recall that Canada is uniquely open to two great world linguistic groups, the anglophone and the francophone. Moreover, the diversity of our sources of immigration is constantly creating or reinforcing ties with countries in Asia, Eastern Europe, and Latin America. The tradition of multilateralism has also encouraged the search for diversified partnerships not limited to any particular geographic grouping. From this viewpoint, the Canadian university system is one of the most open in the world, not only to internationalization but also to globalization.

245

Finally, a fifth characteristic of Canadian universities is the diversity of attitudes toward learning a foreign language. More and more, the francophone universities, like those in Europe, encourage students to learn at least three languages. This pressure is far less evident in anglophone Canadian universities, which in this respect are more like American institutions. Whereas openness to multilateralism and globalization is particularly strong in Quebec and is closely linked to multilinguism (as in all countries with a minority language) it is far less strong in the rest of Canada. This difference is not surprising by any means, and it opens up the debate on the role of internationalization as a channel of cultural uniformity or diversification.

These, then, are the features that stand out from our snapshot of the system in its current state. It is clear that all university functions are now directly involved in the internationalization process and that integrating all these changes into a coherent and shared framework within our institutions remains a major challenge. Moreover, as it is increasingly impossible to divorce the local from the international, openness to the world raises a series of complex issues directly related to the future of each institution. We shall address a few of these issues and try to grasp their implications.

The likely evolution of internationalization and its effects

Internationalization of disciplines and programs

As we have seen, the internationalization of disciplines tends to follow a pattern that changes from one field of science to another. This fact emerges clearly from Gingras et al.'s analysis of research (Chapter 4) and from indications of internationalization in postgraduate programs. The international dimension may differ within the same discipline, and every discipline may have its own paradigm and its own pace of internationalization. This situation is likely to continue and to be reinforced in coming years in all areas, as a result not only of the need to relate local realities more closely to international ones but also of the growing numbers of international topics of study. Whether we are thinking of research on the emergence of continental trading blocs, the greenhouse effect, peace, the role and limits of international institutions, or the impacts of the Internet on learning, we face a whole new set of questions and new fields of study that will inevitably speed up the internationalization of research and lead to a sharper differentiation among postgraduate programs. We must also expect to see more rapid growth in courses, options, and programs with international content. This process will not necessarily occur quickly. As Sheryl Bond and Jacquelyn Thayer Scott (Chapter 3) and Howard Clark (Chapter 5) have reminded us, departments and faculties are often reluctant to address questions of internationalization for fear of the immediate implications it may have for the evaluation of their teaching staff. Nonetheless, the numbers of academic initiatives with an initial international focus are clearly growing. We can already see in several Canadian universities new institutional structures emerging in the form of centres or institutes to study not only geopolitics in its traditional form but also the new focus on economic trading blocs, for example.

The growing institutionalization of partnerships

Because many activities, particularly in the areas of teaching and student mobility, involve projects of limited duration, new projects must constantly be put forward from one year to the next. Despite the great adaptability shown by Canadian universities, the majority of their internationalization initiatives remain fragile, particularly those for student mobility. Without denying the benefits of individual initiatives at the local level, there is a need to ensure continuity and stability so that more structured and durable actions can be taken. One way of dealing with this problem is to put partnerships on a more solid institutional basis.

Increasing evidence of the trend to institutionalization can be seen within the university community itself in the growing number of rules governing the international equivalence of courses and degrees, which reflects the greater mobility of students. This institutional thrust is even more clear in the cases of double-degree and joint programs and the institutional mechanisms to foster the cosupervision of theses.

Networking is becoming the predominant approach to research. Whereas individual collaborative arrangements can now extend worldwide, thanks to the Internet, we also find that researchers are engaging ever more frequently in regular and ongoing collaboration, whether at the instigation of national research policies or at that of new international programs. Research teams of truly transnational composition are a concomitant to the increasingly international nature of research topics. Although the natural sciences are the ones most immediately affected, the point applies just as surely and with increasing force to all other disciplines. Along similar lines, Howard Clark (Chapter 5) has pointed to the emergence of consortia, or formal and structured networks, set up with clearly stated, common objectives and often supported by their own management structure. Consortia are also making headway on the multilateral front. Whether the Agence universitaire de la Francophonie (AUF, university office for francophone people) or the Commonwealth of Learning (COL), which are both based on linguistic and cultural affinity, whether the Inter-American Organization for Higher Education or the Consortium for North American Higher Education Collaboration, which both have a regional geographic focus, universities are forming broad groupings with shared objectives that may relate as much to teaching as to research.

247

Collaboration with institutions in developing countries is expanding with a similar thrust. In some cases, university or government partners may send their scholarship holders to study at the same institution, hoping thereby to promote development through a close form of linkage. All fields of an institution can gradually be brought in so as to benefit from such support. But such partnerships can also take on a business cast when the Canadian university and its foreign partner cooperate to offer new programs that did not exist locally and that might be sold for mutual profit. The proliferation of MBA programs offered abroad is a good illustration of these new permanent alliances.

Canadian universities are also seeking to build stable partnerships with business, as seen in the introduction of international-studies chairs, financing of particular projects by foundations, and development of international research partnerships to pursue medium- and long-term projects. The engineering and biotechnology sectors are replete with examples of this type. Without intending to detract from the importance of personal initiatives, we remark that more and more universities are looking for initiatives leading to stable, ongoing partnerships. This is one way of ensuring that the dimensions of teaching, research, and community service remain solidly and durably open to the world and that Canada secures comparative advantage at a time when competition now extends far beyond national borders.

We should also point out that although it may not be expected of academics, some universities that rate themselves among the best (rightly or wrongly) see international involvement as an opportunity to reinforce their position of leadership at home. We hear more and more in Canada of the ranking of universities on a scale of prestige that often involves a curious mix of perception and reality. Under these conditions, international partnerships become political tools that universities can use locally in extracting financial and material advantage or in enhancing their reputation among the student population.

Toward a globalization of interuniversity competition and cooperation

Canadian universities find themselves faced with a sharp contradiction between their traditional values of solidarity, derived from their unique experience with development assistance, and the new imperative of marketing their institutions and expertise. The aim today is to seek mutual advantage through partnerships in research and student exchange. Granted, it is difficult at times not to find this confusing; it is becoming clear that the dynamics of globalization are making themselves felt at nearly all levels of activity, particularly in Canada.

Student exchanges with Europe in particular, such as through the Conference of Rectors and Principals of Quebec Universities (Conférence des recteurs et principaux des universités du Québec) agreements, but also with certain countries in Asia, are now common, and work terms abroad to gain professional experience are sought out in increasing numbers of countries, especially in the field of management science. All of Canada's universities now participate in worldwide student flows, which would be impossible if this cooperation was not based on mutual trust. However, the recruitment of students today falls clearly within the realm of competition, not only with other local institutions but also and increasingly with those in other countries (Australia, France, United Kingdom, United States), which one by one are adopting national policies or strategies of active recruitment. We are witnessing, in effect, the globalization of competition.

Development assistance has been the supporting framework for the development of local training to meet the needs of developing countries. Canadian universities have contributed to the creation of many programs, often at the master's-degree level, in a great many countries while helping to develop a teaching body to ensure the local university a maximum of autonomy. Today, in a growing number of developing countries, programs in such areas as management and health sciences are aimed at taking advantage of a market that is even more profitable because there are no local alternatives for human-resource development. Consequently, international collaboration with institutions in developing countries designed to respond to the demand for training is becoming less cooperative and more competitive.

249

Competition extends to universities in developed countries as well. Many foreign universities now offer their programs in Canada (University Affairs 1998). One can now take training anywhere, in any country, and Canadian universities are not the only ones finding room for expansion in this regard. This new situation may pose a serious threat to our own universities, which used to be able to count on the steady enrollment of students from their own immediate vicinity. If foreign universities can now offer better or more prestigious programs in Canada, this implies that the internationalization of universities outside Canada may act as an impetus for a reexamination of our own system. The emergence of new technologies serves to highlight these changes even further.

Technological development is in many ways spearheading this new trend. The ability of nearly all universities in the North to offer their programs abroad, via the Internet, raises the question of whether all universities will eventually offer distance programs and if so, under what conditions. University choices and decisions depend on many factors. As we have seen, the question of intellectual property over course content is now an issue that never existed before. The same is true of the risk of losing academic and teaching resources to the private sector. The Fédération québécoise des professeures et professeurs d'université (Quebec federation of university professors) has thus opposed the incorporation of the Multimedia University Press, comprising Quebec universities and certain private partners (CIRST–ENVEX 1997). Moreover, some universities make the content of all their courses accessible, and others face stricter minimum teaching requirements in structuring such exchanges. With the advent of new multimedia possibilities, it is becoming increasingly necessary to develop specialized teaching courses. Teaching methods constitute another important issue. Must there be tutors in place in each country, for example? Should students be able to meet together? How and under what conditions? These are new and unanswered questions. Costs are another essential factor. Who should pay? Who should have free access to instruction? Universities are reluctant to commit themselves on these points. Some will seize the opportunity to increase their revenues while simply avoiding such issues. Others will see the chance to spread information more broadly to countries where infrastructure is inadequate to meet the national challenges of educating their younger generations. But many would like to combine both aspects and are torn between the demands of generating new revenues and making knowledge — humanity's legacy — as widely available as possible. Now that it is possible, moreover, to distribute information publicly over the Internet and privately through intranets, it is technologically feasible to disseminate the same course content under entirely different financial arrangements. This may in fact be a way of adapting to circumstances without having to make the choice of meeting one or another of contradictory demands. In any case, internationalization is sharpening the debate about the social function of the university (see, for example, Freitag 1995).

It should be noted that the language of dissemination is also an unavoidable factor. Canada is in the unique position of hosting the headquarters of two multilateral agencies for distance education, from distinct language groups, AUF and COL. Within these linguistic precincts, which are incidentally often rivals, we find that programs are being offered on both a competitive and a cooperative basis. The two approaches coexist, and the choice of one or the other is made on a case-by-case basis in light of the circumstances governing each project.

It must also be seen that the question of how much to charge has never been posed so sharply, depending on the academic sector. In the professional disciplines, which are synonymous with good prospects for a well-paid career, it is tempting and easy to demand fairly high tuition fees. This is true in management studies, health sciences, law, and engineering, for example. However, it is difficult to imagine such an approach in the arts and social sciences or the humanities, or generally speaking in those disciplines with a high cultural content, which, in the end, treat knowledge, not as a marketable product, but as an instrument of human development. This gap — unfortunately more and more pronounced — points to the urgent need to reconsider the comparative worth of careers devoted to fostering economic output and those with a social calling. Failure to do so will invite the risk of legitimizing the elitist and dominant mercantilism to the detriment of social cohesion and democracy. It is easy to see why university management is so frequently ambivalent on these points.

The situation is no different in research. The science policies of states have long been focused on forging alliances that are in some cases only justifiable in terms of achieving a competitive edge within a given sector. University research takes on a clearly competitive cast, however, when the results are likely to lead to economic advantage. Whereas cooperation is the uppermost consideration in such areas as astronomy or astrophysics, bitter international rivalries between competing laboratories are common in such areas as biotechnology. Although the race for prestige has always been a feature of research to some extent, it is now turning into a race for innovation, with strong encouragement from governments, particularly in the areas targeted for research funding. The universities are thus becoming caught up in this dual dimension of cooperation and competition, with the emphasis depending on the discipline and the economic interest. But it also depends on the researchers themselves, who are after all the prime players. In any case, our institutions are aware that innovations can bring in royalties and bolster their revenues, and the universities are increasingly disposed to enter into formal partnerships or consortia to systematically generate returns in a particular sector. From this viewpoint, it is difficult to build an international presence without a sound national strategy, such as the one that led to the Networks of Centres of Excellence. The national and international dimensions are inextricably linked.

251

This competitive logic is even more apparent in the relationship between universities and the private sector. There seems no limit to the budding of partnerships with foreign companies to develop new products. Universities compete among themselves to win contracts with national or multinational corporations. By doing so, they become fully engaged, not only in competition among themselves, but also in the broader struggle among businesses seeking to find or maintain a foothold in one market or another.

No part of the university is now spared from this globalization of cooperation and competition. The two are found everywhere, and the boundaries between them are becoming more and more blurred. These types of relationship coexist, depending on the particular features of each discipline or the type of activity involved. The same institutions can be at once allies and rivals; their relationships change constantly according to the goal at hand. Generosity competes with a mercantilism that is in full flight and perhaps even stronger than suggested by Slaughter and Leslie (1977) in their analysis of academic

capitalism. The frontiers of shared interests follow outlines as tortu-
ous as those of a jigsaw puzzle. We cannot avoid serious questions
about the values that will shape the world of tomorrow. Questions
are also raised about the new conditions of knowledge creation and
dissemination and the new hierarchy of university disciplines. It is
time to identify and spell out the issues, recognize what is at stake,
and devise the most appropriate course of action.

252

All of this may well serve to speed up governments' thinking
about appropriate levels of intervention. Thus, after a period in
which the recruitment of foreign students was its only concern with
respect to internationalization, the Australian government is now
making subtle changes to reintroduce a more global policy for internationalizing education (Back et al. 1995). The reverse is true in the
case of France, which — in pursuit of a strategy of international influence, strictly through cooperation — has now set up an international
agency to recruit foreign students (CIES n.d.). We may say that
although the paths taken by various governments may diverge, this
tension between academic and commercial objectives in education
exists everywhere. In this sense, the stakes in the field of teaching and
instruction ever more closely resemble those in research. It is imperative that universities contribute directly to this debate and help to
shape new policies.

Management and internationalization by universities

Internal differentiation of management and coordination structures

Most universities have equipped themselves with specialized structures to manage their international activities. Following the creation
of services for foreign students and the subsequent broadening of
their mandate to include student-mobility issues, international cooperation offices were set up essentially to manage contracts. Today,
international cooperation offices carry an ever broader range of
responsibilities. They are expected to receive foreign delegations, prepare agreements for signature, and arrange for the circulation of
international information within the institution — all functions well
described in the *Profile of International Collaboration by Canadian
Universities* (AUCC 1995b). But they have also been assigned the even
more comprehensive responsibility of elaborating and implementing
policies for internationalizing their universities. However, as Howard

Clark points out (Chapter 5), they are not yet in a position to effect rapid change in their university's state of internationalization, as these offices have no direct influence over academic reality.

It is not only that the institutional leadership is not always on side. Even if most universities adopted policies and strategic plans for internationalization, institutional change would likely be slower than hoped, because it is clear that the major focus of decision-making lies at the faculty or departmental level. And as Jane Knight has shown (Chapter 9), only a few departments have established their own international goals. Under these conditions, the key to success lies in making profound changes in a number of internal practices.

253

Another — not uncontroversial — recommendation would be to appoint a vice president for internationalization to be responsible for the much needed coherence of internal initiatives. At present, only the University of British Columbia has such a position. We frequently find in Canadian universities that some services are the responsibility of one vice president but others are in the bailiwick of another vice president, a situation that makes it difficult to ensure internal coordination and a common perspective. Does this point to the need for a new, centralized structure? Several considerations must be addressed before a definitive answer can be offered.

If each Canadian university is following its own model of internationalization, this has to do in large part with the range of disciplines offered. Even within the same university, we find that the concept of internationalization varies according to academic sector or discipline, thereby at least opening the door to different approaches. As Jane Knight notes (Chapter 9), the underlying motive for internationalization may be economic, cultural, or political. All of these motives coexist in a broad diversity of patterns that makes it nearly impossible to identify a single objective for the institution as a whole. If it is true to say that every discipline or academic sector has its own approach to internationalization, then we may also say that the rationale for internationalization in each academic sector is distinct. In every university, its internationalization efforts are linked to specific fields of knowledge and its development; thus, each university's internationalization efforts directly depend on its range of disciplinary fields and specializations. It is understandable that a vice president for internationalization will need to have a deep involvement in academic affairs.

This role is a delicate one, moreover, in several respects, as sharp internal conflicts can arise from failure to understand the rationale for internationalization in each sector. In the social sciences, generally speaking, internationalization will be seen as a tool for promoting understanding among peoples, reinforcing values of solidarity, or perhaps promoting basic human rights worldwide. In the management sciences, most often stress will be placed on enshrining the laws of the marketplace, earning profits, fostering competition and the worldwide spread of consumerism, winning respect for international marketing, and finding an acceptable way of Americanizing business relationships. Some insist on globalizing mercantilism, whereas others counter this with an appeal for globalizing the culture of differentiation. Some seek a return to the days when development assistance represented at least 0.07% of Canada's gross domestic product, whereas others target their MBA programs squarely at the future elites of developing countries. From this viewpoint, the major societal debates are fully reflected within the university, which is also perhaps the best place to reconcile these divergent viewpoints.

This disciplinary split is deepened by the universities' ambivalence about the merits of the cooperative and the competitive approaches. Neither option should be excluded a priori, of course, if institutional development can benefit from both. It would be just as risky to support any initiative that might upset the internal balance. This situation may make the creation of a vice president of internationalization all the more useful. But it also demonstrates the potential limitations of such a position.

Other issues complicate the choice of the best way to manage the internationalization of the universities. As the task has become more complex internal roles and structures have become more diversified. Foreign-student services and international cooperation offices have now been joined by foreign-student recruitment bureaus, which may or may not be attached to those earlier offices. This development raises yet further questions about the coordination of units that may have contradictory objectives.

Doubts are also raised about contract-management functions. The changes that CIDA has made in the way it awards contracts and the reduced volume of contracts reserved exclusively for universities (CIDA's new bidding system, with limited funding for the University Partnerships in Cooperation and Development [UPCD] program) have led several institutions to conclude that the only way to maintain their current contract volume or increase it with funding from international financial agencies, such as the regional banks or the World Bank, is to equip themselves with a more flexible management structure, free of the encumbrances so well described by Howard Clark (Chapter 5). Alliances have been struck with private-sector partners, and some universities have even set up private corporations in an effort to meet their objectives. What would be the best organizational and management models to enable a university to maintain its contract work at a level it deems consistent with its capacities and its expertise? To what extent should the contractual dimension be located outside the university? And, in this case, what kind of relationship will be needed to ensure the academic advantages, without the drawbacks? What will be the impact on university governance? Some have suggested that such questions may even cast doubt on the appropriateness of the collegial system for the management of universities (Buchbinder and Newson 1990). Whatever the case, it is no longer possible to consider questions of international revenue outside the broader context of the growing entrepreneurial character of universities and the structural conditions they need to enable them to generate their own revenue from whatever source. As more and more universities adopt economic objectives, the resulting complexity of their structures will more and more resemble those of holding companies.

Valuing all international activities

The current criteria for the appraisal of professors have frequently been cited as an obstacle to the proper valuation of international initiatives. Although in the case of research great store is placed on faculty members belonging to an international network or publishing in an international journal as offering clear and unquestioned proof of her or his excellence, this does not necessarily hold for those working to secure international training for their students or to strengthen university institutions in developing countries. These cases clearly require better measures of excellence, and it might be useful to clarify some of the more specific evaluation criteria and make more use of such mechanisms as peer juries. A teacher of intercultural relations may be a splendid pedagogue in theory, practice, and person. Yet, even the director of his or her department may have no evidence of this from a credible peer. Profound discrepancies in an evaluation procedure work to the systematic disadvantage of faculty who are interested in building new teaching or social relationships. This tends to inhibit innovation, and only those with tenure can afford to persist in developing an expertise not recognized in their own department. Many forms of appraisal can be established to compel those teachers most concerned to spell out the particular challenges they face and thereby demonstrate the excellence of their work. This would be at least one route to stimulating new thinking and possibly original contributions to the process of internationalization.

One advantage of this approach would be to bring teaching concerns back into the centre of the debate about the quality control of international education and, more broadly, of internationalization. The Europeans have established a credit-transfer system, based essentially on syllabus descriptions. Even if we feel that these methods smack of efforts to impose uniformity, they in fact amount to no more than efforts to control the minimum content of the knowledge to be transmitted. This is certainly not a negligible consideration, but the notions of quality and excellence go far beyond that. The evaluation of a university's internationalization should include output as well as input indicators (see annex A, "Self-evaluation checklist," in CERI–IMHE 1998). In short, the assessment of faculty members' international activities could be a suitable complement to other efforts to enhance the quality of university work. It should be noted that these concerns have not found much reflection in Canada. Although the Canadian Information Centre for International Credentials (CICIC 1995) deals with questions concerning the credit-transfer system, this does not mean that Canadian universities have shown much interest in taking this route.

Internal financing of international activities

The discussion of contractual aspects has served to highlight the organizational problems universities face in resorting to international activities as a source of revenue. Whereas most university presidents favour internationalizing their institutions, a survey would probably show that their support for this varies inversely with its costs to the institution. We may legitimately ask whether any Canadian university has introduced a system of budgeting for international activities. Although we might suppose that part of any operating budget should be used in support of this effort, it is far from clear that in the majority of cases Canadian universities are convinced of this. Certainly, the sorry state of university financing tends above all to preserve the status quo, and the funds earmarked for development are generally modest. It would be interesting, however, to measure the commitment of universities to maintaining such budget envelopes and their relative weight in relation to those established for the teaching and research functions. In fact, it would appear that the major concern of universities is to cover the infrastructure costs for existing services, which the universities are under increasing pressure to make self-financing, either directly or through their generating greater general revenues for the university. We may consider it unfortunate that in Canada, as opposed to Europe, government budgets do not cover or only partially cover the infrastructure costs for managing international cooperation.

To sum up, managing the internationalization of universities is becoming an increasingly complex affair. On one hand, it raises essentially political questions of balance and values, both internally and externally — as well as academic questions, which often seem to receive too little serious consideration to generate new evaluation practices or support for a new departmental dynamic. On the other hand, structures for managing international activities are becoming more diverse and require more and more specialized expertise and a closer identification with academic objectives. Pressure is increasing therefore to ensure a better synergy through new structures or new forms of coordination. But, for the most part, these structures have so far been inadequate to the configuration of individual institutions, their intended projection of themselves on the international scene, or their efforts to adapt to ever-changing circumstances in an increasingly fractured internal and external institutional environment. In effect, in addition to having to take account of their own dynamic, universities must also take account of government interventions, which in this area tend to promote dispersal, rather than coherent, well-integrated action.

257

The role of governments

In the course of a few years, the universities have undergone some fundamental changes as a result of sizable budget cuts. Relatively independent of government in matters affecting their management, they have been obliged to overcome their revenue shortfalls in a variety of ways, primarily by taking on new research contracts financed by the private sector and by seeking greater revenues from international sources. Some studies suggest that in the area of research and development, Canadian universities are now more tightly bound than their American counterparts to the private sector (CIRST–ENVEX 1998).

This need for universities to earn income results directly from government decisions to reduce public funding for higher education. Depending on the province, governments are retreating in a number of ways. The issue of privatization, a term that covers a wide variety of situations, has come to the fore. In Alberta, government funding received by the University of Calgary has shrunk from 90% of its operating budget 10 years ago to 39% today (Kant 1998). The Ontario government, for its part, allows universities to set tuition fees for all professional programs — such as medicine, law, and administration — and in nearly all provinces students have seen major hikes in tuition fees (as noted in Chapter 1), and this has had a direct impact on the levels of enrollment at Canadian universities.

The disinvestment of provincial governments in higher education has been dramatic, and universities have been forced to increase their revenues to survive; they have had to be ready to either embrace the logic of the knowledge marketplace or reduce their activities and risk disappearing completely. From this viewpoint, governments bear a large responsibility for the tensions described above. At the same time, the senior level of government has shown indifference to, and a lack of understanding of, the importance of internationalization and its effects on the universities.

From a strictly financial viewpoint, federal government funding for international education, not including the UPCD program of CIDA, stood at barely $20 million in 1997/98 (AUCC 1998; also see AUCC's web site [listed in Appendix 1]). But nearly $14 million is destined for foreign partners and about $6 million is granted to Canadian students. If we add the $33 million for the UPCD program, the federal contribution to international education is $53 million. These amounts are absurdly low. Moreover, as we have seen, international grants from the funding councils are very modest, despite the recent appearance of new programs. For example, the Social Sciences and Humanities Research Council, in partnership with CIDA, has just established a new program called Canada in the World, aimed at promoting studies in developing countries, and the Natural Sciences and Engineering Research Council has announced the creation of its International Initiatives Fund, which will help Canadian researchers join international networks. It is understandable, too, that AUCC and other organizations recently presented a memorandum to the federal government, urging it to devote funding of the order of $100 million annually to international education (AUCC 1998[1]). Despite the shift in the magnitude of the requested funding, we still must recognize that the proposal remains modest by comparison with the European project, SOCRATES, which alone represents spending of about $1 530 billion between 1995 and 1998.

Although new funding is clearly required, the pertinence of these recommendations can certainly be debated. In fact, as we shall

---

[1] AUCC (Association of Universities and Colleges of Canada). 1998. Scotia Bank–AUCC Awards for Excellence in Internationalization. AUCC, ON, Canada. Unpubished document.

see, we may ask whether it would not be better to address the question of support for internationalization more generally, rather than focusing on a set of programs or subprograms. This also explains why several provincial governments would like to see major initiatives mounted but mainly under the category of recruiting foreign students. We can only regret that the provinces take such a narrow view of their constitutional responsibilities. Quebec is an exception, but resources are scarce there, too.

With their eyes firmly fixed on their budget balances, governments have no medium- or long-term perspective to offer, other than that of supporting commercial initiatives. In fact, no comprehensive vision guides their actions in higher education or with respect to the role internationalization might play in support of development and higher education. The piecemeal approach is the rule, however contradictory it may be.

Jane Knight's article (Chapter 9) draws attention to a series of studies pointing to the absence of a policy framework and the (partly related) lack of coordination among stakeholders. In Canada, we face a curious situation in which the provinces, which are responsible for education and make the most influential decisions in this area, evince little or no interest in policy or vision for the internationalization of the universities; and in which the federal government, which has no constitutional role in education, involves itself in international education but, for political reasons, studiously avoids any direct intervention.

This situation explains the creation of intermediary institutions, such as the Canadian Bureau for International Education, the World University Service of Canada, and more recently the CECs, which were established thanks to a sizable grant from the Asia–Pacific Foundation. Under these circumstances, the obvious lack of coordination is the direct result of the political divide between the federal government and the provinces, but it also reflects differing philosophies among bodies within the federal government itself. Moreover, as we saw in Chapter 3, some bodies, such as the World University Service of Canada and the Canadian Bureau for International Education, which have played a positive and important role in training related to development assistance, are now entering increasingly into competition with the universities themselves to win contracts or to undertake recruiting. The fragmentation is institutionalized by the proliferation of these intermediaries, which are ever more frequently in a conflict of interest with the very institutions that they are supposed to serve.

How can we hope to achieve better coordination when the prevailing pattern is that of proliferation and fragmentation in the higher education system and in the forms of internationalization? It is time for governments to realize that universities have significant stakes in the broader panorama of international relations. It is essential to appreciate the scope of these stakes and to think seriously about the steps that might enable Canadian universities to make long-term commitments to cooperation, as well as to competition, which are of such strategic importance not only for the universities themselves but also for the economic and cultural leadership of our country.

Rather than going ahead with large, standardized programs that lead to increases in uniformity and adhere to an existing pattern, would it not be wiser to support the institutions' proposals, which are aimed at targets of a suitable scale in the international areas in which each institution can hope to be effective with appropriate methods, including, of course, student exchanges and recruitment? How can we move from a program approach to one that is strategically targeted and that reconciles consistency with effectiveness? This calls for a radical rethinking of the ways governments are providing support in the new setting taking shape. The major risk is that by pursuing a strategy of differentiation we may promote proliferation and oblige universities, if they want access to funding, to deal with so many different institutions and on so many different issues that they cannot hope to manage them all coherently. In such a confusing context, how will it be possible to develop strategic plans that represent anything more than good intentions? One way to support the universities may be to give each of them the means to carry out a comprehensive plan in which all facets of internationalization are present to varying degrees, according to their particular institutional strengths, the originality of their contribution, and their international networks. It is not a question here of local or regional resistance to internationalization, perceived as a leveling force, as it was sometimes in Europe (de Wit and Callan 1995), but one of strengthening the capacity of Canadian universities to create and diffuse knowledge internationally.

Internationalizing the production and dissemination of knowledge

It is clear that we are well on the way to a state of globalized "production" and dissemination of knowledge. As a locus for the production of knowledge, the universities many years ago lost whatever monopoly they may have once had. Universities must now come to terms with various specialized public or private research centres and new forms of producing and diffusing knowledge, which Gibbons et al. (1995) referred to as Mode 2. This mode may be characterized — at the risk of caricature — as one in which knowledge is immediately placed in context in direct response to the concerns of users. This mode is essentially interdisciplinary and marked by the globalization of economic interests. It thus takes an international perspective from the very outset. Moreover, as the number of universities is growing throughout the world, it is clear that no one institution can pretend to cover all areas of knowledge with equal success. The globalization of production, the transformation of modes of production, and the dissemination of knowledge itself call for some profound questioning and inevitable adaptation:

261

> Knowledge producing, knowledge mediating and knowledge diffusing institutions have proliferated since 1945. Universities and university-like establishments of higher education, professional societies, government and corporate R&D [research and development] laboratories, consultancy firms and think tanks, nongovernmental organizations and other advocacy groups have multiplied and continue to create their own market for knowledge. They have been driven essentially by developing links with new clients, reflecting the socially distributed aspects of Mode 2 knowledge production.
>
> Gibbons et al. (1995, p. 137)

The question is whether universities, either the established or the new ones, can adapt to the new knowledge demands and the various conditions the users associate with them. To this question, Gibbons et al. (1995, p. 151) replied, "Yes, through further change and diversification of both form and function, and the surrender of their monopoly position in world knowledge production."

In fact, there are many ways for universities to adapt. Everywhere in the world we find reforms of higher education systems, which have often had the effect of diversifying teaching institutions as much by sector (technical or professional institutions) as by level (undergraduate programs or advanced studies) or even by legal status (public institution, private, mixed). Universities are thus under pressure to change. Some will choose to give priority to more traditional research (what Gibbons et al. [1995] called Mode 1), whereas others will pursue activities more like those of Mode 2, that is, activities more directly related to scientific and technological development, including technology transfer. Every university, depending indeed on its institutional personality, can include both modes to a certain degree, particularly as more and more government support is devoted to Mode-2 activities. But as we have seen in Canada, the recently created Canadian Innovation Fund contributes only 40% of total eligible project costs.

We may legitimately expect to see an overall intensification of research activities, a growing degree of diversification, and the creation of new structures to produce and manage knowledge. In the United States, a new class of universities is emerging, as revealed in a recent study conducted by Graham and Diamond (1997) on the development of US research universities. Based essentially on the per capita ratio of research grants and on published articles by discipline, the study proposes a reclassification of American universities. More refined classifications are emerging and creating new frames of reference for the international presence of the major universities. The Carnegie classification will need to be revised to some extent. The Carnegie system classifies US higher education institutions into seven broad categories and draws a distinction between doctoral and research universities. One of the criteria for this distinction is the number of doctorates granted each year, along with the importance of research activities and budgets. In Canada, there is no similar classification, but *Maclean's* magazine, for example, has proposed grouping institutions into three categories: medical–doctoral universities, which include medical sciences; comprehensive universities without medical faculties; and primarily undergraduate universities. The question of differentiation according to degree of research has proven divisive for the university community. Some universities in Canada refuse to compare themselves with other Canadian universities alone and look instead to North America as a whole. National boundaries are no longer the frame of reference for institutions that see themselves in a continental or global setting.

The differentiation of universities can be based not only on the "vertical axis" of knowledge creation (favoured by universities that view themselves as prestigious) but also on the "horizontal axis" of dissemination. Particularly in the area of teaching, it is now possible to offer programs to ever greater numbers of students, even across several continents. Some American universities have established campuses abroad. What was once an exception may now become the model. Distance education is also part of this expansionary approach, allowing universities to offer highly diversified training, ranging from individual courses, to program options, to full programs on virtual campuses.

Universities reserved exclusively for young people finishing high school are a thing of the past, and we find more and more adult students in our universities, either in regular studies or, increasingly, in specialized programs. In addition, distance teaching can reach out to groups in the workplace and to individuals at home who are unavailable during regular hours. Internationalization is contributing directly to the diversification of the student population, a population that not only seeks continuous learning but also is increasingly independent of the limits imposed by physical location. It is worth noting that this diversification can bring about an even greater dispersal of activities and, in fact, drive the universities toward institutional fragmentation. The increasing diversity poses a threat in terms of disintegration of training and an increasing individualization of learning. In the end, the university might be no more than a data bank of programs and didactic self-learning materials (packages). The successor of the mass university may be a new form of technology-mediated mass education, in which the student is increasingly isolated. The "virtualization" of the university may in fact be bringing about a sort of knowledge consumerism, in which the students may not be the winners!

Finally, even beyond the issue of institutional development along the vertical or horizontal axis, questions are raised, particularly in developing countries, about the link between knowledge and local and regional development. The relevance of certain knowledge coming from the North can often be challenged, and we are witnessing (most notably in Africa) a growing and perhaps irremediable schism between local and regional communities and their university institutions. These communities can in fact question the relevance of knowledge from the North on two levels: first, in terms of the need for indigenous development; and second, in terms of redefinition of the role, as well as of the structures, of national universities. Increasing direct access to knowledge from the North can only accelerate the disintegration of higher education systems in the South and inhibit the development of new, local modes of knowledge production and dissemination.

In this way, the complex dynamics of internationalization are substantively different in countries of the North and in those of the South. In each case, however, the effect on the organization of higher education systems and universities will be profound. This process is unfolding precisely at a time when other forces are pushing the universities toward ever greater levels of self-funding. Hence, the world's higher education systems — already intertwined through networks, alliances, and competition — are becoming even more inextricably linked. Practically everywhere, universities are doing their best to create their own medium- and long-term sources of revenue. In the South, privatization is often seen as a life raft, but for universities in industrialized countries, the challenge is somewhat different. Whereas in recent years research and development were seen as the key to self-financing, now it is education and training (as commercial services) that are introducing the idea of the "service university" (Newson 1994). The entrepreneurial character of the university is spreading and taking root. Universities are no longer merely academic campuses with clearly defined boundaries and well-categorized activities but are progressively becoming new learning and cognitive business complexes, part of the knowledge economy. They are emerging as new organizational forms for the quaternary economy and thereby bringing some fundamental questions to the fore about, for example, intellectual property, the role of professors in research and teaching, collegiality and institutional governance, and even the status of students within the context of continuous education.

Canadian universities are experiencing these forces of change, at times involuntarily, and like all other institutions they are working hard to equip themselves to master their ongoing restructuring. It is clear, however, that the universities' success will be closely linked to our shared perception of what is at stake. The universities and the various governments need to establish a convergence of outlook on objectives, and programs must ensure coherence and cohesion of action in the medium term. Canadian universities still possess real assets: their variety, flexibility, and openness to the world (not just to certain regions); their sense of initiative and organization and their devotion to public service; and their concern for equality, particularly when it comes to access. For anyone who views higher education as an essential instrument of the wealth and culture of a country, these assets are convincing arguments that the time has come for important and innovative change. With and only with such change can we hope to simultaneously sustain the outreach of our universities, increase our capacity to create innovations in research and development that are relevant to those in need, actively promote a successful pedagogy, and show the way to a humane appropriation of information technologies. Achieving these goals will be necessary to ensuring strong intellectual leadership in Canada for the world of tomorrow, when knowledge will be the source of both wealth and global citizenship.

Canadian University and Other Web Sites on Internationalization

The following are the addresses of Canadian university web sites and their international pages (as of 1 March 1999). These pages provide information on one or more of the following: general and specific international programs, international cooperation activities, and international students and education. Some institutions have no international page, but the relevant information on these institutions is readily accessible via each institution's main web-site address.

Table A1. Addresses of Canadian university and other web sites on internationalization.

Institution	Program etc.	Web address
Acadia University	International Centre	admin.acadiau.ca/internat/intcent.htm
University of Alberta	University of Alberta International	www.international.ualberta.ca/
Athabasca University		www.athabascau.ca/
Augustana University College	Canadian Prairies Mexico Rural Development Exchange	www.augustana.ab.ca/departments/international/contents.htm
Bishop's University	Information for International Students	www.ubishops.ca/international/index2.htm
Brandon University	Office of International Activities	www.brandonu.ca/OIA/
University of British Columbia	International Liaison Office	www.interchange.ubc.ca/ubcintl/
	International Student Services	www.international.ubc.ca/
	Bridge to the 21st Century: Internationalization at UBC	www.vision.ubc.ca/bridge
British Columbia Open University		www.ola.bc.ca/
Brock University	International Services	www.BrockU.CA/international/
University of Calgary	University of Calgary International Centre	www.ucalgary.ca/UofC/departments/IC/
	Progress of the 13 Initial Curriculum Fellows	www.ucalgary.ca/commons/ucr/Progress
University College of Cape Breton	University College of Cape Breton's Centre for International Studies	www.uccb.ns.ca/international/
University College of the Cariboo	International Programs and Services	www.cariboo.bc.ca/intered/index.html
Carleton University	Carleton International	www.ci.carleton.ca/

(continues)

Concordia University	International Students Office	relish.concordia.ca/Advocacy_Support_Services/internat.html
Concordia University College of Alberta		www.concordia.edmonton.ab.ca/
Dalhousie University	Lester Pearson International	www2.dal.ca/lpi/index.html
Collège dominicain de philosophie et de théologie		www.op.org/Canada/college.htm
University College of the Fraser Valley	International Education	www.ucfv.bc.ca/intl_ed/
University of Guelph	Centre for International Programs	www.uoguelph.ca/CIP/index.htm
École des hautes études commerciales	HEC International	canarie.hec.ca/hecinter/
King's University College		www.kingsu.ab.ca/
University of King's College		www.ukings.ns.ca/
Lakehead University	International Activities	www.lakeheadu.ca/~internat/
Laurentian University of Sudbury		www.laurentian.ca/
Université Laval	Bureau de coopération internationale	www.ulaval.ca/vrr/internat/
University of Lethbridge	International Students at the University of Lethbridge	home.uleth.ca/reg-adn/visa.htm
University of Manitoba	University of Manitoba International	www.umanitoba.ca/student/ics/uminternational/
	International Centre for Students	www.umanitoba.ca/student/ics/
McGill University	International Perspectives	www.mcgill.ca/international/
McMaster University	Office of International Affairs	www.mcmaster.ca/oia/
Memorial University of Newfoundland	International Centre	www.mun.ca/international/

Table A1 continued.

Institution	Program etc.	Web address
Université de Moncton		www.umoncton.ca/
Université de Montréal	Bureau de la coopération internationale	www.bci.umontreal.ca/
Mount Allison University	International Students' Guide	www.mta.ca/eli/guide.htm
Mount Saint Vincent University		www.msvu.ca/
University of New Brunswick	UNB Research and International Co-operation	www.unb.ca/ric/
Nipissing University		www.unipissing.ca/
University of Northern British Columbia	Office of International Programs	quarles.unbc.ca/keen/international/
Nova Scotia Agricultural College	International Centre	www.nsac.ns.ca/ic/index.html
Nova Scotia College of Art and Design		www.nscad.ns.ca/
Okanagan University College	International Education	www.ouc.bc.ca/international/
University of Ottawa	University of Ottawa International	aix1.uottawa.ca/international/
École polytechnique de Montréal	Renseignements généraux pour les étudiants étrangers	www.polymtl.ca/2510etra.htm
University of Prince Edward Island	Centre for International Education	www.upei.ca/~cie/
Université du Québec	Université du Québec Relations internationales	www.uquebec.ca/uqss/rel-int-public/index.html
Université du Québec en Abitibi–Témiscamingue		www.uqat.uquebec.ca/
Université du Québec à Chicoutimi		www.uqac.uquebec.ca/

(continues)

Institution	Description	URL
École nationale d'administration publique	Administration internationale	enap.uquebec.ca/enap-ai/
École de technologie supérieure	Relations internationales	webp.etsmtl.ca/coop/coop-int.htm
Université du Québec à Hull	Guide pour étudiants non Canadiens	www.uqah.uquebec.ca/registra/venezetudier/page_guinoncan.html
Institut national de la recherche scientifique		www.inrs.uquebec.ca/
Université du Québec à Montréal	Bureau de la coopération internationale	www.unites.uqam.ca/bei
Université du Québec à Rimouski		www.uqar.uquebec.ca/
Télé-Université	Coopération nationale et internationale	www.teluq.uquebec.ca/Alice/est/m_eni.htm
Université du Québec à Trois-Rivières		www.uqtr.uquebec.ca/
Queen's University at Kingston	International Studies	www.queensu.ca/intstudy.html
Redeemer College		www.redeemer.on.ca/
University of Regina	International Liaison Office	www.uregina.ca/gradstud/internat/
Campion College		www.uregina.ca/campion/
Luther College		www.uregina.ca/luther/
Royal Military College of Canada		www.rmc.ca/rmca.html
Ryerson Polytechnic University	Ryerson International	www.ryerson.ca/R_International/
Université Sainte-Anne		ustanne-59.ustanne.ednet.ns.ca/
Collège universitaire de Saint-Boniface		www.ustboniface.mb.ca/
St Francis Xavier University	Coady International Institute	www.stfx.ca/institutes/coady/

Table A1 continued.

Institution	Program etc.	Web address
Saint Mary's University	Saint Mary's International	www.stmarys.ca/administration/international/
Saint Paul University		www.ustpaul.ca/
St Thomas University	International Students	www.stthomasu.ca/international/international.htm
University of Saskatchewan	University of Saskatchewan International	www.usask.ca/registrar/Current_Calendar/Gen_Info/gi_uofs_international.html
Saskatchewan Indian Federated College	International Indigenous Program	www.sifc.edu/int/
Université de Sherbrooke	Bureau de la recherche et de la coopération international	www.usherb.ca/PP/rech.html
Simon Fraser University	Office of International Cooperation	www.sfu.ca/international/
University of Sudbury		alumni.Laurentian.Ca/www/uofs/
University of Toronto	Research and International Relations	utl2.library.utoronto.ca/www/rir/hmpage/index.htm
University of St Michael's College		www.utoronto.ca/stmikes/
University of Trinity College		www.trinity.utoronto.ca/
Victoria University		vicu.utoronto.ca/
Trent University	Trent International Program	www.trentu.ca/admin/tip/
Trinity Western University		www.twu.ca/
University of Victoria	University of Victoria's Office of International Affairs	www.oia.finearts.uvic.ca/

University of Waterloo	International Student Office	www.adm.uwaterloo.ca/infoiso/
St Jerome's University		www.usjc.uwaterloo.ca/
University of Western Ontario	International Student Services	www.sdc.uwo.ca/int/index.html
Brescia College		www.uwo.ca/brescia/
Huron College	International Education	www.uwo.ca/huron/huron7.html
	International Student Exchanges	www.uwo.ca/huron/exchange.html
King's College		www.uwo.ca/kings/
Wilfrid Laurier University	Wilfrid Laurier International	www.wlu.ca/~wwwlinte/
University of Windsor	Office of International Affairs	www.uwindsor.ca/international/
University of Winnipeg	International Students Admission Bulletin	www.uwinnipeg.ca/~admissio/internat.htm
York University	York International	international.yorku.ca/

Other related web sites

Association of Universities and Colleges of Canada	Canadian University Exchange Agreements	www.aucc.ca
	Canadian University Projects in International Development	www.aucc.ca/english/international
Centre for Curriculum, Transfer and Technology	Internationalizing the Curriculum	ctt.bc.ca/curric.BP/index.html

Table A1 concluded.

Institution	Program etc.	Web address
Royal Melbourne Institute of Technology	Internationalizing the Curriculum across RMIT University	www.rmit.edu.au/departments/epi/cpaper2
Tom Wholley	Best Practice Guidelines for Internationalizing the Curriculum	www.cttbc.ca/curr/BP/whatcons
University of Minnesota	Working Papers on Internationalization of the Curriculum surrounding the internationalization of undergraduate education	www.isp.umn.edu

Contributors

Jonathan Baggaley

Jon Baggaley is a professor of educational technology at Canada's open distance-education university, Athabasca University, in Alberta. He graduated in psychology at the University of Sheffield and has since taught at the University of Liverpool, Memorial University of Newfoundland, and Concordia University in Montréal. He is the author or editor of several books and articles on the psychology of television, educational media, media production and evaluation, health promotion, and community development. As an educational media consultant, Dr Baggaley has advised governmental, non-governmental, and broadcasting organizations in 14 countries. Recent projects of his include an ongoing consultancy with the US Centers for Disease Control and Prevention, involving the design and evaluation of national educational media campaigns; and assistance to the Government of Ukraine in reviving and updating its early traditions of media use in rural-community development. Dr Baggaley is also a professional actor and director in stage, radio, film, and television.

Sheryl Tatlock Bond (coeditor)

Sheryl Tatlock Bond earned her doctorate in higher education at Indiana University and has been working in the field as an educator for more than 25 years. First as the founding Director of the Centre for Higher Education Research and Development at the University of Manitoba and more recently as associate professor of higher education at Queen's University at Kingston, she has personally and academically focused on academic leadership, education, gender and development, and international educational policy. For nearly 20 years, Dr Bond has worked as a consultant to a wide range of non-governmental organizations, including the Association of Universities and Colleges of Canada, Canadian International Development Agency, International Development Research Centre, Commonwealth Secretariat, World Bank, British Council, International Federation of University Women, Inter-American Association of Higher Education, and government ministries both in Canada and abroad. Her field work and research, carried out in collaboration with partners in a variety of cultural contexts, have taken her throughout Africa, India, Latin America, Malaysia, and Sri Lanka.

Fernand Caron

Fernand Caron is a consultant in the management of international projects, with such duties as providing support to institutions and the private sector in international development. Dr Caron obtained a doctoral degree in physical education from the Université catholique de Louvain in Belgium. He has been a professor and head of international cooperation at two universities in the Université du Québec network and has also been responsible for the International Cooperation Division of the head office of the Université du Québec. Dr Caron served as Deputy Director of the International Division of the Association of Universities and Colleges of Canada in the late 1980s. He has written more than 70 monographs, reports, and scientific articles, including many on international cooperation and development. Dr Caron is now President of EFC International Inc. in Montréal.

Howard C. Clark

Born in New Zealand, Howard Clark earned his PhD from the University of Auckland. He has also been awarded both PhD and ScD degrees from Cambridge University. Dr Clark has been a chemistry professor at the University of British Columbia and the University of Western Ontario. He served in senior positions at Western and then the University of Guelph, where he was appointed the Academic Vice

President (1976–86). He oversaw the university's international endeavours and helped establish a university-based corporation to carry out international development projects on a contractual basis. Dr Clark was President of Dalhousie University from 1986 until his retirement in 1995. During that time, he reestablished the Lester Pearson Institute, strengthening its international mandate, and encouraged debate on the need for the university to internationalize. He was involved in, or visited, most of Dalhousie's projects. He also encouraged the international marketing of the university's faculties of dentistry and medicine. Dr Clark is President Emeritus of Dalhousie University.

Martine Foisy
Martine Foisy is the Assistant to the NSERC/Alcan Chair for Women in Sciences and Engineering in Quebec. She is also pursuing her PhD in history at the Université du Québec à Montréal. Her thesis is on the establishment of structures to support research at Quebec universities.

Yves Gingras
Yves Gingras is a professor of the history and sociology of science at the Université du Québec à Montréal. He obtained his PhD in history and the sociopolitics of science at the Université de Montréal and was a postdoctoral researcher at Harvard University. An author of many publications, including more than 40 articles, Dr Gingras focuses on the history and evaluation of university research, science policy, and the history and sociology of science. He has been a consultant to several organizations and government ministries, is Editor-in-Chief of *Scientia Canadensis*, and is a member of the scientific committees of the European magazines *Didaskalia, Culture technique,* and *Actes de la recherche en sciences sociales*. Dr Gingras and Benoît Godin are cofounders of the *Observatoire des sciences et des technologies* and members of the Centre inter-universitaire de recherche sur la science et la technologie (interuniversity centre for science and technology research).

Benoît Godin
Benoît Godin is a professor at the Institut national de la recherche scientifique (national institute for scientific research) in Montréal, where he specializes in scientific policy and evaluation of science. Dr Godin earned his PhD at Sussex University. He has published several articles, including those in *Research Policy and Social Studies of Science,* and has recently published a book on scientific culture.

Dr Godin is also an active member of the Centre inter-universitaire de recherche sur la science et la technologie (interuniversity centre for science and technology research). Along with Yves Gingras, he is a cofounder of the *Observatoire des sciences et des technologies*.

Jane Knight

Jane Knight is head of International Affairs in the Office of the President at Ryerson Polytechnic University. Dr Knight was the Director of the China Partnership Program at Ryerson and led a university-wide task force to develop an internationalization strategy. Earlier work with United Nations Educational, Scientific and Cultural Organization in Paris and a development organization in India helped her to bring policy and practical experience to the study of international education. On the research front, she is currently involved with an international project of the Organisation for Economic Co-operation and Development's Programme on Institutional Management in Higher Education on the quality assurance of internationalization and a comparative study of internationalization strategies. Dr Knight has conducted several national studies on the status and issues of internationalization in Canada.

Jean-Pierre Lemasson (coeditor)

Jean-Pierre Lemasson began working at the Université du Québec à Montréal in 1976, first in the Bureau de recherche institutionnelle (institutional research bureau), then as Assistant to the Dean of Graduate Studies and Research. In 1988, Mr Lemasson established the university's International Cooperation Office, and he remains its Director. In this position, he participates in the work of several university organizations, such as Conference of Rectors and Principals of Quebec Universities (Conférence des recteurs et principaux des universités du Québec), Association of Universities and Colleges of Canada, and Montréal International. Mr Lemasson holds a master's degree in psychosociology from the Sorbonne and did his doctoral studies in the history and policy of science at the Université de Montréal. In 1995/96, he took a sabbatical and worked at the International Development Research Centre's Montevideo office, where he studied the place of university research in higher education systems in Latin America. Various studies resulted in a joint publication produced by the International Institute for Higher Education in Latin America and the Caribbean and the United Nations Educational, Scientific and Cultural Organization. Mr Lemasson is currently conducting comparative research on the higher education systems in the Americas.

James Shute

James Shute is Director of the Centre for International Programs and professor of rural extension studies at the University of Guelph. His undergraduate and postgraduate degrees were earned at Queen's University at Kingston and Michigan State University. Dr Shute has been a visiting professor at the University of Melbourne, Lincoln University, and the University of Bath. He has been an adviser or consultant to the Canadian International Development Agency, International Development Research Centre, International Maize and Wheat Improvement Center, Canadian nongovernmental organizations, and recently the Commonwealth Higher Education Management Service. He has studied and worked in many countries, including Australia, Barbados, China, Ghana, Indonesia, Jamaica, Kenya, Malaysia, New Zealand, Nigeria, Pakistan, Sierra Leone, Sri Lanka, Thailand, Trinidad, several European countries, and those of the Southern African Development Community. Dr Shute is author or editor of more than 100 publications in applied communication, rural extension, human-resource development, evaluation, and the internationalization of higher education.

Jacques Tousignant

Jacques Tousignant is a consultant in international cooperation and university affairs, working primarily since 1995 for the Vice President (Academic and Research) at the head office of the Université du Québec. Earlier experience includes consulting for the Inter-American Organization for Higher Education and the International Cooperation Bureau of the head office of the Université du Québec and serving as the latter's Director of Planning and Institutional Research. Mr Tousignant holds two master's degrees, one in arts and the other in theology, obtained in Paris and Montréal. He has taught in Brazil, Quebec, and Manitoba. He took part in the United Nations Educational, Scientific and Cultural Organization's mission to Rwanda in 1997. Mr Tousignant is a member of the University Teaching and Research Commission of the Conseil supérieur de l'éducation in Quebec and is on the board of Collège François-Xavier-Garneau.

Jacquelyn Thayer Scott

Jacquelyn Thayer Scott is President and Vice-Chancellor of University College of Cape Breton, in Sydney, Nova Scotia. Before assuming her current post in 1993, Dr Scott served as Director of the School of Continuing Studies at the University of Toronto. She has also been on the faculty at the University of Manitoba, has operated her own

278

public-relations and management consulting firm, and has worked as a journalist for the Canadian Press and Colombian Newspapers. Dr Scott serves on a number of governing boards and advisory committees, including the Prime Minister's Advisory Council on Science and Technology, Management Consortium on Environmental Technologies for the Province of Nova Scotia (Vice Chair), and the Canadian Network for the Advancement of Research, Industry and Education, Ltd. Dr Scott has been awarded a number of professional honours in her field and is the author of numerous scholarly and popular articles and books on voluntary-organization management and policy and higher education policy.

Catherine Vertesi

Catherine Vertesi joined the University of British Columbia in 1980 as a lecturer in the Faculty of Commerce and Business Administration. In her role as Program Director and, later, Assistant Dean, first for Undergraduate Studies and then for the MBA program, she initiated student-mobility programs through exchanges, study abroad, and summer field schools overseas, which have benefited a significant number of students. Ms Vertesi has carried out several campus-wide initiatives, including the establishment of an adult-learner centre, curriculum revision in English as a second language for degree students, and student recruitment. She served on the British Columbia government advisory committee on the future of Royal Roads Military College, is the cochair of the Canada Special Interest Group for the International Association for Foreign Student Affairs, and serves on the Board of the Canadian Bureau for International Education. Ms Vertesi is the Director of External Relations for Continuing Studies at the University of British Columbia.

Acronyms and Abbreviations

ACA	Academic Cooperation Association
ACCC	Association of Canadian Community Colleges
AIESEC	Association for International Exchanges of Students in Economics and Commerce
APEC	Asia–Pacific Economic Cooperation
AUCC	Association of Universities and Colleges of Canada
AUF	Agence universitaire de la Francophonie (university office for francophone people)
CBIE	Canadian Bureau for International Education
CEC	Canadian Education Centre
CHEG	Canadian Higher Education Group
CIDA	Canadian International Development Agency
COL	Commonwealth of Learning

CREPUQ	Conférence des recteurs et principaux des universités du Québec (Conference of Rectors and Principals of Quebec Universities)
CUPID	Canadian University Projects in International Development
CUSO	Canadian University Service Overseas
DFAIT	Department of Foreign Affairs and International Trade
ECTS	European Credit Transfer System
EIP	Educational Institutions Program [CIDA]
ERASMUS	European Community Action Scheme for the Mobility of University Students
ETS	École de technologie supérieure (school of advanced technology)
GNP	gross national product
ICDS	Institutional Cooperation and Development Services [CIDA]
IDRC	International Development Research Centre
IFI	international financial institution
IMHE	Programme on Institutional Management in Higher Education [OECD]
IOHE	Inter-American Organization for Higher Education
IQRP	Internationalization Quality Review Process
MRC	Medical Research Council of Canada
NAFTA	North American Free Trade Agreement
NCE	Network of Centres of Excellence
NGO	nongovernmental organization
NRC	National Research Council of Canada
NSERC	Natural Sciences and Engineering Research Council of Canada
OC	Order of Canada (Officer)
ODA	official development assistance

OECD	Organisation for Economic Co-operation and Development
SAP	structural-adjustment program
SPB	Special Programmes Branch [CIDA]
SSHRC	Social Sciences and Humanities Research Council of Canada

TOEFL	Test of English as a Foreign Language
UBC	University of British Columbia
UISP	University Initiated Scholarship Program [CIDA]
UMAP	University Mobility in Asia and the Pacific
UNB	University of New Brunswick
UNESCO	United Nations Educational, Scientific and Cultural Organization
UPCD	University Partnerships in Cooperation and Development [CIDA]
UPEI	Univeristy of Prince Edward Island
UQAM	Université du Québec à Montréal
UQTR	Université du Québec à Trois-Rivières
UVF	Université virtuelle francophone (virtual francophone university)
UWI	University of the West Indies
UWO	University of Western Ontario
WETV	Global Access Television
WUSC	World University Service of Canada

Bibliography

ACA (Academic Cooperation Association). 1997. Making the case for international cooperation in higher education: the Meise consensus. ACA, Brussels, Belgium.

ACIE (Alberta Centre for International Education). 1999. Alberta Centre for International Education. ACIE, Edmonton, AB, Canada. Internet: www.acie.ab.ca. Cited May 1999.

ACPAU–CAUBO. 1998. Distribution of university revenues by sources — 1973/74–1995/96. Bulletin CIRST/ENVEX, 3(2–3).

Altbach, P.G.; Lewis, L.S. 1998. Internationalism and insularity: American faculty and the world. Change: The Magazine of Higher Learning, 30(1), 54–55.

Arum, S.; Van de Water, J. 1992. The need for a definition of international education in U.S. universities. *In* Klasek, C., ed., Bridges to the future: strategies for internationalizing higher education. Association of International Education Administrators, Carbondale, IL, USA. pp. 191–203.

AUCC (Association of Universities and Colleges of Canada). 1977. The role of Canadian universities in international development. AUCC; Royal Society of Canada, Ottawa, ON, Canada. Mimeo.

———— 1980. Canadian university experience in international development projects. AUCC, Ottawa, ON, Canada. 78 pp.

283

————— 1995a. Internationalization and Canadian universities. AUCC, Ottawa, ON, Canada.

————— 1995b. Profile of international collaboration by Canadian universities. AUCC, Ottawa, ON, Canada.

————— 1995c. A year of transitions: AUCC activities 1995. AUCC, Ottawa, ON, Canada.

————— 1996a. Internationalization of higher education: a common vision? Report of a survey of the private sector, governments and educational institutions on the internationalization of higher education in Canada. AUCC, Ottawa, ON, Canada. 49 pp.

————— 1996b. Orientations 1996. Portrait of the university in Canada. AUCC, Ottawa, ON, Canada.

————— 1998. Canadian University Projects in International Development (CUPID). AUCC, Ottawa, ON, Canada.

Back, K.J.; Davis, D.M.; Olsen, A. 1995. Internationalization of higher education in Australia. *In* de Wit, H., ed., Strategies for internationalization of higher education: a comparative study of Australia, Canada, Europe and the United States of America. European Association for International Education, Amsterdam, Netherlands. pp. 33–46.

————— 1996. Internationalization of higher education: goals and strategies. IDP Education Australia, Canberra, Australia.

————— 1997. Strategies for internationalization of higher education in Australia. *In* Knight, J.; de Wit, H., ed., Internationalization of higher education in Asia Pacific countries. European Association for International Education, Amsterdam, Netherlands. pp. 33–45.

Baggaley, J. 1997. Cross-cultural uses of media research technology. *In* Goldberg, M.; Fishbein, M.; Middlestadt, S., ed., Social marketing: theoretical and practical perspectives. Erlbaum, Hillsdale, NJ, USA.

Baggaley, J.; Anderson, T.; Haughey, M., ed. 1998. Partners in learning. Proceedings of the 14th Annual Conference of the Canadian Association for Distance Education (2 vols.). Athabasca University, Athabasca, Alberta.

Barnard, A.K. 1988. North–South collaboration: a Canadian perspective. *In* Shine, G.L.; Gopinathan, S.; Cummings, W.K., ed., North–South scholarly exchange. Mansell Publishing Ltd, London, UK. pp. 164–178.

BCCIE (British Columbia Centre for International Education). 1997. British Columbia Centre for International Education. BCCIE, Victoria, BC, Canada. Internet: www.bccie.bc.ca. Cited May 1999.

Beaver, D. de B.; Rosen, R. 1978a. Studies in scientific collaboration. Part I: The professional origins of scientific co-authorship. Scientometrics, 1(1), 65–84.

————— 1978b. Studies in scientific collaboration. Part II: Scientific co-authorship, research productivity and visibility in the scientific elite, 1799–1830. Scientometrics, 1(2), 133–149.

Berry, J.W. 1995. Cooperation for capacity building: improving the effectiveness of university linkage projects. J.W. Berry & Associates, Ottawa, ON, Canada.

Bond, S. 1998. Perspectives on graduate employment: Canada. *In* Holden-Ronning, A.; Kearney, M.L., ed., Graduate prospects in a changing society. UNESCO Publishing, Paris, France. 394 pp.

Blumler, J.G.; Katz, E. 1974. The uses of mass communications. Sage, London, UK.

Brodhead, T.; Pratt, C. 1994. Paying the piper: CIDA and Canadian NGO's. *In* Pratt, C., ed., Canadian international development assistance policies: an appraisal. McGill – Queen's University Press, Montréal, PQ, Canada; Kingston, ON, Canada. pp. 87–119.

Bruneau, T.C.; Jorgensen, J.J.; Ramsay, J.O. 1978. CIDA: the organization of Canadian overseas assistance. Centre for Developing Area Studies, McGill University, Montréal, PQ, Canada. 50 pp.

Buchbinder, H.; Newson, J.A. 1990. Corporate–university linkages in Canada: transforming a public institution. Higher Education, 20(4), 355–379.

Campbell, D.D. 1978. Western Canada. *In* Sheffield, E.; Campbell, D.D.; Holmes, J.; Kymlicka, B.B.; Whitelaw, J.H., ed., Systems of higher education in Canada. International Council for Educational Development, New York, NY, USA. pp. 133–187.

CERI–IMHE (Centre for Educational Research and Innovation; Programme for Institutional Management in Higher Education). 1998. Programme pour la gestion des établissements d'enseignement superieur : qualité de l'internationalisation. CERI–IMHE, Paris, France. Mimeo, CERI–IMHE–DG 98–8. 19 pp.

Chartrand, L.; Duchesne, R.; Gingras, Y. 1987. Histoire des sciences au Québec. Boréal, Montréal, PQ, Canada.

CICIC (Canadian Information Centre for International Credentials). 1995. Canadian Information Centre for International Credentials. CICIC, Toronto, ON, Canada. Internet: www.cicic.ca.

CIDA (Canadian International Development Agency). 1995. Canada in the world: government statement. CIDA, Ottawa, ON, Canada.

CIES (Centre international d'enseignement supérieur). n.d. Higher education, research and professional training … Choose France. CIES, Paris, France. Internet: www.cies.fr. Cited Jun 1999.

CIRST/ENVEX (Centre interuniversitaire de recherche sur la science et technologie; l'Environnement externe de l'Université du Québec) (Robitaille, J-P.; Gengras, Y., ed.). 1997. Les NTIC dans le réseau universitaire québecois. Bulletin CIRST/ENVEX, 2(2).

———— 1998. La restructuration des universités canadiennes. Bulletin CIRST/ENVEX, 3(2–4).

CMEC (Council of Ministers of Education). 1996–97. Post secondary education systems in Canada. Vol. 1: Overview. 23 pp. Internet: www.cmec.ca.cicic.postsec/vol1.overview

COU (Council of Ontario Universities). 1997. Presentation to the Standing Committee on Finance and Economic Affairs. COU, Toronto, ON, Canada, 6 Mar 1997.

CREPUQ (Conférence des recteurs et principaux de universités du Québec). 1998. Characteristics and remuneration of career professors in Quebec universities. Report of a teaching staff survey, 1995/96 and 1996/97. CREPUQ, Montréal, PQ, Canada. 55 pp.

Crowley, T. 1988. The new Canada movement: agrarian youth revolt and adult education in the 1930's. University of Guelph, Guelph, ON, Canada. Occasional Papers in Rural Extension, No. 4, Nov.

285

Cunningham, S.; Tapsall, S.; Ryan, Y.; Stedman, L.; Bagdon, K.; Flew, T. 1997. New media and borderless education: a review of the convergence between global media networks and higher education provision. Commonwealth of Australia, Canberra, Australia.

Daniel, J. 1997. Mega-universities and knowledge media. Stylus, Herndon, VA, USA.

Delage, P.B. 1987. Assessing the impact of the Ghana–Guelph project on institutionality at the University of Ghana. Institute for International Development and Cooperation, University of Ottawa, Ottawa, ON, Canada. Working Paper NR/874.

———— 1988. Human resources development and institution-building: the Ghana–Guelph project. Institute for International Development and Cooperation, University of Ottawa, Ottawa, ON, Canada. Working Paper NR/882.

de Wit, H., ed. 1995. Strategies for internationalization: a comparative study of Australia, Canada, Europe and the United States of America. European Association for International Education, Amsterdam, Netherlands.

de Wit, H.; Callan, H. 1995. Internationalization of higher education in Europe. *In* de Wit, H., ed., Strategies for internationalization of higher education: a comparative study of Australia, Canada, Europe and the United States of America. European Association for International Education, Amsterdam, Netherlands. pp. 67–95.

de Wit, H.; Knight, J. 1997. Asia Pacific countries in comparison to Europe and North America: concluding remarks. *In* Knight, J.; de Wit, H., ed., Internationalization of higher education in Asia Pacific countries. European Association for International Education, Amsterdam, Netherlands. pp. 173–179.

DFAIT (Department of Foreign Affairs and International Trade). 1994. The international dimension of higher education in Canada: collaborative policy framework. DFAIT, Ottawa, ON, Canada.

———— 1998. Marketing Canadian education — 1998. DFAIT, Ottawa, ON, Canada. Internet: www.dfait-maeci.gc.ca/culture/educationmarketing/menu.html

Dupuy, M. 1980. The Canadian university's role in international development. *In* Canadian university experience in international development projects. Association of Universities and Colleges of Canada, Ottawa, ON, Canada. 78 pp.

EduQuébec. 1998. Studying in Québec. Government of Quebec, Québec, PQ, Canada. Internet: www.eduquebec.gouv.qc.ca/anglais/Etudier/Etudier.htm?3

Ellingboe, B.J. 1996. Evidence of internationalization and recommendations for future campus-wide strategies. *In* Working papers on internationalization of the curriculum. University of Minnesota, Minneapolis, MN, USA.

ETS (Educational Testing Service). 1994–95. TOEFL test and score manual supplement 1994–95. ETS, Princeton, NJ, USA. Internet: www.etsis1.ets.org/pub/toefl/9495sumpdf

Faris, R. 1975. The passionate educators. Peter Martin Associates, Toronto, ON, Canada. 202 pp.

Fielden, J. 1997. Benchmarking university performance. A Bulletin of Current Documentation, 131, 20–25.

Flowerdew, J.; Miller, L. 1995. On the notion of culture in L2 lectures. TESOL Quarterly, 29, 345–373.

Fogelberg, P.; Pajala, K., ed. 1997. An internationalisation quality review process: University of Helsinki, 1996. University of Helsinki, Helsinki, Finland. 36 pp.

Freitag, M. 1995. The drowning of the university. Nuit Blanche editeur; Éditions La Découverte, Québec, PQ, Canada.

Fuller, A.M.; Waldron, M.W. 1989. Outreach in agriculture and rural development. *In* van den Bor, W.; Shute, J.C.M.; Moore, G.A.B., ed., South–North partnership in strengthening higher education in agriculture. PUDOC, Wageningen, Netherlands. pp. 101–119.

GGA (Goss Gilroy Associates). 1991. Report on the evaluation of the Educational Institutions Program. GGA, Ottawa, ON, Canada. Executive summary.

Gibbons, M.; Limoges, C.; Nowothy, H.; Schwartzman, S.; Scott, P.; Trow, M. 1995. The new production of knowledge. Sage Publications, London, UK.

Gingras, Y. 1991. Physics and the rise of scientific research in Canada. McGill – Queen's University Press, Montréal, PQ, Canada.

Goldring, J. 1984. Mutual advantage: report on the Committee of Review of Private Overseas Student Policy. Australian Government Printing Service, Canberra, Australia.

Graham, H.D.; Diamond, N. 1997. The rise of American research universities. Johns Hopkins University Press, Baltimore, MD, USA. 296 pp.

Gwyn, S. 1972. Cinema as catalyst. Memorial University of St. John's, St. John's, NF, Canada.

Hamlin, D.L. 1964. International studies in Canadian universities. Canadian Universities Foundation, Ottawa, ON, Canada.

Harari, M. 1992. The internationalization of the curriculum. International Education Administrators, Carbondale, IL, USA. 208 pp.

Harris, R.S. 1973. A history of higher education in Canada: 1663–1960. University of Toronto Press, Toronto, ON, Canada.

HCSCEAIT (House of Commons Standing Committee on External Affairs and International Trade). 1987. For whose benefit? Report of the Standing Committee on External Affairs and International Trade on Canada's Official Development Assistance Policies and Programs. Supply and Services Canada, Ottawa, ON, Canada. Winegard report.

Hersh, J. 1997. Internationalization of education. Paper presented at the International Conference on Inter-university Cooperation and Exchanges, Aug 1997, Peking University, Beijing, China.

Hughey, A; Hinson, D. 1993. Assessing the efficacy of the Test of English as a Foreign Language. Psychological Reports, 73, 187–193.

Huntington, S. 1996. The clash of civilizations and the remaking of world order. Simon and Schuster, New York, NY, USA.

287

IDRC (International Development Research Centre). 1993. Empowerment through knowledge: the strategy of the International Development Research Centre, Ottawa, 1993. IDRC, Ottawa, ON, Canada.

IIE (Institute of International Education). 1998. International student enrolments at U.S. colleges and universities remain flat, as U.S. study abroad numbers grow. Open Doors 1996/97. IIE, New York, NY, USA. Press release, Jan 1998.

IMHE (Program for Institutional Management in Higher Education). 1997. Internationalization quality review process guidelines. IMHE; Organisation for Economic Co-operation and Development, Paris, France.

Innis, H. 1950. Empire and communication. Clarendon, Oxford, UK.

Irvine, I. 1998. International office benchmarking survey. Australian International Education Foundation, Canberra, Australia. 11 pp.

James, S. 1996a. Educational media and Agit Prop: I. The legacy of Vertov. Journal of Educational Media, 22(2), 111–122.

———— 1996b. Educational media and Agit Prop: II. The Vertov Process repatriated. Journal of Educational Media, 22(3), 161–173.

Jones, G.A. 1997. Higher education in Canada: different systems, different perspectives. Garland Publishing, New York, NY, USA.

Kalvemark, T. 1997. Sweden. *In* Kalvemark, T.; van der Wende, M., ed., National policies for the internationalization of higher education in Europe. National Agency for Higher Education, Stockholm, Sweden. pp. 174–188.

Kalvemark, T.; van der Wende, M., ed. 1997. National policies for the internationalization of higher education in Europe. National Agency for Higher Education, Stockholm, Sweden.

Kant, I. 1998. Essential presuppositions and the idea of a Canadian university. Interchange, 29(1), 84.

Kehm, B.; Last, B. 1997. Germany. *In* Kalvemark, T.; van der Wende, M., ed., National policies for the internationalization of higher education in Europe. National Agency for Higher Education, Stockholm, Sweden. pp. 91–152.

Kerr, M.G. 1996. Partnering and health development. University of Calgary Press, Calgary, AB, Canada; International Development Research Centre, Ottawa, ON, Canada. 250 pp.

Knight, J. 1994. Internationalization: elements and checkpoints. Canadian Bureau for International Education, Ottawa, ON, Canada. 15 pp.

———— 1995. Internationalization of Canadian universities: the changing landscape. Association of Universities and Colleges of Canada, Ottawa, ON, Canada. 65 pp.

———— 1996. Internationalizing higher education: a shared vision? Canadian Bureau for International Education; Association of Universities and Colleges of Canada, Ottawa, ON, Canada. 46 pp.

———— 1997. Internationalization of higher education: a conceptual framework. *In* Knight, J.; de Wit, H., ed., Internationalization of higher education in Asia Pacific countries. European Association for International Education, Amsterdam, Netherlands. pp. 5–19.

Knight, J.; de Wit, H. 1995. Strategies for internationalization of higher education: historical and conceptual perspectives. *In* de Wit, H., ed., Strategies for internationalization of higher education: a comparative study of Australia, Canada, Europe and the United States of America. European Association for International Education, Amsterdam, Netherlands. pp. 5–32.

———— ed. 1997. Internationalization of higher education in Asia Pacific countries. European Association for International Education, Amsterdam, Netherlands.

———— ed. 1999. Quality assurance of the international dimension. Organisation for Economic Co-operation and Development, Paris, France.

Lacroix, R.; Shapiro, B; Tavenas, F. 1998. The strategic role of the university in the age of the knowledge economy. La Presse, 24 Nov.

Latchem, C. 1998. NIME International Forum on Building International Educational Networks: issues and prospects (concluding address). National Institute of Multimedia Education, Tokyo, Japan.

Lawrence, R. 1997. How Asian students buy. International Educator, 1(4), 18–19, 30.

Leclerc, M; Miquel, J.-F.; Narvaez, N.; Frigoletto, L.; Okubo, Y. 1991. La coopération scientifique France–Québec : une analyse des cosignatures. Interface, 12(5), 19–23.

Leidenfrost, J.; Fiorioli, E; Johnson, L. 1997. Austria. *In* Kalvemark, T.; van der Wende, M., ed., National policies for the internationalization of higher education in Europe. National Agency for Higher Education, Stockholm, Sweden. pp. 42–58.

Lemasson, J.-P. 1993. La coopération institutionnelle avec les pays du Tiers Monde. Le cas des universités canadiennes. Communication. Assemblée annuelle de l'Association européenne pour l'éducation internationale, The Hague, Netherlands.

Luukkonen, T.O.; Persson, O.; Sivertsen, G. 1992. Understanding patterns of international scientific collaboration. Science, Technology and Human Values, 17(1), 101–126.

Luukkonen, T.O.; Tijssen, R.J.W.; Persson, O.; Sivertsen, G. 1993. The measurement of international scientific collaboration. Scientometrics, 28(1), 15–36.

MacKinnon, A.R. 1975. Canadian programs in Third World education development: an overview of Canadian programs. Canadian and International Education, 4 (2), 1–16.

McAllister, I. 1993. Towards 2000: sustaining development cooperation. *In* McAllister, I., ed., Windows on the world. Dalhousie University, Halifax, NS, Canada. 439 pp.

———— 1996. Working with neighbours: university partnerships for international development. Association of Universities and Colleges of Canada, Ottawa, ON, Canada. 104 pp.

———— 1998. The university as a partner in international and regional development. Association of Universities and Colleges of Canada, Ottawa, ON, Canada. 48 pp.

McKinnon, J.D. 1998. University's cyber classes spark faculty concerns. The Wall Street Journal, 15 Jul, p. F1.

McLeod, S. 1997. Alumni survey summary. Paper presented at the New Waves Conference, 13–16 Mar, Bali, Indonesia. Capilano College, North Vancouver, BC, Canada.

McLuhan, M. 1962. The Gutenberg galaxy: the making of typographic man. University of Toronto Press, Toronto, ON, Canada.

———— 1964. Understanding media: the extensions of man. McGraw-Hill, New York, NY, USA.

McLuhan, M.; Fiore, Q.; Angel, J. 1967. The medium is the message: an inventory of effects. Bantam, New York, NY, USA.

McWhinney, B.; Godfrey, D. 1968. CUSO. *In* Developing countries. Ryerson Press, Toronto, ON, Canada. pp. 461.

Mestenhauser, J.A. 1996. The portraits of international curriculum: an uncommon multidimensional perspective. *In* Working papers on internationalization of the curriculum. University of Minnesota, Minneapolis, MN, USA. 31 pp.

Miquel, J.-F.; Shinozaki-okubo, Y.; Narvez, N.; Frigoletto, L. 1989. Les scientifiques sont-ils ouverts : la collaboration internationale? La recherche, 206, 116–118.

Morris, E. 1996. Internationalize the curriculum by internationalizing the faculty. *In* Working papers on internationalization of the curriculum. University of Minnesota, Minneapolis, MN, USA. 13 pp.

Morrison, D.R. 1994. The choices of bilateral aid recipients. *In* Pratt, C., ed., Canadian international development assistance policies: an appraisal. McGill – Queen's University Press, Montréal, PQ, Canada; Kingston, ON, Canada. pp. 23–155.

———— 1998. Aid and ebb tide: a history of CIDA and Canadian development assistance. Wilfred Laurier Press, Toronto, ON, Canada. 842 pp.

Newson, J.A. 1994. Subordinating democracy: the effects of fiscal retrenchment and university business partnerships on knowledge creation and knowledge dissemination in universities. Higher Education, 27(2), 141–161.

Nova Scotia. 1998. Study in Nova Scotia, Canada. Nova Scotia Department of Education and Culture, Halifax, NS, Canada. Internet: www.ednet.ns.ca/educ/study/

NUFFIC (Netherlands Universities Foundation for International Cooperation in Higher Education). 1995. Quality in internationalization: guidelines for the assessment of the quality of internationalization in higher professional education. NUFFIC, Amsterdam, Netherlands.

OECD (Organisation for Economic Co-operation and Development). 1996a. The development of an internationalisation quality review process at the level of higher education institutions. OECD, Paris, France. Draft. 20 pp.

———— 1996b. The internationalization of higher education. OECD, Paris, France.

O'Neil, M. 1998. Area studies is dead: long live area studies. Paper presented at the Canadian Council for Area Studies Conference, Ottawa, ON, Canada. Mimeo. 14 pp.

Patterson, B. 1996. The public relations dilemma of internationalization — on campus and off. Paper presented at the From Rhetoric to Reality Conference, 21–22 Nov, Ottawa, ON, Canada. Association of Universities and Colleges of Canada, Ottawa, ON, Canada.

Pratt, C. 1994a. Canadian development assistance: a profile. *In* Pratt, C., ed., Canadian international development assistance policies: an appraisal. McGill – Queen's University Press, Montreal, PQ, Canada; Kingston, ON, Canada. pp. 3–24.

291

———— 1994b. Humane internationalism and Canadian development assistance policies. *In* Pratt, C., ed., Canadian international development assistance policies: an appraisal. McGill – Queen's University Press, Montreal, PQ, Canada; Kingston, ON, Canada. pp. 334–370.

Quebec. 1998. Universities and the future: government policy options regarding Québec universities. Quebec Ministry of Education, Montréal, PQ, Canada. Consultation document, 20 Feb.

Rasmussen, A. 1990. Jalons pour une histoire des congrès internationaux au XIXᵉ siècle : régulation scientifique et propagande intellectuelle. Relations internationales, 62, 115–133.

Rawkins, P. 1994. An institutional analysis of CIDA. *In* Pratt, C., ed., Canadian international development assistance policies: an appraisal. McGill – Queen's University Press, Montreal, PQ, Canada; Kingston, ON, Canada. pp. 156–185.

Robertson, H.-J. 1998. No more teachers, no more books: the commercialization of Canada's schools. McLelland & Stewart, Toronto, ON, Canada. 360 pp.

Roblin Commission (Manitoba). 1994. Post-secondary education in Manitoba: doing things differently. University Education Review Commission, Winnipeg, MB, Canada.

Salewicz, S; Dwivedi, A. 1996. Project leaders tracer study. Evaluation Unit, International Development Research Centre, Ottawa, ON, Canada. 58 pp.

Schroeder-Güdehus, B. 1978. Les scientifiques et la paix. Presses de l'Université de Montréal, Montréal, PQ, Canada.

———— 1990. Les congrès scientifiques et la politique de coopération internationale des académies des sciences. Relations internationales, 62, 135–148.

Shute, J.C.M. 1970. The professional school looks abroad: a case study. *In* Walmsley, N., ed., International education. Canadian Bureau for International Education, Ottawa, ON, Canada. pp. 53–57.

———— 1972. Canadian university technical assistance programs in Africa. Canadian Journal of African Studies, 6(3), 491–500.

———— 1979. The Ghana project: a story of international cooperation. University of Guelph, Guelph, ON, Canada. 61 pp.

———— 1980. The Ghana–Guelph project in retrospect. *In* Canadian university experience in international development projects. Association of Universities and Colleges of Canada, Ottawa, ON, Canada. pp. 39–44.

————— 1995. Assessing the medium-term impact of an institutional strengthening project. Canadian and International Education, 24(2), 85–94.

————— 1996. Canada. *In* Caston, G., ed., The management of international cooperation in universities: six countries case studies and an analysis. UNESCO New Papers on Higher Education, No. 16. pp. 39–58.

Shute, J.C.M.; Grieve, G.D.; Jenkinson, G.M.; Protz, R. 1985. Evaluating the impact of an undergraduate program. NACTA Journal, 29(1), 56–58.

Shute, J.C.M.; van den Bor, W. 1994. South–North university cooperation: a Netherlands–Canada example. *In* Aarts, H.; Flatin, K., ed., Europe and beyond. European Association for International Education, Amsterdam, Netherlands. EAIE Occasional Paper 5. pp. 45–52.

Slaughter, S.; Leslie, L. 1997. Academic capitalism: politics, policies and the entrepreneurial university. Johns Hopkins University Press, Baltimore, MD, USA. 276 pp.

Smillie, I. 1985. The land of lost content: a history of CUSO. Deneau Publishers and Co., Toronto, ON, Canada.

Snellman, O., ed. 1995. Internationalization of higher education: goals, prerequisites and quality assurance. Centre for International Mobility, Helsinki, Finland.

SSHRC (Social Sciences and Humanities Research Council). 1979. Annual report, 1978–79. SSHRC, Ottawa, ON, Canada.

————— 1984. Annual report, 1983–84. SSHRC, Ottawa, ON, Canada.

Stanbury, W.T. 1998. Interim report of the Faculty of Commerce Review Committee. University of British Columbia, Vancouver, BC, Canada.

Stanley, D.; Mason, J. 1998. Preparing graduates for the future: international learning outcomes. British Columbia Centre for International Education, Victoria, BC, Canada.

Statistics Canada. 1995–96. Number of full-time professors by province — 1992/93 to 1995–96. Government of Canada, Ottawa, ON, Canada. Publication Catalogue No. 81-2290XPB.

————— 1998. Effectifs à temps plein et à temps partiel des universités. Government of Canada, Ottawa, ON, Canada. CANSIM, statistics tables 00580701, 00580702.

Strong, M. 1996. Connecting with the world: priorities for Canadian internationalism in the 21st century. International Development Research Centre, Ottawa, ON, Canada. 33 pp.

Teichler, U. 1996a. Comparative higher education: potentials and limits. Higher Education, 32(4), 431–465.

————— 1996b. Student mobility in the framework of ERASMUS: findings of an evaluation study. European Journal of Education, 31(2), 153–179.

Therien, J.-P. 1994. Canadian aid: a comparative analysis. *In* Pratt, C. ed., Canadian international development assistance policies: an appraisal. McGill – Queen's University Press, Montréal, PQ, Canada; Kingston, ON, Canada. 314–333.

Tickner, A.W. 1991. The NRC postdoctorate fellowships, 1948–1978. Scientia Canadensis, 15(2), 145–154.

Tillman, G. 1997. Internationalization of advanced learning: toward a planning framework. Association of Canadian Community Colleges;

Association of Universities and Colleges of Canada; Canadian Bureau for International Education, Ottawa, ON, Canada.

Tossell, W.E. 1980. Partnership in development: Canadian universities and world food. Science Council of Canada, Ottawa, ON, Canada. 145 pp.

Tretheway, M. 1992. Island programs: the UBC experience with a summer program in France. *In* Rugman, A.M.; Stanbury, W.T., ed., Global perspective: internationalizing management education. University of British Columbia Centre for International Business Studies, Vancouver, BC, Canada. pp. 345–352.

293

UBC (University of British Columbia). 1997. Think about it: President's address. Bridge to the 21st century: internationalization at UBC. UBC, Vancouver, BC, Canada. Internet: www.vision.ubc.ca/bridge
———— 1998. Universitas 21. UBC, Vancouver, BC, Canada. Internet: www.interchange.ubc.ca/ubcintl/U21.html

Umakoshi, T. 1997. Internationalization of Japanese higher education in the 1980's and early 1990's. Higher Education, 34, 259–273.

UNESCO (United Nations Educational, Scientific and Cultural Organization). 1997. European Convention on the Academic Recognition of University Qualifications. Council of Europe, Strasbourg, France. Internet: www.coe.fr/eng/legaltxt/32e.htm
———— 1998. World Conference on Higher Education in the 21st Century, 5–9 Oct, Paris, France. UNESCO, Paris, France.

University Affairs. 1998. University report: Phoenix rising in BC. University Affairs, Oct, p. 20.

van den Bor, W.; Shute, J.C.M. 1991. Higher education in the Third World: status symbol or instrument for development. Higher Education, 22(1), 1–5.

van der Wende, M. 1997. Internationalising the curriculum in Dutch higher education: an international comparative perspective. Universiteit Utrecht, Amsterdam, Netherlands.

Vertesi, C. 1992. Roles and methods of student exchanges in internationalizing management education. *In* Rugman, A.M.; Stanbury, W.T., ed., Global perspective: internationalizing management education. University of British Columbia Centre for International Business Studies, Vancouver, BC, Canada. pp. 329–344.

Vroeijenstijn, A.I. 1995. Improvement and accountability: navigating between Scylla and Charybdis. Jessica Kingsley Publishers, London, UK. 188 pp.

Walmsley, N. 1970. Canadian universities and international development. Association of Universities and Colleges of Canada, Ottawa, ON, Canada. 330 pp.

Welch, A.R. 1997. The peripatetic professor: the internationalization of the academic profession. Higher Education, 34, 323–345.

Whalley, T.; Langley, L.; Villarreal, L. 1997. Best practice guidelines for internationalizing the curriculum. Douglas College, Vancouver, BC, Canada. Internet: www.cttbc.ca/Curr/BP/whatcons.html

Whitelaw, J.H. 1978. Postsecondary systems in Quebec. *In* Sheffield, E.; Campbell, D.D.; Holmes, J.; Kymlicka, B.B.; Whitelaw, J.H., ed., Systems of higher education in Canada. International Council for Educational Development, New York, NY, USA. pp. 65–100.

Wilson, D. 1998. Defining international competencies for the new millennium. Canadian Bureau for International Education, Ottawa, ON, Ontario.

Wilson, J.D.; Stamp, R.M.; Audet, L.-P. 1970. Canadian education: a history. Prentice-Hall, Scarborough, ON, Canada. 528 pp.

294 Wodehouse, D. 1996. Quality assurance: international trends, preoccupations and features. Assessment and Evaluation in Higher Education, 21(4), 347–356.

———— ed. 1997. Certification manual. Global Alliance for Transnational Education, Washington, DC, USA.

World Bank. 1996. Electronic seminar, education and the role of technology. World Bank, Washington, DC, USA, Oct–Nov.

Zarek, P. 1999. Co-op Ontario. Mohawk College, Hamilton, ON, Canada. Internet: coopont.mohawkc.on.ca

About the Institution

The International Development Research Centre (IDRC) is committed to building a sustainable and equitable world. IDRC funds developing-world researchers, thus enabling the people of the South to find their own solutions to their own problems. IDRC also maintains information networks and forges linkages that allow Canadians and their developing-world partners to benefit equally from a global sharing of knowledge. Through its actions, IDRC is helping others to help themselves.

About the Publisher

IDRC Books publishes research results and scholarly studies on global and regional issues related to sustainable and equitable development. As a specialist in development literature, IDRC Books contributes to the body of knowledge on these issues to further the cause of global understanding and equity. IDRC publications are sold through its head office in Ottawa, Canada, as well as by IDRC's agents and distributors around the world. The full catalogue is available at http://www.idrc.ca/books/index.html.